THE OVERSHADOWED PREACHER

The Overshadowed Preacher

Mary, the Spirit, and the Labor of Proclamation

Jerusha Matsen Neal

WILLIAM B. EERDMANS PUBLISHING COMPANY
GRAND RAPIDS, MICHIGAN

Wm. B. Eerdmans Publishing Co.
4035 Park East Court SE, Grand Rapids, Michigan 49546
www.eerdmans.com

Printed in the United States of America

26 25 24 23 22 21 20   1 2 3 4 5 6 7

ISBN 978-0-8028-7653-9

Library of Congress Cataloging-in-Publication Data

Names: Neal, Jerusha Matsen, 1972– author.
Title: The overshadowed preacher : Mary, the Spirit, and the labor of proclamation /
    Jerusha Matsen Neal.
Description: Grand Rapids, Michigan : William B. Eerdmans Publishing Company,
    2020. | Includes bibliographical references and index. | Summary: "Homiletic
    theology that reclaims the preacher's particular, embodied identity in proclaiming
    the Word of God"—Provided by publisher.
Identifiers: LCCN 2020015397 | ISBN 9780802876539 (hardcover)
Subjects: LCSH: Preaching. | Mary, Blessed Virgin, Saint. | Holy Spirit. | Human
    body—Religious aspects—Christianity.
Classification: LCC BV4211.3 .N43 2020 | DDC 251—dc23
LC record available at https://lccn.loc.gov/2020015397

For my mother,
Patricia Dunagan Matsen,

You who . . . abide in the shadow of the Almighty will say to the Lord,
"My refuge and my fortress; my God, in whom I trust."

Psalm 91:1-2

Contents

Foreword

"The preaching event itself . . . is a living, breathing, flesh-and-blood expression of the theology of the Holy Spirit."[1] These penned words from James Forbes in his Lyman Beecher Lectures at Yale in 1986 strike me every time I read them. Living. Breathing. Flesh and blood. The Holy Spirit. These words remind me that although the church as we know it may be dying, preaching is living because the Word of God is not dead. God is still speaking and the Holy Spirit is still breathing through the crucified and risen flesh and blood of Jesus Christ and our very own human bodies. This hopeful promise and initiation of breath blows all the way from the first days of creation over waters (Gen. 1) to a valley of dry bones (Ezek. 37)—a context of contamination—to a Lenten wilderness in 2020, a COVID-19 global pandemic. There is still breath, and where there is breath, there is life and echoes of linguistic proclamatory resurrection hope—"you shall live" (Ezek. 37). The Spirit is life and the one in whom, according to Jürgen Moltmann, "our life wakes up."[2] In the Spirit, preaching wakes up and becomes fully alive with resurrection power.

But so often the Spirit has been a second- or third- or no-thought-at-all in relation to the ministry of preaching. This is ironic because there would be no preaching, no word, no Word of God, no Jesus Christ, the anointed one, without the anointing Spirit of life, the breath of life, the power and presence of God hovering over and overshadowing humankind. Yet preaching, in many seminary classrooms, is typically presented,

1. James Forbes, *The Holy Spirit and Preaching* (Nashville: Abingdon Press, 1989), 19.
2. Jürgen Moltmann, *The Source of Life: The Holy Spirit and the Theology of Life* (Minneapolis: Fortress Press, 1997), 11.

even if implicitly, as a Spiritless task, something totally dependent on human power, intelligence, and rhetoric. Jerusha Matsen Neal is one of those homiletics professors who avoids this pedagogical humanism, because she teaches that preaching is reliant on a living relationship with a living, risen Jesus, in the power of the Spirit. She urges readers to embrace one critical shadow, and that is being overshadowed by the Holy Spirit as was Mary. This is a refreshing reminder not to allow technology (*technē*, our technique) to overshadow theology in homiletics.

This does not mean that human beings, flesh and blood, do not matter, because we do in the gracious economy of God. How could it be otherwise when God became human in Jesus to love the human world? Preaching is definitely not all about our power, but at the same time, we preachers are still present in body, flesh, and blood. God is present and we are present, too. Our humanness is not erased because it is embraced by an incarnate God made flesh through the agency of the Spirit. As Neal writes, preaching "is a willingness to show up in one's own skin. . . . " Flesh and blood, human skin, matter because the Spirit matters, and Spirit matters are fleshy, human matters like a pregnant Mary.

When you take the Spirit seriously, you have to take the human body seriously because pneumatology implies materiality. The Spirit works physically, materially, earthily, bodily, and bloodily. She does not try to run and escape from incarnation but moves God toward it, as we see in the incarnation of God in Christ. Thus, in homiletics and the church more broadly, somatic amnesia is an indication of pneumatic amnesia, because the Spirit uses human flesh and blood, earthly means for heavenly purposes.

Preaching is a clear sign of the Spirit's incarnational work. But Neal offers a faithful witness that the embodied sermon we should remember and that is vital when considering embodiment in preaching is the resurrected body of Christ, alive in the power of the Spirit. That flesh-and-blood risen body, often neglected in teaching preaching, is at work through our homiletical bodies in the Spirit.

And in preaching, the Spirit embraces all bodies, all flesh, all humanity. The Spirit falls like fire and ignites human beings to become more fully human in order to proclaim a word in and through our brokenness and blessedness. The Spirit breathes on and through broken flesh to offer the hope and truth of God. In Toni Morrison's novel *Beloved*, the Spirit calls Baby Suggs, holy, an "unchurched preacher," to preach to a collective black body in the clearing of the woods, despite having "busted her legs, back, head, eyes, hands, kidneys, womb and tongue" through the grind of slavery. In her heartfelt sermon, she tells her congregation that theirs is a "flesh that needs to be loved" and they should "love it hard." This is quite an extraordinary expression of a somatic sermon, for at the end of this proclamation, there are no words but only bodies dancing and making music to articulate the gospel in that context. Baby Suggs, "saying no more, . . . stood up then and danced with her twisted hip the rest of what her heart had to say while others opened their mouths and gave her the music. Long notes held until the four-part harmony was perfect enough for their deeply loved flesh."[3]

To be clear, this somatic scene, this individual and communal embodied proclamation, is a work of the Spirit, where we see the interrelationship of the somatic, sonic, and pneumatic. The vulnerable ministry of the homiletical body, expressed culturally as black bruised bodies, is, according to M. Shawn Copeland, a "liturgy of Spirit"[4] because it is a literary example of the relationship between the Spirit and human flesh in preaching. The embrace of the Spirit's presence through an embrace of the human body is an embrace of incarnational homiletics. To acknowledge the Spirit in preaching should lead one to honor the human body, to love the flesh and blood of God's creation.[5] To proclaim a living, breathing gospel in the Spirit requires a whole human person, even a wounded one, like Baby Suggs or Mary or Jesus.

All types of diverse bodies overshadowed by the Spirit in pulpits will dance and make music, because flattened words alone cannot fully express the sermonic bearing of Christ as preachers themselves are reborn through gospel proclamation. This book and the gospel will lead you to sing and make harmony like Mary, intoning a human song magnifying God through your living, breathing, flesh and blood. This is a literary invocation for the Spirit to breathe on and overshadow you that you and your preaching might be born again. As you read, let the Spirit midwife the living Word of God through you that in the end, you and your congregation can sing, "My soul doth magnify the Lord."

Luke A. Powery
Lent 2020

3. Toni Morrison, *Beloved* (New York: Vintage, 2004 [1987]), 102–104.
4. M. Shawn Copeland, *Enfleshing Freedom: Body, Race, and Being* (Minneapolis: Fortress Press, 2010), 51–52.
5. See Stephanie Paulsell, "Honoring the Body," in *Practicing Our Faith: A Way of Life for a Searching People*, ed. Dorothy C. Bass (San Francisco: Jossey-Bass Publishers, 1997), 14–15.

Preface

The book you hold in your hand is a tightrope stretched across shark-infested waters. It takes three of the most romanticized and misused categories in Christian theology—the body, the Spirit, and Jesus's mother, Mary—and attempts to say something meaningful, careful, and credible through them in relation to Christian preaching.

It is a book of theology about practice. More tricky, it is a book that gets practical about theology. It tries to describe the mystery of God's anointing. And that is dangerous business.

The homiletic discipline is littered with tin models of sermon types and typologies. Worse, it is filled with ghosts that are anything but holy. Particularly in my specialization of pulpit performance, when the church has tried to get concrete about what Spirit-filled preaching looks like, people get hurt. Teasing out the power of the Spirit from the power of persuasion, populism, or prosperity is hard, as is releasing the power of the Spirit from the regulatory grip of the church. The church's manifestos on the body's importance for preaching have been tools for norming *certain* bodies and ridiculing others. The church's talk of the Spirit has been co-opted, too often, by the spirits of the age.

And yet here we stand, balancing on a wire. Sometimes, what is at stake in a performance is worth the risk. Sometimes, the only way to the other side is a treacherous crossing.

And we, as preachers, need to get to the other side.

Preachers are burning out, trying to embody what they were never meant to be. Preachers around the world who do not fit a given mold continue to be silenced or shamed. Those who *do* fit that mold, frail and fallible, claim undue power over their congregations and the congregations of others as their pulpit performances beam a globalized gospel around the world. Any one of these reasons would be reason enough to justify the discussion. But I have another.

I believe that preaching bodies are revelatory signs—frail and fallible, yes, but faithful—by the Spirit's power. They are signs that there is an Other body among those gathered. They are signs witnessing to the risen body of Jesus—alive not only in the church or in the proclaimed word but living outside of both. They are signs because the Spirit continues to do what she has done for centuries: bring the bodies of preachers into living relation with Christ's own. It's been part of the Holy Ghost's job description since at least the day an angel relayed an annunciation to a Nazareth teenager.

Which brings us to Mary—arguably the most romanticized and misused of the three subjects named. The ways that her body's "over-shadow[ed]" (Luke 1:35) labor intersects with the Spirit-mediated labor of preaching is the subject of this book. I do not plan to hand preachers any tin models at the end—no archetypes or universal symbols. Instead, I hope to give them a metaphor that, like a tightrope across a cavern, points the preacher in a direction, asks her to find the Spirit's center of gravity, and step out in faith.

In a global season when human witnesses to Jesus's resurrected body are especially needed, the metaphor's trajectory matters. Its endpoint is not proper exegetical technique, pristine performance, or raw rhetorical power. Its goal is living, embodied relation to Jesus. It's on him that our eyes are fixed and *to* him that this tightrope points.

It better be. He's the One promising to catch us if we fall.

Acknowledgments

In my living room hangs a painting by a Fijian artist named Ledua Peni. It shows a cluster of figures in a small boat, silhouetted against a dark sky. The travelers are rowing in deep water. Their faces are in shadow, and it is unclear whether the day's light is fading or dawning. The painting is called, *Follow Me*.

What is most arresting about the painting is not the boat or its figures. What holds the viewer's eye is all that happens beneath the water. The boat floats near the top of Peni's frame, and underneath, we see what the figures in the painting do not—schools of fish and turtles glowing in sea foam. The light missing from the sky shines in the currents. The travelers are held, buoyed, and directed by hidden communities. In the midst of an uncertain journey, Peni's painting sings of grace.

Our family has done a great deal of traveling over the past ten years. We relocated to New Jersey after a decade of pastoral ministry in Southern California so that I could start a doctoral program. We moved to the South Pacific to train pastors at Davuilevu Theological College at the request of the Fijian Methodist Church. We returned three years later to North Carolina, trying to make sense of theological education and ministry in the ambivalent light of a divided church. What I remember most about those moves is not the questions they raised or how small they made us feel. What I remember are the communities, teeming with color and life, that held us in the deep.

This book took shape in the midst of these transitions and was the labor of multiple communions. I am grateful for my Princeton Theological Seminary teachers and doctoral colleagues—particularly my advisor, Sally A. Brown, who shepherded this project from its infancy to its defense. Her eye for structure, careful feedback, and love of metaphor have been foundational to my formation. Michael Brothers graciously pressed the work toward accessibility and clarity. Beverly Gaventa steered the discussion of Acts away from theological generalities and toward textual descriptions of the risen Jesus—a trajectory that changed the course of the book. All the while, a precious, struggling congregation supported our family and invested in our call. Wesley United Methodist Church was a sacramental witness to the resurrected Christ during those growing years.

To write about theories of relationship and hospitality is one thing. To move around the world and live in the tender crucible of Christian community is entirely different. Our colleagues and students at Davui-levu Theological College stretched the scope and depth of this book through their witness of welcome. I am humbled when I remember the privileges of morning and evening worship and the sweet prayers shared by our *matasiga* small group. I am grateful for the courage of church leaders who invited our family to be a part of the Fijian Methodist community and invited a woman to teach preaching at the oldest pastoral training school in the country. Davuilevu embodied the labor described in these pages.

Through the years, Charles Campbell had eyes for the book's deep DNA. He kindly joined my dissertation committee when the need arose and continued to serve as mentor and guide during our time overseas. He has read more versions of this manuscript than I can count, and his insight and encouragement have been vital to its completion. Chuck's foolish wisdom points me to greater hope, and his truth-telling fuels my love of this vocation. Our years working together at Duke Divinity School have been too few.

It is an honor that Luke Powery, Dean of Duke Chapel, pens the forward. Powery's writing on the intersection of Spirit and sermon was catalytic in the book's early stages and instrumental to the field. His pulpit artistry and wise leadership serve as testimonies to his theological passion. I am grateful to call him a colleague and friend. I'm grateful, as well, for the numerous Duke Divinity School colleagues who have shaped these pages through their feedback. Anathea Portier-Young and Brittany Wilson gave the book's biblical sections particular care. My thinking was strengthened by their helpful critiques and continuing work on biblical embodiment. Debbie Wong has been an excellent research assistant, and Christine Parton Burkett, an attentive conversation partner. Christine and Tracie Ashlie pointed me toward the poem that opens the epilogue.

The book would have not been possible without the team at Wm. B. Eerdmans and its investment in the work of homiletic theology. Given the quickly changing landscape of the United States church and increasingly global conversations within our guild, I have been blessed to work with a publisher that recognizes the urgency and practical significance of the theological affirmation at preaching's heart. I am grateful for its witness.

And of course, I have not been alone in the boat. There are dear souls who have sat beside me in the unknowing. Many have prayed this work into the world, listening carefully over cups of Fijian coffee, calling long-distance, and sending prophetic care packages like navigational stars. My gratitude swells for Annie Dominguez, who read the unreadable drafts, and for my sister Amy Matsen, who held vigil with me following the death of our mother. I thank God for my curious, courageous father, Luther Matsen, who taught me to follow the golden thread. Words fail when I think of my children, Mercy and Josiah, who said yes to God's call when they could have said no. I am humbled by their bravery. Their kindness has made me a better woman, scholar, preacher, and mother. My husband, Wesley, took my hand twenty-two years ago, and he has held it faithfully. He has carried this work with me. He has listened patiently as I pondered ideas aloud in our bed at night and awoken to my clicking fingers on the keyboard. He has edited and edited again. He is my compass and my closest companion. I have tasted the goodness of God in Wesley's overshadowed sermons these many years.

But not in Wesley's sermons alone. In each season of our journey, ordinary preachers in ordinary classrooms and congregations have been my guides. To write a theology of Spirit-filled preaching is not to look to big steeples. It is to be surprised by the Spirit's work in hidden places. It has been my great joy to celebrate the abundance thriving beneath the surface of choppy ecclesial waters. The preachers I have taught and interviewed have been living signs to me of God's faithful presence. Their words have held me like a womb, and together, we have found a brooding Spirit and Savior.

CHAPTER 1
....

Uneasy Borders, Tricky Definitions

∿

*It is morning at Davuilevu Theological College, the oldest pastoral
training school in the Fiji Islands. The wooden "lali" beats a slow, distinctive rhythm, as the preacher walks with measured steps from the
back of the chapel and takes his place at the pulpit. The drum beat
stops. Except for the wake-up calls of birds, there is no noise. The community is still and holds a collective breath. The choir leader gives a
soft, vocal pitch, and a four-part chord rises from every corner of the
room. "Ni voleka mada na Karisito," the students sing, slow and certain. Their eyes are shut. Their bodies, seated. It is a song they have
sung in morning and evening devotions since childhood. I join them,
finding my way. Expectancy hums in the tight harmonies, like hope
held close to the chest. The words are an iTaukei translation of a hymn
brought to Fiji by Methodist missionaries over 180 years ago. "Jesus,
stand among us in Thy risen power," the hymn begins. And on this
particular morning, I believe he does.*

Reflections on a chapel service at Davuilevu Theological College

∿

I came to Fiji as a mission partner during a season when my own country, the United States, was in turmoil. During the years of Ferguson
and Charleston, the exhausting whirlwind of the 2016 election, the

1

2017 Women's March and ICE immigration raids, I sat every morning in the chapel service described in the epigraph and wondered what it meant that *"Jesus stands among us in his risen power."* In certain ways, those services seemed far removed from the angst in my own nation. The communal performance of faith, the careful repetition of words passed down, and the present-day promise of gospel hope seemed a world set apart.

But, of course, beneath their performances of morning worship, these future leaders of the Fijian church had their own fears, brought about by turmoils of similar scale. In the nation of Fiji, things once taken for granted—things like tides and seasons—were shifting because of climate change. Globalization created new conversations but also new divisions and silences, as communal traditions struggled to remain relevant. Distrust between the largely Christian indigenous population and their Hindu and Muslim neighbors had erupted in a series of political coups. A military dictatorship created doubt in the trustworthiness of the political process. Even in the hymn so beautifully rendered by the Davuilevu students that morning, borders of identity, agency, and tradition were shifting. The hymn was a reminder of the community's Western missionary past, but also a resistance to the encroaching cultural *otherness* of social media, secularity, and foreign-funded megachurches. It was a performance of adaptation and stability in light of a vulnerable community's ambivalence about change.

Davuilevu performed more than singing technique that morning. Through its worship, it was negotiating complicated questions about the community's autonomy, freedom, and vocation, questions that are deeply theological. When I speak of a preacher's performance in the pulpit, I speak of a similar labor. A preacher's performance is more than elocution and eye contact. Performance is what Ronald Pelias calls the "dialogical engagement" between text, performer, audience, and event.[1] It pays attention to bodies not only as objects in space but as events in time. It attends to their contexts and commitments, and in so doing, it makes visible the uneasy, relational borders that give definition and

---

1. Ronald Pelias, *Performance Studies: The Interpretation of Aesthetic Texts* (New York: St. Martin's Press, 1992), 15. This "dialogical engagement" between text, performer, audience, and event is not disconnected from materiality. It mediates between understandings of subject and object as objectively severed or subjectively collapsed—arguing instead for an uneasy, relational boundary that connects the two in time, even as it maintains their distinction.

movement to human persons and histories.[2] Preaching's performative borders press us toward a rearticulation of the Holy Spirit's critical role in the work of proclamation and toward a fully human embrace of God's world. More than this, the uneasy borders of performance become sites of physical testimony to an embodied Savior. His presence is the vibrating hope at the heart of that Fijian hymn.

The Uneasy Promise of Resurrection

Ours is a world of uneasy borders. We live in a season marked by global migrations, religious and nationalistic violence, and the hegemony of a larger-than-life economy. Rising sea levels erode island coastlines, and higher temperatures compress the acreage of arable farmland. But geographic borders are not the only borders shifting. Over the course of a generation, the borders that separate self and other, subject and object, normative center and exotic edge have blurred.[3] Borders of race and gender, once thought self-evident, have been refigured as provisional and performative.[4] Human agency seems overrun by discourses of power.[5]

2. My description of bodily borders as "uneasy" does not carry a negative connotation. It names the participatory dynamism that accompanies performative action and therefore accompanies our understanding of others and ourselves. I do not seek to prove this epistemological "unease" through philosophical, hermeneutic argument; there is a long history of projects that attempt that task. For one example, see Paul Ricoeur's discussion of the self and narrative identity in *Oneself as Another*, trans. Kathleen Blamey (Chicago: University of Chicago Press, 1992), 140–68. My goal is to name the theological significance—and indeed, necessity—of preaching's "uneasy" performative borders for homiletic theology. For another example of a theologian who uses a personal, emotionally evocative term to describe a physical performative border, see Kristine Culp's description of the church's borders as "vulnerable" in *Vulnerability and Glory: A Theological Account* (Louisville: Westminster John Knox, 2010).

3. Ricoeur speaks of the "amazing oscillations that the philosophies of the subject" have undergone in recent history. See Ricoeur, *Oneself as Another*, 4.

4. See Judith Butler, "For a Careful Reading," in *Feminist Contentions: A Philosophical Exchange*, ed. Judith Butler, Seyla Benhabib, Drucilla Cornell, and Nancy Fraser (London: Routledge, 1995), 127–43, for her resistance to ontological categories of gender in favor of performative categories. She states, "there need not be a 'doer behind the deed' . . . the 'doer' is invariably constructed through the deed."

5. Pierre Bourdieu, *The Logic of Practice* (Cambridge: Polity Press, 1992), 56, for example, describes a cultural "habitus" that shapes the self, even as it is enacted by the self.

The borders of our natural world and the borders of our own understanding cannot be taken for granted.

It is from this uneasy place that the Davuilevu community sings its witness: Jesus stands among us on these borders of change. This is more than just a pretty turn of phrase. Jesus's bodily presence in Christian worship is the Spirit-mediated solace of the faithful. It is the promise that sets Christian preaching apart from preaching in other traditions or, for that matter, in the ubiquitous TED Talks.[6] *Jesus stands among us*. It's not that Jesus doesn't show up in other rhetorical performances. But Christian preaching promises something specific. The promise may be parsed differently by different traditions, but it is tangled deep in the roots of our faith. Through the ordinary actions of human preachers and the faith of those gathered, the Spirit makes the risen Jesus present—as surely as he's present in the Eucharist.[7] It's why preaching was so precious to the Protestant Reformers. And it's what we mean when we say that Christian preaching is grounded in resurrection. It's not just that Christian preachers proclaim that the resurrection happened. They preach in relation to a risen Lord.

But affirming Jesus's bodily resurrection has a cost. It means that Jesus stands among us in an uneasy, performative way. To have a body is to be both known and hidden; bodies cannot be conjured or stripped of their mystery. Jesus is no shape-shifting ghost—nor is he simply communal memory, as if our talk of "presence" was a manner of speech. Resurrection means that Jesus is not safely enclosed in tombs of tradition and narrative so that "ecclesiology smothers eschatology."[8] We do not own him, nor do we replace him. To claim that Jesus stands among us as a resurrected body is to claim that he is both *present with us* and *absent from us*, that he is Other than us while performing in relation to us.

A great deal is at stake for preachers in figuring out what this presence and absence mean for their sermon performances. Even more is at stake

---

6. For an explanation of TED Talks, see https://www.ted.com/about/our-organization.

7. In Fred W. Meuser's *Luther the Preacher* (Minneapolis: Augsburg Press, 1983), 13, he summarizes Luther's view on the matter: "In the sermon, one actually encounters God."

8. Douglas Farrow, *Ascension and Ecclesia: On the Significance of the Doctrine of the Ascension for Ecclesiology and Christian Cosmology* (Grand Rapids: Eerdmans, 1999), 260.

for the church. This book will not come at that problem through a rehashing of sacramental debates,[9] though one can discern their echoes. Nor will it parse the issue by comparing theologies of ascension[10] or analyzing biblical examples of divine embodiment across the Judeo-Christian tradition.[11] Instead, it will describe the mystery of Christ's presence and absence by comparing the biblical narratives of Acts's preachers and Mary's pregnancy—both examples of how Christ's body marks the borders of faithful human action through the Spirit's power.

These biblical descriptions of Spirit-empowered action are critical because the consequences of Jesus's presence and absence are not always clear, particularly when it comes to the simple question of what the preacher is to *do* in the sermonic act. What is her job description? The preacher, like those Fijian seminarians, also stands in shifting borderlands of identity, agency, and communal norms. She is also vulnerable and, quite often, ambivalent. What does it mean to embody the promise of Jesus's risen power in her performance? My fear is that homiletic instruction has not always provided preachers appropriate training to the task.

It is a frightening thing when the boundaries that establish who we are, what we can accomplish, and where we belong grow visibly uneasy. Nationalist politics and quests for ecclesial purity respond by building walls on these borders, trading vulnerable relation for rigidity. Homiletic training—particularly in relation to the messy work of rhetoric—has its own version of this trade. It can respond to the uneasy borders of the world and the uneasy borders of Christ's resurrected presence by flattening a preacher's performance into practices that can be mastered, passed down, and counted on. These human definitions of "excellence" create manageable descriptions of an impossible job. But time-honored practices can also exclude preachers who do not fit the mold. They can make the church's borders and homiletic practices invulnerable to time and context, and more critically to Jesus himself. The danger is not only that a preacher's Spirit-filled witness will be muted by these homiletic norms

9. For comparison of Calvin's sacramental touchstones and his treatment of sermon rhetoric, see Jerusha Neal, "The Overshadowed Preacher: Mary, the Spirit and the Body of the Word" (PhD diss., Princeton Theological Seminary, May 2014).

10. See Farrow's excellent treatment of this subject in *Ascension and Ecclesia*.

11. Brittany E. Wilson's work in *Embodied God: Seeing the Divine in Luke-Acts and the Early Church* (New York: Oxford University Press, forthcoming) presses this project forward in significant ways.

or even that a changing world will leave preachers behind, sequestered in increasingly outdated homiletic forms. The danger is that the promise of Jesus's resurrected body, present in power and inaccessible to our manipulations, will be replaced with a body safe and solid—an unchanging body of knowledge that is more statue than flesh. If that is the preacher's comfort, then Jesus is truly absent, for this body resembles no-*body* at all. Jesus's living performance of salvation is replaced by rhetorical norms that are crisply under our control, and we are left substituting our performances for his.

The gamble at the heart of this book is the performative gamble that the Reformers took centuries ago in their reconfiguration of sacramental theology—a gamble we will touch on in this opening chapter. In letting go of an ecclesial guarantee of Christ's bodily presence, the Reformers put their trust in a lived-in-time, Spirit-mediated relationship. What would a similar risk look like in the labor of preaching? How might this posture shape the questions of our discipline, the expectations of our congregations, and the testimonies of our lives?

Given what is at stake, it's only fair that I show you my cards. Defining one's terms is tricky business, and before you sign on for the journey, you should know where I stand.

Tricky Definition 1: Preaching

I am standing in front of my speech communications class in a United States seminary—a required course for all incoming students.

"Are there any questions?" I ask.

It is March. We have been together for over six months. We have talked about performative exegesis and the vocal interpretation of Scripture. We've talked about inflection and emphasis, phrasing and rate. We've talked about volume, poise, and internalization; about eye contact, gesture, and stage fright. But now the question comes.

A woman in the front row raises her hand and asks it—tentatively, almost sheepishly—as if she should know the answer and doesn't.

"What do you think we are doing when we preach?" she asks. "I mean—what are we really doing? What do you think it means when we say that we speak God's Word?"

The entire class turns to me with expectant eyes and pencils poised.
They have been waiting for someone to have the courage to ask.

Journal entry, March 22, 2011

It should be an easy question for a preaching instructor to answer.

But the student isn't looking for isolated doctrinal principles. She has asked her question in a practical theology classroom, not in the systematic theology course she took last term. Her question grows out of her bodily frustrations with preaching and the unchartable borders of text and body, Word and words, Spirit and flesh that make up preacherly performance.

Heinrich Bullinger wrote the definition of preaching I learned as a seminary student: "The preaching of the Word of God is the Word of God."[12] It's a terrifying claim for congregations, as there are any number of bad sermons. But I think the claim is more terrifying for the preacher, particularly when the great *dis*claimer at the statement's heart is laid bare. Be clear. Preaching is not the Word of God. Preaching *of the Word of God* gets that distinction, which means that what preachers *do*—what they discern, translate, apply, show, promise—in the course of a sermon matters profoundly. The Word of God is not taken for granted.

And the stakes are high. John Calvin says it this way. "It is a settled principle that the sacraments have the same office as the Word of God [i.e., the proclamation of the sermon]: to offer and set forth Christ to us, and in him the treasures of heavenly grace."[13] In other words, *Jesus stands among us* when proclaimed—but only if the preacher does it right. Of course, this is a horrible way to interpret Bullinger. It misses the primacy of God's gracious act and makes preaching into a "works-righteousness" exercise—or worse, a warlock's evocation. For the Reformers, God is free: Giver and Gift. And yet the point emphasizes the importance of *performance* in Reformed theology.

To be precise, performance, as I am using the term, doesn't mean pretense or play-acting, and it isn't a matter of "works righteousness." It

12. Heinrich Bullinger, The Second Helvetic Confession, 5.004.
13. John Calvin, *Institutes of the Christian Religion*, Library of Christian Classics 20-21 (Philadelphia: Westminster, 1960), 2:953.

is a way to describe the lived-in-time relationality of revelation in Protestant thought. It describes salvation that is imputed (and imparted), not by church fiat but through faith.

Thomas J. Davis charts Martin Luther's movement from the Catholic understanding of the sacrament as an *opus operatum* (literally "a work done") to an understanding grounded in event and time—an *opus operantis*, "a work being done, in process, in which one is intimately involved."[14] There are two issues at stake in this shift away from a localized, guaranteed, sacramental Presence to a sacramental understanding grounded in event. The first pushes back against a taken-for-granted efficacy of the ritual on its own, independent of the church's active dependence on the Word. The second takes issue with the concept of a sacrament as a human work at all. Brian Gerrish stresses that for Reformers like Calvin, the sacrament is "by definition a gift, . . . not something to be done."[15] The sacrament is the gracious act of a living Lord, not the oblation of a priest or congregation.

My grandmother might explain this kind of "actively passive"[16] dependence through the hymn "Leaning on the Everlasting Arms."[17] Divine arms are strong to save, but the leaning matters. It's what leads Karl Barth to say that "without ambivalence, the liability to misunderstanding and the vulnerability [of preaching], . . . it could not be real proclamation."[18]

Of course, there is ambivalence—and then there is *ambivalence*. Ev-

14. Thomas J. Davis, *This Is My Body: The Presence of Christ in Reformation Thought* (Grand Rapids: Baker Academic, 2008), 22. Even more literally, one might translate the Latin phrase as "a thing done by one who is in the process of doing." In attributing the efficacy of the sacrament to the finished work of Christ, Augustine's original distinction between *ex opere operato* and *ex opere operantis* made clear that the sacrament's efficacy could not be undermined by any fault or flaw in the priest's performance. The Reformers agreed but stressed that Christ's sacramental presence was always a present-tense gift of grace "through faith" (Eph. 2:8), not something that could be objectified and independently dispersed by the church. For a Catholic perspective on the importance of divine guarantee, see Cathal Doherty, *Maurice Blondel on the Supernatural in Human Action: Sacrament and Superstition* (Leiden: Brill, 2017).

15. B. A. Gerrish, *Grace and Gratitude: The Eucharistic Theology of John Calvin* (Minneapolis: Fortress Press, 1993), 149–50.

16. An *actio mere passiva*. See Calvin, *Institutes*, 2:1303.

17. Elisha A. Hoffman, "Leaning on the Everlasting Arms," 1887.

18. Karl Barth, *Church Dogmatics*, I/1, ed. Geoffrey W. Bromiley and T. F. Torrance, trans. Geoffrey W. Bromiley (Edinburgh: T&T Clark, 1975), 94.

ery age thinks itself uniquely challenged, perhaps. But I don't blame contemporary preachers for concluding that the opacity of "the preaching of
the Word of God" has increased exponentially in the last century. There
was a time when theological knowledge seemed smooth like marble, cool
and hard to the touch. There was a time when students of the Bible believed a text's meaning could be isolated in time, frozen and objectified.
There was a time when tradition was used as a singular noun. For anyone
paying attention, that time is long gone.

Preachers are negotiating a morass of uneasy borders between text
and exegete, manuscript and performance, communal role and personal
identity—not to mention the uneasy borders of a hurting world.[19] How
do these ambiguities intersect the most uneasy border of all: the border between the commissioned preacher and God? My starting place in
this journey is the problematic—some would say naive—doctrinal assurance that through a living relationship with God the event of preaching
makes present an absent Person. Disclaimers and definitions are needed.
But first, take stock of the radical claim and the conundrum it presents.
Preachers know the devil is in the details.

How does this relationship impact the other uneasy borders of the
preacher's performance? When Davuilevu students sing of Jesus standing among us, there is only one person visibly standing: the preacher
of the Word. And this is the challenge. What does the preacher "do" in
relation to this Jesus? How does his presence impact our relationship with
the people we serve, the bodies we inhabit, and the world we interpret?
How do his body and his performance—his "real presence"—relate to
our own?[20]

---

19. For descriptions of this changing landscape, see Edward Farley's classic de-
scription of *habitus* in "Theology and Practice Outside the Clerical Paradigm," in
Practical Theology, ed. Don Browning (San Francisco: Harper & Row, 1983), Richard
Osmer's argument that rhetorical practice offers a starting place for a twenty-first-
century rationality in "Rhetoric and Practical Theology: Toward a New Theological
Paradigm," in *To Teach, Delight, and to Move*, ed. David Cunningham (Eugene, OR:
Cascade, 2004), or Elaine Graham's insistence that theological disclosure "emerges
from the contingency of human practice" in *Transforming Practice: Pastoral Theology
in an Age of Uncertainty* (London: Mowbray Press, 1996), 10.

20. The heated eucharistic debates of the Reformers were shaped by a common
commitment to Christ's Spirit-mediated presence, despite his ascended absence.
Even Huldrych Zwingli, who emphasized the absent part of that equation, makes
space for a "functional" presence of Christ's natural body. See Thomas Davis, *This*

Tricky Definition 2: Body

The young preacher shuffles the pages of her manuscript nervously. She has been working on this sermon all week. She doesn't get to preach often—so she wants to get it right. She's studied the passage in its original language. She's done her exegetical study. She's quoted a lot of theologians. She's prayed that she might "fade away" and let God speak God's words through her. She prayed it just this morning in her quiet time: "Let me disappear, so they can see Jesus."

But she knows that everything she does is distracting to her congregation because who she is, is distracting! Her voice will never sound like the senior pastor's. She has to stand on a wood box to see over the pulpit. Her robe swallows her up like a cloud.

When her congregants shake her hand on the way out, they don't comment on her words—they comment on her new haircut. One man says, "It's nice seeing your pretty smile up there."

It seems they didn't see Jesus, at all . . . which makes her wonder if she was really called in the first place.

Journal entry describing the
experience of a female theological student
in her field-education church, November 3, 2017

Embodiment is a bit of a buzzword in seminaries these days, regularly invoked to make up for centuries of antibody bias in Christian theology. Bodies have been regularly distrusted and patronized in Western epistemologies, trotted out as an afterthought to first principles and predetermined truth.[21] J. Kameron Carter has pointed out the violent

---

Is My Body: The Presence of Christ in Reformation Thought (Grand Rapids: Baker Academic, 2008), 158.

21. While acknowledging divergent streams in Western thought, Jonathan Sacks, in *The Dignity of Difference* (London: Continuum Press, 2002), 48, argues that "Plato's ghost" has haunted much of the West's scholarship, leading to an understanding of truth that prioritizes disembodied universality over "empirical reality with all its messy and chaotic particulars."

consequences of such bodily "forgetting": the universalizing tendency of modernity and a racializing of the other.[22] In other words, the West's "forgetting" of the body corresponds to an enduring obsession with bodily categorization and regulation. Carter's point is underscored by contemporary culture, where the body appears coddled, primped, and worshiped, but where real bodies are picked over and picked apart, malnourished and overfed. Real bodies are measured against idealized projections on the billboards of our consciousness. And when real bodies diverge from those ideals, the consequences are serious—sometimes deadly. In a culture obsessed with the body, the government debates giving children equal access to health care.[23] In a culture that prioritizes bodily preservation, the color of an unarmed man's skin increases his risk of being shot by a police officer.[24] It would seem the greatest consequence of "bodily forgetting" is that bodies matter quite a lot.

It's a paradox that any preacher who does not fit the ideal of their community's expectations knows. The same traditions that encourage a preacher's "fading away" are the traditions that take careful note of clothes worn, emotion shown, gender performed, and any number of other bodily markers of pulpit authorization. Students in my homiletic classroom were recently discussing the importance of the body for the work of preaching. A young female preacher, grappling with her own #MeToo history, said simply, "I actually wish my body didn't matter quite so much."

The question, of course, is the tricky definition of *body*. What are a "real" body's characteristics? Is it frozen in time, static and autonomous? Is it related to identity or determined by discourse? Is it a da Vinci ideal? Some scientifically observable norm?

I venture three descriptive characteristics.

Real bodies are *particular*. They exist in space, materially bounded,

22. J. Kameron Carter, *Race: A Theological Account* (Oxford: Oxford University Press, 2008), 373. Work revalorizing the body continues to emerge among feminist thinkers and critical race theorists.

23. Annie Lowrey, "The Damage to Children's Health Insurance Is Already Being Done," *Atlantic*, November 22, 2017, https://www.theatlantic.com/politics/archive/2017/11/the-threat-to-childrens-health-insurance/546662.

24. Aldina Mesic, et al., "The Relationship between Structural Racism and Black-White Disparities in Fatal Police Shootings at the State Level," *Journal of the National Medical Association* 110, no. 2 (April 2018): 106–16. https://doi.org/10.1016/j.jnma.2017.12.002.

which gives them a certain mystery. There are things we cannot know about the bodies outside of ourselves. They stand on different patches of earth, and so our careful observations of them are always an interpretation. Bodies remind us that there is an unknowableness to the world. Dan Stiver, describing the philosophy of Paul Ricoeur, says, "We are not transparent texts, whose meaning is self-evident and singular."[25] We know in part. We prophesy in part—at least on this side of that great getting-up morning. For Ricoeur, this is true even in discerning the mystery of our own selves.[26] Bodies do more than reveal our specificity. They limit what we can see.

But real bodies are also *permeable*. They interact with the world. Because of the material limits of bodies, I can touch another's hand. I can feel the sun on my cheeks. I can also experience a flush of shame, a slap, a bullet. Bodies are vulnerable to the interpretations, actions, and contexts that surround them. Maurice Merleau-Ponty describes us as "involved in the world and with others in an inextricable tangle."[27] We are vulnerable to others, dependent on others, implicated by others. Bodies appear to provide the possibility for action and autonomy in the world, but at the same time, they tether us to scripts, forces, and actors outside our control.

Finally, real bodies are *provisional*. They change. They move. They exist not only in space but in time. If they would hold still and certain, we might be able to discover rules to name and train them—but bodies are moving targets, uneasy borders. One might say a body is a border that is performing. It underscores the limits of our knowledge, our goodness, our independence, and our mortality. And finally, it raises the question of trust. In a world that limits what we can see and control, in a world that shifts beneath our feet, *what can we count on?*

It is no wonder that the West has avoided conversations that take the depth and breadth of bodily experience seriously. Bodies create and articulate change, and in the words of James Baldwin, "Any real change implies the breakup of the world as one has always known it, the loss of

25. Dan Stiver, *Theology after Ricoeur: New Directions in Hermeneutical Theology* (Louisville: Westminster John Knox, 2002), 164.

26. Paul Ricoeur, *Oneself as Another*, trans. Kathleen Blamey (Chicago: University of Chicago Press, 2002).

27. Maurice Merleau-Ponty, *Phenomenology of Perception*, trans. Colin Smith, International Library of Philosophy and Scientific Method (New York: Humanities Press, 1962), 454.

all that gave one an identity, the end of safety."[28] Yet there are moments when followers of Christ have risked that change. There are moments when the church has taken seriously the implications of these bodily characteristics, even at the risk of disrupting the theological world they have always known.

The sacramental debates of the Reformers are an example. Protestant theology can be caricatured as "body-denying" when compared to the sensory richness of Catholic tradition. But the driving force behind Luther, Zwingli, and Calvin's debate about eucharistic practice was a question about the nature of materiality: in particular, the nature of Christ's risen body. They worked out the problem differently, each stressing different aspects of that body's *particular*, *permeable*, and *provisional* character. But they agreed that there was an absence of Christ's body in eucharistic practice, alongside its presence. For all of Luther's talk of "ubiquity," a believer could not access the benefits of Christ's body without discerning that body through the Spirit's gift of faith.[29] For Zwingli and Calvin, the absence was underlined further. Jesus's body had ascended into heaven, which meant that his presence was always a gift given in time through faithful practice and—once again—the Spirit's power.[30]

The Reformers were walking into dangerous territory with this acknowledgment. By allowing for the *provisional* nature of eucharistic practice, they were facing head-on what Devin Singh describes as the "traumatic" experience of "abandonment" created by Christ's ascension.[31] They were deconstructing the desire to replace Christ's bodily absence with the body of the church, the materiality of sacramental elements, the bodies of charismatic leaders, or a body of cultural knowledge. All the

---

28. James Baldwin, *Nobody Knows My Name: More Notes of a Native Son* (New York: Vintage, 1993), 117.

29. Gerhard Ebeling, "The Beginning of Luther's Hermeneutics," *Lutheran Quarterly* 7, no. 3 (Autumn 1993): 317, states that, for Luther, "The spiritual is not . . . a realm of . . . inwardness and invisibility. Instead, the spiritual is a category of understanding."

30. For a summary of early Reformers' sacramental positions, see David Steinmetz, "The Eucharist and the Identity of Jesus in the Early Reformation," in *Seeking the Identity of Jesus*, ed. Beverly Roberts Gaventa and Richard B. Hays (Grand Rapids: Eerdmans, 2008), 271.

31. Devin Singh, "The Trauma of Ascendency as Abandonment," paper presentation for the "Race, Coloniality and Philosophy of Religion" panel, American Academy of Religion, Boston, November 18, 2017.

while, each insisted that Christ's presence was, in some form, salvation's ground. Their starting place for a discussion of Christian practice was the necessary intervention of a risen, embodied Person whose presence could not be controlled, denied, or guaranteed.

Preaching walks into this dangerous territory, as well—at least when the *particularity*, *permeability*, and *provisionality* of bodies are allowed to inform preaching's sacramental character. Claire Waters summarizes the dilemma in her discussion of the first medieval preaching handbooks. Written centuries prior to the Reformation debates, these *ars predicandi* manuals dealt primarily with the preacher's rhetorical training and the uneasy borders of audience, interpretation, and delivery. The very need for the subject matter reinforced that "[Christ] is both present, in the form of his representative [the preacher], and also absent, and thus unable to immediately guarantee that representative's appropriateness" without instruction and authorization.[32] The same implicit dilemma haunts contemporary homiletic classrooms and puts working preachers in a double bind. As much as they might try to mirror Christ's presence, preachers' performances themselves undercut the authority of their words, for there is no ignoring that their bodies are forever getting in the way. They cannot make present any absent Person or risen power unless their greatest fear is true: unless that Person and power are nothing more than the potent performances of preachers themselves. In which case, they stand in the pulpit alone.

Tricky Definition 3: Spirit

I am standing in the pulpit of one of the oldest continuously meeting congregations in the Northeast. It is Sunday morning, and light pours across the pews from stained-glass windows. Scattered throughout the cavernous space, twenty people have gathered for worship. We represent nine native languages. If not for first-generation immigrants from

---

32. Claire M. Waters, *Angels and Earthly Creatures: Preaching, Performance, and Gender in the Later Middle Ages* (Philadelphia: University of Pennsylvania Press, 2004), 28.

around the globe—denominational loyalists, all—the congregation would have died years ago.

These people, my church family, are weary. They have worked too much overtime this week, afraid of the layoffs that have affected many in the community. They sit far from each other in silence. I know enough of their stories to recognize the grief that hangs in the shadows.

Visitors are sitting in the back pew: a man who has been sleeping on the streets, now sleeping off a hangover, and a woman with nervous eyes. A recent widower slips in late; his teenage children have stayed home. A woman struggling with mental illness sits in front of another who is in an abusive marriage. Across the aisle is a recovering addict who recently had a fistfight in the fellowship hall.

My speech feels strange and stilted in my mouth. The Scripture hangs above my head, just out of reach. My words fall heavy on the floor. I struggle to speak across borders of language and culture and socioeconomic class. I struggle to create an atmosphere of intimacy and welcome. But mostly I struggle to say something faithful in this difficult place.

I feel my inadequacy and their disappointment. I have let them down. Or I have let God down. Or maybe—it is God who is to blame.

Journal reflections
on a sermon given January 31, 2010

On days when Christ's absence feels palpable, we search for substitutes. We take over for him. We disappear into our role, finding safety in routine. We tell ourselves that it doesn't matter what we do anyway—or perhaps we just need to do it (whatever "it" is) better. We may even stop believing that he was supposed to show up in the first place. *Disappearing* preachers, those who aspire to fade away and are inevitably "splinched," share something in common with *disillusioned* preachers, those dear souls ready to throw in the towel.[33] Both have given up hope that the

33. Thanks to Anna Carter Florence for *splinched*, this apt Harry Potter reference. See Anna Carter Florence, *Preaching as Testimony* (Louisville: Westminster John Knox, 2007), 114. *Splinching* is when a witch or wizard "disapparates" to a new location unsuccessfully and leaves part of her or his body behind.

resurrected body is present and particular—a body marked by the uneasy borders of a living thing that cannot dissolve us or be dissolved away. Both have stopped engaging with an embodied, resurrected God in and through the sermon.

I have a hunch about this *bodily* forgetting. I think it is linked to a *pneumatological* forgetting in the ways we teach and practice preaching. For all their differences, Luther, Calvin, and Zwingli shared a commitment to the vital role of the Holy Spirit in making divine and human participation possible. *The Holy Spirit working through faithful, performative action was what made engagement with Christ's body possible.* The Spirit allowed human actors to remain themselves while they performed as Christ's "body" in the world (or for Luther and Calvin, when *mediating* that body to the faithful). Human actors did not disappear or dissolve in Spirit-empowered performance. Nor was the particularity of their action dismissed. The Spirit was how Christ became present in ways that honored those bodily particulars. Even the particularity of the bread mattered to the Reformers![34] Reducing it to an "accident" was as problematic to them as divinizing it. The Spirit was the theological means through which the bread could remain fully itself—even as it made Christ's body known.

When I read Barbara Brown Taylor's celebrated memoir *Leaving Church* as a young mother and preacher, I was grateful for her stark articulation of the difficulty she found in remaining in the pastoral role. Finally, the "central revelation" that caused her to leave parish ministry was that the "call to serve God is first and last the call to be fully human."[35] I agreed. I also remember betting my ministry on the hope that Taylor's choice between "full humanity" and the pastoral role was a false one—at least for me. I had not been called to leave the church. I had been called to stay.

But her point rang true. There was something not "fully human" in Protestant practices of proclamation. An idealized shadow kept finding its way into church pulpits. It was hinted at in Pablo Jiménez's description of a friend's praise of a fellow Caribbean preacher. "If you close your

---

34. The particularity of the sign is theologically meaningful to Calvin: "his life passes into us and is made ours—just as bread when taken as food imparts vigor to the body." See Calvin, *Institutes*, 2:1365. "The figure of bread" is a gift, not a "mask to prevent our eyes from seeing the flesh [of Christ]." See Calvin, *Institutes*, 2:1374.

35. Barbara Brown Taylor, *Leaving Church: A Memoir* (Norwich, UK: Canterbury Press, 2011), xi.

eyes, you'd think Billy Graham is preaching!" the colleague intoned.[36] It was seen in the tears of a woman called to serve a tradition where few female preachers had gone before, wondering if her manner—her body— was "masculine enough" to meet the needs of her community.[37] It played out in a congregation's expectation of a pastor's long-suffering power, her ever-available spiritual energy, and her ability to bring dead congregations to life with carefully crafted, relevant words. More importantly, it was revealed in the paradox of preachers' own expectations that they must "get out of the way"—and yet, simultaneously, "save souls" with rhetoric that "brings home" the Word with fire.

The consequences of such idealisms reach farther than individual crises of authenticity. As is often the case, the personal becomes political. When false shadows convince preachers that ecclesial practices are adequate substitutes for Christ's particular, permeable, provisional body—in other words, when those practices are separated from the Spirit's mediating gift—preaching becomes *dangerous*. The cultural performance of one corner of the world gains hegemonic authority. The good news for all is redefined through a nationalistic lens. Individual preachers can protect their institutional authority at all costs.[38] They can take up abusive rhetoric in their quest for persuasive power—often using the language of the Spirit to do so. The Christian dominionist movement in the United States serves as one example. In sermons advocating for a Christian state and asserting believers' "anointing as kings," Reverend Rafael Cruz describes a God-given "anointing to go to the battlefield . . . to go to the marketplace and occupy the land. To go to the marketplace and take dominion."[39] But, of course, such conflation of worldly power,

36. Pablo Jiménez, "If You Just Close Your Eyes: Post-Colonial Perspectives on Preaching in the Caribbean," *Homiletic* 40, no. 1 (2015): 22–28.

37. This particular example is based on two female seminary students who expressed similar fears over a decade apart. The fact that one expressed her concerns in 1998 and one in 2012 shows the stubborn staying power of this issue for women preachers—and for women rhetors in traditionally male roles more generally.

38. The cover-up of sexual abuse in various denominations is a case in point. See Curtis Freeman, "Southern Baptists and Roman Catholics Face Similar Crises," *News and Record*, February 24, 2019, https://www.greensboro.com/opinion /columns/curtis-freeman-southern-baptists-and-roman-catholics-face-similar-crises /article_4fca4890-6613-5705-99b5-1dc7d1a8ed35.html.

39. Reverend Cruz's sermon is described at length in Morgan Guyton, "The Theology of Government Shutdown," *Huffington Post*, December 6, 2017, https://www .huffingtonpost.com/morgan-guyton/the-theology-of-governmen_b_4020537.html.

ecclesial power, and the power of the Christ is nothing new. Singh argues that the Western imperial project itself can be traced to the theological crisis created by Jesus's ascension and the church's inability to face up to the implications of a body it could not grasp.[40] Unable to evoke or contain that body, the church displaced it into Tradition (with a capital T), fueling a cultural colonialism that continues to marginalize diverse practices of faith.[41] Indeed, sifting "Tradition's" definition, authority, and function is a recurring flash point in contemporary theological classrooms.[42]

I am not attempting to create a comprehensive pneumatology out of whole cloth. My goal in these chapters is specific. In relation to preaching, the role of the Spirit is reasserted in bringing the preacher's performance into embodied relation with Christ's. That may seem like small, provincial potatoes. The project risks falling into what Kirsteen Kim describes as the "dialogical" rut in Western Protestant pneumatology—making the work of the Spirit an "in my heart," interecclesial matter.[43] I recognize the danger and affirm the broad reach of the Spirit's wings in the world. But this "dialogical" understanding of the Spirit also has profound implications for the church's public witness. Significant, real-world injustices result when one breezes by the practical implications of this most basic affirmation about Christian preaching. When the role of the Spirit is not acknowledged, preachers spend their ministries unwilling to face their own vulnerability and humanity in the pulpit, which means that churches learn to do the same. In this denial of their bodily particularity, permeability, and provisionality, their need for Christ's body— as crucified, resurrected Savior—is also denied. Indeed, if the Reformers were right, when the Spirit's role is eclipsed,

40. Singh, "Trauma of Ascendency."

41. See Douglas Farrow's "In Support of a Reformed View of Ascension and Eucharist," in *Reformed Theology: Identity and Ecumenicity*, ed. Wallace M. Alston Jr. and Michael Welker (Grand Rapids: Eerdmans, 2003), 360, for a critique of Graham Ward's ecclesial vision of "radical orthodoxy" for its inability to explain "how or in what way the savior can be distinguished from the church."

42. Kenyatta Gilbert, "A Promising, Trivocal Hermeneutic for Twenty-First-Century Preaching: Justice, Transformation and Hope," *Toward a Homiletical Theology of Promise*, ed. David Schnasa Jacobsen (Eugene, OR: Cascade, 2018), 46, discusses the ways the theological formulations that framed his seminary training were not "prejudice-free" and, in fact, were limited theological methods "indigenous to one's particular, ecclesial habitat."

43. Kirsteen Kim, *The Holy Spirit in the World: A Global Conversation* (Maryknoll, NY: Orbis, 2007), 144.

there is no access to that Savior. The preacher and her people lean on shadows instead.

And here the political becomes personal again. *Dangerous* preachers keep doing what they do, to devastating effect. *Disappearing* preachers burn out or walk away, trying to be more than they are and feigning to know more than they know. They pretend that all is well when it is not. "I play the role," one says, "but have lost my voice." And then there is the *disillusioned* preacher, who isn't sure she believes any of it anymore. "I can preach to make them better people," one pastor says to me, "but how do I preach to make them new creations?" "Nothing I say in the pulpit makes any difference." If Christ is present and active, "why does he feel so far away?"[44]

Reclaiming a Fully Human Homiletic

This book affirms the seemingly impossible promise that by the Spirit's power, Jesus is in the room when preachers preach the Word. He is embodied—not as tradition, words on a page, or even as the preacherly power of performative speech, but as himself, risen and reigning. In this way, he stands out of our control, absent from our performances even as he is present through them. Reclaiming the full humanity of preachers starts with a homiletic theology that reclaims the absence and presence of this fully human Word.

But what does this affirmation mean for what preachers *do*? What would it mean to move out from under the shadow of false ideals and be overshadowed by the Spirit instead? This is the purpose of the chapters that follow: to describe the rhetorical performance of preachers in a way that takes the Spirit's mediating work seriously. The practical translation is critical because, while our performances can never substitute for Christ, human performance matters. Fully human performance bears the marks of vulnerable encounter, both with others and with the ultimate Other. Indeed, it is through such imperfect labors of love that the Spirit reveals Christ among us.

And so I come to the Spirit-empowered labor of Mary, Jesus's mother.

When I was thirty, pregnant with my second child and pastoring a

---

44. Personal interviews with pastors about the challenges and joys of preaching, April 23 and May 6, 2012.

Southern Californian congregation, I went on a spiritual retreat to a local Catholic monastery. The brothers were gracious and hospitable, but I found myself hungering for some sign that my female witness had value in this very masculine space. When I came across their lovely chapel dedicated to the Virgin Mary, I discovered where the community's veneration of femaleness had been localized. There was only one problem. This Mary did not remind me of my own female witness. She was so silent and removed from the world. I remember thinking at the time that I wished she could leave her podium and stretch her wooden arms and legs. I wished she could get behind the pulpit and preach—revealing the secrets she had learned over years of watching and waiting in her alcove.

Over the next ten years, I embarked on an extended study of what Mary might teach preachers in the pulpit. When I first became interested in comparing the Spirit-empowered pregnancy of Mary to the work of preaching, I was interested in the question of divine and human agency in the Word's mediation. I was interested in God's work and our work in the practice of preaching and how Mary's labor informed that mystery. I came to my research as a Protestant, convinced of Mary's flawed and finite nature, despite her faithfulness. I came as a mother aware of how an emphasis on Mary's submission and passivity in pregnancy was only half of the story. Pregnancy and birth, while not something that one controls, are in fact called *labor* for a reason. But I also came to this research as a practicing preacher who found very familiar baggage in traditions that stressed Mary's purity, passivity, and power.

Christians have been writing about Mary, the mother of Jesus, for millennia. And she, like many preachers, has often struggled to remain fully human in her role as bearer of the Word. In Catholicism she has become norm and symbol, "co-redemptrix" and Queen—and in Protestantism she has often disappeared from discussion. These tendencies are particularly visible around discussions of Mary's laboring body. Similar to the preacher's performance, Mary's bodily participation in the birth of Christ raises complicated questions for Protestant pillars of grace and revelation. Is the Word born into the world by our purity and effort or by the gracious gift of God? Perhaps for this reason, many Protestant scholars found it easier to avoid the subject of Mary's bearing body altogether. [45] But I think that in avoiding the subject, we have missed a theological opportunity.

---

45. There are multiple reasons for this silence, of course, including a reticence born of propriety. See Jennifer Glancy's discussion in *Corporal Knowledge* (Oxford:

Luke's treatment of Mary's Spirit-empowered pregnancy provides a metaphor for the content of sacramental performance in the pulpit, a description of how our bodies relate to the Spirit's work and Christ's embodied presence in the sermon. This description affects our relationships with human communities and human constructions of authority and power. Luke provides a provocative picture of how Mary's body matters in bearing Christ to the world—and how it doesn't. It is a picture helpful for contemporary debates about the value of embodied performance for theology and the decolonization of culture. It is a picture that provides a resource for describing Christian practice in ways that make space for a living God and living communities. These broader challenges rumble under the foundations of this project. But it is also a picture I find helpful for *disillusioned*, *disappearing*, or *dangerous* preachers—descriptions that, on a given Sunday, might fit any of us.

What I offer is a metaphor—not a model. Again, definitions are key. Metaphors don't reduce the things they describe to literary tropes. They don't substitute flesh-and-blood realities with abstractions. Metaphors are tug-of-wars between an "is" and an "is not."[46] The dissimilarities of the objects being compared are part of what makes a metaphor significant. Metaphors honor the particularity of those objects and don't ask one thing to subsume another.

Pregnancy and preaching are not the same thing. And Mary's pregnancy is distinct from either of those generalized terms. Her experience of pregnancy is as particular as her experience of responding to a call. Mary is not a type or essence of the preacher (or mother). Rather, Luke describes her as a human person. As such, her story—which is finally all we have of her—is held in uneasy, generative relation to the act of proclamation. I proceed with caution, for feminism has learned the dangers of univocal categorizations of experience.[47] But I also proceed boldly, for

---

Oxford University Press, 2010), 82–84. Luke himself provides a scant description. But for Protestants, there is the added concern that giving attention to Mary and her body will "shift attention away from the saving grace of God in Christ alone." See Nancy Duff, "Mary, Servant of the Lord," in *Blessed One: Protestant Perspectives on Mary*, ed. Beverly Roberts Gaventa and Cynthia L. Rigby (Louisville: Westminster John Knox, 2002), 60.

46. Paul Ricoeur, *The Rule of Metaphor: Multi-Disciplinary Studies in the Creation of Meaning in Language*, trans. Robert Czerny (Toronto: University of Toronto Press, 1977), 248.

47. Margaret Kamitsuka, *Feminist Theology and the Challenge of Difference* (Ox-

metaphors matter. They bear insight through their uneasy borders. They shape thought and create space for new conversations.

In this metaphor's push and pull, you will see something of me. The meaning of a metaphor shifts across time and space—as anyone who has lived in an unfamiliar culture will attest. My context and my convictions inform my metaphorical work. I am an ordained woman who stands in a pulpit still denied to many who share my gender. Across millennia, women have responded to that denial in various ways. Some have thrived in spite of it—renaming their proclamation as something other than preaching.[48] Some have broadened their definition of preaching to include activities that require no ecclesial sanction.[49] I celebrate the Spirit's stretching of all expectations. Christian proclamation takes many forms. But my work challenges this denial more simply. I believe it matters to Christ's church that women preach from its pulpits, with full ecclesial blessing. I've seen too many complementarians use the affirmation that preaching can happen in a kitchen (which I believe) to suggest that, in the case of women, this is the only place it should happen.[50] And yet this affirmation of women's ordination leaves me with a dilemma. How do women preach in fully human ways in relation to a tradition that has excluded them for so long? How do they perform faithfully without co-option or perpetuating the tradition's exclusion of others?

The wound at the root of these questions goes deep and reaches beyond categories of gender. Questions of autonomy, power, and authority affect preachers of all sorts. They are tangled deep in the theological DNA of our homiletic practices, which means that attending to those practices requires theological work. If I am correct, the converse is also true. Robust theologies of proclamation attend to the bodies of preachers, for it is

---

ford: Oxford University Press, 2007), 10, discusses how categories of "experience" can marginalize difference within and among groups.

48. Kate Bowler's *The Preacher's Wife: The Precarious Power of Evangelical Women Celebrities* (Princeton: Princeton University Press, 2019) catalogs the various ways that evangelical woman exert spiritual authority outside of the pulpit.

49. Donyelle McCray's description of Pauli Murray's advocacy, poetry, and letters as preaching is a case in point. See Donyelle McCray, "Pauli Murray: Preaching in Many Voices," lecture at Duke Divinity School, April 1, 2019.

50. Cara Bentley, "John MacArthur Says Southern Baptist Preacher Beth Moore Should 'Go Home,'" *Premier*, October 21, 2019, https://www.premier.org.uk/News /World/Pastor-John-MacArthur-says-Southern-Baptist-preacher-Beth-Moore -should-go-home.

in and through those bodies that Jesus is witnessed. They bear his marks by the Spirit's power.

Mary's pregnancy as a metaphor for preaching invites men and women, parents and nonparents, queer preachers and straight, to integrate the surrender of the preaching moment with the significance and particularity of the preacher's work. Correspondingly, the metaphor requires the homiletic discipline to give increased attention to the performing bodies of preachers of all sorts. As chapter two will show, teachers of pulpit performance have a history of privileging certain bodies and excluding others from pulpit norms.[51] For centuries the interplay of theology and rhetoric worked to create rigid borders around who could and who could not preach. The violence leveled against those who dared to publicly proclaim the Word of God without official authorization testifies to the chillingly real barriers surrounding pulpit speech.[52] Perhaps, in conceiving the uneasy border between preacher and Word through a metaphor grounded in a woman's overshadowed body, God's promise to Mary will reconfigure the borders of Christ's church.

51. In Dwight Conquergood, "Rethinking Elocution: The Trope of the Talking Book and Other Figures of Speech," *Text and Performance Quarterly* 20 (2000): 325–41, the author discusses "standards of taste" in nineteenth-century elocution, for example.

52. Waters, *Angels and Earthly Creatures*, 101. See also Beverly Mayne Kienzle, "The Prostitute-Preacher: Patterns of Polemic against Medieval Waldensian Women Preachers," in *Women Preachers and Prophets through Two Millennia of Christianity*, ed. Beverly Mayne Kienzle and Pamela J. Walker (Berkeley: University of California Press, 1998), 99–113.

CHAPTER 2
....

Dangerous Deliveries

The Queen of Heaven and the Pulpit Prince

> All around me floated archetypal mothers, Italian Madonnas—the
> red velvet framing their breasts as unstained as their smiles. . . .
> I could not see through them. My own experience waited blind
> and dumb, unspoken.
>
> Susan Griffin, "Feminism and Motherhood"

I breezed past a rather important sentence in the last chapter, and I want to return to it. As I began my research on Mary's pregnancy as a metaphor for pulpit performance, I found "very familiar baggage in traditions that stressed Mary's purity, passivity, and power." It's a strange claim since Protestants have frequently been doctrinaire in their rejection of Marian idealism. As I noted, the differences between the Catholic and Protestant treatments of Mary seem especially stark when we are dealing with Mary's pregnant labor. Catholics, for their part, have penned many volumes on the subject; Protestants, on the other hand, have a chorus of uncomfortable throat clearing. Protestants take a certain pride in this fact, congratulating ourselves on our biblically attentive reticence and our avoidance of romantic excess. But pride comes before a fall. While we Protestants may have avoided a fixation on Mary's delivery of the baby Jesus, we do carry very *familiar baggage* when it comes to another delivery: the delivery of the sermon.

When I was living in New Jersey, I lived in a heavily Catholic neighborhood. Veneration of Mary—through May Day celebrations, lawn statuary, and rear-view mirror rosary beads—was regularly visible. Catholic facilities would set aside space in their buildings to honor the Virgin

Mother as a matter of course. None of this was out of the ordinary. One day, however, I entered a Presbyterian church and experienced a shock of recognition. In a shadowy alcove of the narthex, there hung a gold-framed, calligraphy transcript of the founding pastor's first sermon. The frame had been set above a table covered with flowers and candles—and looked for all the world like a small Marian shrine.

I'm not the first to have noticed these connections. In Barth's *Church Dogmatics,* the section on preaching and the section on Mary are shaped by very similar arguments and theological concerns. If one were to skip his introductory and concluding remarks and drop into the meat of his discussion, one might mistake one section for the other. The driving force of both is the very Barthian insistence that revelation is independent of the "arbitrary cleverness, capability, or piety of man [*sic*]"—and mothers.[1] Protestants have insisted on this ever since *sola gratia.* But doctrine and practice do not always walk hand in hand. Remaining "fully human" in the vocation of Word-bearing is a challenge that cuts across denominational lines. This chapter will flesh out several strands of Protestant homiletics that have added to the challenge, imaging the performing preacher as a passively powerful *co-redemptrix,* a mediator between Word and flesh, or the embodiment of ecclesial tradition. Surprisingly, the shadows cast by the Catholic Queen of Heaven and the Protestant pulpit prince are remarkably similar.

Barthians are not the only ones to worry about the theological dangers found in those shadows. Catholic feminists like Elizabeth Johnson have noted that traditional Catholic interpretations of Mary eclipse the work of the Holy Spirit. She states, "Mary is called intercessor, mediatrix, helper, advocate, defender, consoler, counselor . . . she is the link between [the believer] and Christ."[2] Does this not, Johnson argues, "dislocate" the work of the Holy Spirit in the world? How strange, she points out, that Gerard Manley Hopkins's words, "She, wild web, wondrous robe, / mantles the guilty globe . . . and men are meant to share / her life as life does air," do not refer to the Holy Spirit but to the Blessed Virgin.[3] This Mary, bearing little resemblance to the young woman found in the

1. Karl Barth, *Church Dogmatics,* I/2, *Doctrine of the Word of God,* ed. Geoffrey W. Bromiley and T. F. Torrance, trans. Geoffrey W. Bromiley (Edinburgh: T&T Clark, 1956), 182.

2. Elizabeth A. Johnson, *Truly Our Sister: A Theology of Mary in the Communion of Saints* (New York: Continuum, 2003), 80.

3. Johnson, *Truly Our Sister,* 89.

Gospels, "wag[es] eternal hostilities against the poisonous serpent, and . . . completely crush[es] his head under her immaculate heel."[4] Christ leaves this Virgin's body "with a body taken from [her] most clean flesh and purest blood."[5] This symbolic Queen, according to Vatican II, is the "ideal representative or type of the church . . . perfectly represent[ing] the qualities of receptivity, humility, obedience and passivity."[6] She is the perfect disciple, symbolizing the "faith, charity and union with Christ that should mark the whole community."[7]

Johnson, and feminists like her, contend that these theological arguments have dangerous ethical consequences. Turning Mary into an idealized norm marginalizes the diverse experiences of women who do not and cannot fit her mold. Marina Warner agrees that "through the very celebration of the perfect human woman, both humanity and women [are] subtly denigrated."[8] The glorification of an idealized feminine archetype mutes the voices of actual female bodies—and compensates for their silence.[9] Johnson insists on the importance of letting Mary be "first and foremost, herself," not just for Mary but also for the women who have been regulated and ignored by the church's fascination with her body.[10]

I think a similar ethical danger lies in the Protestant church's fascination with the body of the preacher—whether that fascination is demonstrated in attempts to harness and silence the body or tap into its persuasive power. The history of pulpit rhetoric is intertwined with the church's wrestling with the implications of embodied, human performance for

4. Pius IX, *Ineffabilis Deus*, 1854, trans. and ed. Ulick J. Bourke. To be fair, this statement includes the modifier "through Christ" in relation to the Virgin's act. But it deliberately replaces Mary for Christ as the agent in the traditional interpretation of, "he will crush your head" in Genesis 3:15.

5. Bridget, *The Word of the Angel: Sermo Angelicus*, trans. John E. Halborg (Toronto: Peregrina, 1996), 18.

6. Johnson, *Truly Our Sister*, 39-40.

7. Johnson, *Truly Our Sister*, 39-40.

8. Marina Warner, *Alone of All Her Sex: The Myth and the Cult of the Virgin Mary* (New York: Vintage, 1983), xxi.

9. Sarah Coakley, "Mariology and 'Romantic Feminism,'" in *Women's Voices: Essays in Contemporary Feminist Theology*, ed. Teresa Elwes (New York: Marshall Pickering, 1992), 106-10, addresses the romantic feminism of Leonardo Boff, arguing that the "feminine 'other'" that he lauds is a "male construct" and a "thinly disguised reorientation of traditional gender stereotypes."

10. Johnson, *Truly Our Sister*, 101.

divine revelation—and indeed, Western philosophy's own debate on how knowledge, context, and persuasion are related.[11] This chapter will provide examples of how inadequate theologies of performance and revelation have led to less than fully human pulpit practices, practices that can cause the preacher to disappear, become disillusioned, or become dangerous. Theology, as Johnson insists, has bodily consequences. Indeed, such consequences can signal when theologies have lost their way.

But before getting to that conversation, we must acknowledge a deeper wound in the homiletic tradition. It is not only that poor practices have risen from underdeveloped (if well-intentioned) theologies of preaching. At times, theologies justifying particular schools of pulpit performance have risen directly from the desire of those in positions of power to maintain their authority and control. Pulpit rhetoric has been used as a justifying tool to silence those unauthorized or untrained by ecclesial hierarchies. It has been used to exclude, marginalize, and disempower those whose bodies do not fit an expected mold. The history of homiletic performance is no benign history. It is a history that requires us to exchange our rose-colored glasses for safety goggles. When the church starts talking about the body, whether it be Mary's body, the preacher's body, the church's body, or a particular body of knowledge, you can bet that more than theory and theology is at stake. Before we can name the shadows that haunt our preaching, then, we'll have to shine some light in a few of the pulpit's dirty corners.

Unholy Ghosts of Homiletics

In his book *The Hidden History of Women's Ordination*, Gary Macy frames the preaching and liturgical reforms of the late Middle Ages as responses to the fear that the exclusivity of the male priesthood was being threatened. Macy argues that liturgical theologies tying the efficacy of the Spirit to the authority of the church and the gender of the candidate were intended to explain away outliers in the tradition, like Hildegard of Bingen, who administered the Eucharist to her community, or female scholars who pursued theological education.[12] Claire Waters sees the influx of

---

11. Richard McKeon, "Rhetoric in the Middle Ages," *Speculum* 17 (1942): 1–32, stresses the complex, shifting influences in medieval definitions of rhetoric.

12. Gary Macy, *The Hidden History of Women's Ordination: Female Clergy in the*

preaching handbooks at the time as reflecting similar anxiety about decentralization in pulpit authorization and women preachers whose testimonies of faith exceeded many of their male counterparts in dynamism.[13] The definition of preaching itself was at stake. Was preaching defined by its context and form or by the authorization of the speaker? And if it was the speaker's authorization that mattered, how was that authorization determined? If that authorization was solely dependent on the Spirit, charismatic women prophets could cause all sorts of trouble. If authorization was dependent on education provided by the church—and those newly minted homiletic textbooks—greater control was possible. The greatest control of all, of course, seemed to lie in the simple argument that preaching was religious speech authorized as such by the church.[14] But that argument left loopholes as well. Readily relinquishing the title of preacher in exchange for the act itself, women like Margery Kemp engaged in public proclamation. Kemp claimed, shrewdly, that her open-air testimonial speech should not bother church authorities since it wasn't "preaching."[15]

Finally, the most airtight theological justification behind an exclusively male priesthood could not draw on misogynistic generalizations about female dullness and impropriety alone. Women of character and learning were belying those claims. Instead, the case was made that a certain verisimilitude was needed between the physical body of the Christ and the body of the preacher. This embodied representation was critical to the preaching act and the anointing it required. The gendered

---

Medieval West (Oxford: Oxford University Press, 2008), 125, sees this marginalization of women as corresponding with a simultaneous marginalization of lay lords and a "larger struggle to define and defend an exclusive claim for sacred power." For examples of prior forms of female leadership culminating in the double monasteries of the twelfth century, see Jo Ann McNamara, *Sisters in Arms: Catholic Nuns through Two Millennia* (Cambridge: Harvard University Press, 1996).

13. Claire Waters, *Angels and Earthly Creatures: Preaching, Performance, and Gender in the Late Middle Ages* (Philadelphia: University of Pennsylvania Press, 2008), 20, notes the 1210 bull of Pope Innocent III as one attempt to "put a stop to this nonsense" of preaching abbesses.

14. Finally, "preaching" and "prophesy" become different categories, "displacing preaching from full participation in the realm of plenitudinous, divine communication," in an attempt to honor social norms. See Waters, *Angels and Earthly Creatures*, 30.

15. Waters, *Angels and Earthly Creatures*, 121. Waters notes Kemp's defense in *The Book of Margery Kempe*: "I preche not, syr, I come in no pulpytt."

body of Christ became an exclusionary criterion for bodily performance in the pulpit.[16]

It's sobering history—but don't miss the crux of Waters's argument. The first flurry of homiletic handbooks in church history was inextricably linked to questions of ecclesial power and exclusion. It's enough to give a homiletician pause.

Catherine Brekus moves this history closer to the present day. She notes how a renewed emphasis on training preachers in nineteenth-century United States worked to sideline women who did not have access to this education and who had previously relied on theological justifications of "warm inspiration" as the foundation of their ministries.[17] Added to this new emphasis on education were the complex ways that elocutionary speech training worked to erect "protocols of taste, civility, and gentility" during the same period.[18] Dwight Conquergood emphasizes the ways that elocution worked as a bodily discipline that excluded and marked "others," particularly racial others. Elocutionary training and minstrel shows shared common assumptions about which performances and traditions were noble—and which were laughable. Even as immigrants and former slaves "raided and redeployed [elocutionary speech training] for their own subversive ends," the traditions themselves were steeped in racist stereotypes that marked bodies outside bourgeois standards of taste as "low-bred" or "vulgar."[19] In contrast, those bourgeois standards were christened as "universal" laws of "truth and propriety," ascribing moral significance to the bodily presentation of speakers.[20] These speech schools shaped the public-speaking norms that undergirded the pulpit training of the time, defining what it meant to speak "naturally." And for women, there existed a double bind. Proper speech

16. Waters, *Angels and Earthly Creatures*, 36–37. The preacher should also be "not evidently deformed, physically strong . . . and not too young," excluding differently abled bodies as well.

17. Catherine A. Brekus, *Strangers and Pilgrims: Female Preaching in America* (Chapel Hill: University of North Carolina Press, 1998), 287.

18. Dwight Conquergood, "Rethinking Elocution: The Trope of the Talking Book and Other Figures of Speech," *Text and Performance Quarterly* 20, no. 4 (October 2000): 326.

19. Conquergood, "Rethinking Elocution," 328.

20. James Rush, *The Philosophy of the Human Voice: Embracing Its Physiological History; Together with a System of Principles, by Which Criticism in the Art of Elocution May Be Rendered Intelligible, and Instruction, Definite and Comprehensive*, 7th rev. ed. (Philadelphia: J. B. Lippincott, 1879), 477.

performances required the proper embodiment of gender norms, which meant that women had no business speaking from the pulpit in the first place.

I offer one more example: the training of South Pacific preachers by overseas missionaries. In his book *Bible-ing My Samoan: Native Languages and the Politics of Bible Translating in the 19th Century*, Mosese Ma'ilo emphasizes the centrality of "language standardization" in the missionary project of Bible translation and its close relationship to colonial authority.[21] In this case, catechetical training dismantled more than diversities of linguistic expression. It dismantled diverse dialects themselves, and with them, diverse understandings of God and human community. This dismantling had a profound impact on contemporary South Pacific preaching. Theologians like Upolu Lumā Vaai connect the theology and practice of Christian missionaries who came to the Pacific with a God of "totality, linearity, and consolidation."[22] The resulting warrant for reducing "everything into one" led to the institutionalizing of "one truth" into Pacific "educational, political, church, and village/tribal systems."[23] In this case, the bodies and tongues of diverse communities were molded into a single ecclesial form rather than coexisting in lived relation. The body was central to theological training—but not as a particular, permeable, provisional site of revelation. It was valued, instead, as a site of standardization. This legacy haunted my own homiletic teaching overseas. Davuilevu Theological College currently conducts its classes in English because of the multiple languages represented in its student body. Students preach in English with facility, but also with grief. They know how much is lost in translation. As their teacher, I could only wonder.

Starting with the Body?

These are the ghosts that loom when a United States colleague turns to me and poses a significant question: "How would one teach preaching in a way that starts with the body?" Preaching is a messy, bodily business. There are no easy answers or catchall formulas. Preaching takes place in

21. Mosese Ma'ilo, *Bible-ing My Samoan: Native Languages and the Politics of Bible Translating in the 19th Century* (Apia, Samoa: Piula, 2016), 114.

22. Upolu Lumā Vaai, "A Theology of Talalasi: Challenging the 'One Truth' Ideology of the Empire," *Pacific Journal of Theology* 2, no. 5 (2016): 50.

23. Vaai, "A Theology of Talalasi," 51.

a material world subject to our interpretation, even as it confronts and interprets us. *What if we took that embodied performance seriously?* How might homiletics look different if we started with the question of what we really *do* when we preach, instead of with theoretical abstractions? The colleague asks the question earnestly, wanting to reclaim the significance of living flesh in the Christian tradition. He is underlining the significance of *practical* in practical theology. I share his concerns.

But "starting with the body" is no easy thing. And it is not new. The homiletic tradition has tried it before, sometimes with calculated deliberation, sometimes without even knowing. And more often than not, preachers have ended up the worse for wear. "Starting with the body" can imply romantic essentialism. It can treat the body as if it were autonomous or transparent, all-powerful or purely passive. "Starting with the body" can lead to the cultural values, knowledges, and practices of *certain* bodies being projected as natural, universal ideals. *But does it have to?* That's the question at the heart of this book. Could the Protestant Reformers' commitment to the particular, permeable, provisional nature of human bodies—and the body of Christ—be translated into the teaching of preaching? Could their commitment to the necessary work of the Spirit in that relationship inform a preacher's practice?

The Reformers were quite clear about the sacramental nature of the sermon, and they penned volumes describing a believer's "passively active," Spirit-inspired performance of faith in the Eucharist.[24] But how these two affirmations intersect the practice of the preacher is underdeveloped in Reformation thought. It's clear that rhetoric matters. Luther has deep suspicions about dialectic theology's usefulness when separated from a rhetorical context and function.[25] Calvin agrees. More than this, Calvin draws on theories of rhetoric to explain his theology of revelation and sacramental signs.[26] And yet both display an ad hoc

24. An *actio mere passiva*. See John Calvin, *Institutes of the Christian Religion*, Library of Christian Classics 20–21 (Philadelphia: Westminster, 1960), 2:1303.

25. Carl Springer, *Cicero in Heaven* (Boston: Brill, 2018), 78–79. Springer discusses Luther's respect for Ciceronian oratory, in particular.

26. For good introductions to the role of rhetoric in Calvin's preaching, teaching, and theological thought, see William James Bouwsma, *John Calvin: A Sixteenth-Century Portrait* (New York: Oxford University Press, 1988); David Wright, "Calvin's Accommodating God," in *Calvinus Sincerioris Religionis Vindex: Calvin as Protector of the Purer Religion,* Sixteenth Century Essays & Studies 36, ed. Wilhelm Neuser and Brian Armstrong (Kirksville, MO: Sixteenth Century Journal Publishers, 1997); and

approach to performative practice. Perhaps the overlap between Christ's Word and the words of the preacher was easier to imagine than the overlap between body and bread. Sound, after all, can cross borders of difference in a way that material objects cannot. Maybe the Reformers thought that less needed to be explained. But preaching is more than sound. If pulpit rhetoric points toward and mediates the body of Christ through the power of the Spirit, complicated questions about the borders of the preacher's body, voice, agency, and communal relationships emerge. The question of "what we really do" when we preach comes to the fore. Frankly, the description of "passive action" sounds more convincing as an explanation of eucharistic practice than the public labor of sermonizing. But if preaching is sacramental in nature, if it is God's very Self who speaks in and through the sermon as grace and gift, what other description could apply?

Three Metaphors for the Preacher's Performance

There is a "relational ontology" at the center of Protestant thought.[27] For Luther and Calvin, *being* was not a static noun to which a predicate was added. The self was defined in lived relationship to Christ. We are who we are because we are in relation to Another—and it is in that Other that we "live and move and have our being" (Acts 17:28). This relational identity isn't something to be taken for granted or objectified, like a stone carried around in one's pocket. It is lived out in time, performed in the world. And yet, it is grace and gift. It is only possible because of the Spirit's power.

Beautiful stuff, for sure, but confusing in practice. Frustrating even, if on a given Saturday night one has yet to be "gifted" tomorrow's sermon. It's no wonder that, in lieu of practical descriptions as to how this relational ontology impacted the preacher's Sunday morning performance, Protestant rhetorical models emerged that grew increasingly distant from the Reformers' sacramental understandings.[28] Human experience,

---

Randall C. Zachman, *John Calvin as Teacher, Pastor, and Theologian: The Shape of His Writings and Thought* (Grand Rapids: Baker Academic, 2006).

27. Julie Canlis, *Calvin's Ladder: A Spiritual Theology of Ascent and Ascension* (Grand Rapids: Eerdmans, 2010), 72.

28. Models, of course, are slippery things. They are, by definition, less nuanced than the realities they purport to represent. A given preacher's practice may touch

skill, and communities began standing in for Christ's body and for the Spirit that provides access to that body. Such things are rarely attested to directly, of course. These rhetorical models don't show up as major changes in theological doctrine. Instead, they emerge in the metaphors used to describe the function, content, and value of the preacher's performance. They show up as pictures trying to make sense of mystery. But sometimes metaphors reveal a lot about how theological doctrines are actually translated in practice.

The following metaphors for the preacher's performance have led to dangerous pulpit deliveries. This is hard to admit because I don't think these metaphors are in the same category as the homiletic power plays described previously. I don't think they were crafted in order to exclude people from the pulpit. To the contrary—though in a way this is even more concerning—they were often well-intentioned attempts to "start with the body" in the teaching of preaching. They were attempts to make practical sense of Protestantism's theology of the Word—which is the work of my life and the subject of this book. But over time, these metaphors led to idealizations of a preacher's *agency*, *identity*, and *communal role*. They became shadows promising more than could be delivered, exacting a toll on preacher and gathered community alike. Pulpit rhetoric became viewed as (1) a human skill only tangentially related to the Spirit's work, (2) revelation itself, fused to and thereby identified with the Word, or (3) the cultural vocabulary of the community, mediating the Word through a repository of traditions and narratives. In each case, the uneasy borders of Christ's presence and absence, his *standing among us* without being *replaced by us*, lost its characteristic Protestant tension. The presently active *opus operantis* of God's gracious, relational gift was undermined, and Christ's body lost its particular, permeable, provisional character.

There is an irony here. These attempts to "start with the body" have, in different ways, asked the preacher to leave behind the limits, vulnerabilities, and beauties of embodied life. And in so doing, they have obscured preachers' need for a very different shadow: the shadow of the Spirit. No longer seen as a necessary mediator between divine and human performance, the Spirit is underplayed as an afterthought, outsourced to an ecclesial body, or located within the skill set of a gifted

---

down in several of the following categorizations. But each represents a distinct homiletic approach to the preacher's performance, and each is prone to specific ethical challenges.

speaker. In practice if not theory, human bodies eclipse the Spirit's power, standing in for a Savior. And as any Catholic feminist will tell you, that sort of embodied idealism leads to trouble.

Metaphor One: Rhetoric as the Word's Persuasive Handmaid

It's not as though Calvin never gave advice to preachers. But his rhetorical advice is strangely ambivalent. On the one hand, he is like Paul. In his commentary on 1 Corinthians 1:17–18, Calvin states, "The preaching of Christ crucified is simple and unadorned, and hence it ought not to be obscured by false ornaments of speech."[29] While Calvin asserts that the Holy Spirit could make use of scholarly arts "founded on just principles," the goal for rhetoric is to "be in subjection to [the Word], yielding service to it, as a handmaid to her mistress."[30]

On the other hand, this handmaid wielded power. Calvin describes rhetoric's potency, often ascribing power to artful words and metaphors that would normally be ascribed to Holy Spirit. Figures of speech, for Calvin, are "living things full of hidden power which leave nothing in man untouched."[31] They "arouse the mind" and "penetrate the soul."[32] Simple exposition of a passage is not enough. Preachers "who want to discharge the ministry of the gospel aright learn not only to speak and declaim but also to penetrate into consciences, so that men may see Christ crucified and that His blood may flow."[33] Unlike a passive handmaid, the "good and faithful shepherd is not barely to expound the scripture, but . . . use earnestness and sharpness to give force and virtue to the Word of God."[34]

Calvin's description of rhetoric as the handmaid of truth has a long

29. John Calvin, "1 Corinthians 1:17–18," *Commentary on the Epistles of Paul the Apostle to the Corinthians* (Grand Rapids: Eerdmans, 1948), 76.

30. Calvin, "1 Corinthians 1:17–18," 75.

31. John Calvin, "Hebrews 4:11–13," *Commentary on the Epistle to the Hebrews* (Grand Rapids: Eerdmans, 1949), 102.

32. John Calvin, "True Partaking of the Flesh and Blood of Christ," in *Tracts Relating to the Reformation*, vol. 2 (Edinburgh: Calvin Translation Society, 1844), 567.

33. John Calvin, *The Epistles of the Apostle Paul to the Galatians, Ephesians, Philippians, and Colossians*, vol. 11 of *Calvin's New Testament Commentaries*, ed. David Torrance and T. J. Torrance (Grand Rapids: Eerdmans, 1973), 47.

34. John Calvin, *A Selection of the Most Celebrated Sermons of John Calvin, Minister of the Gospel, and One of the Principal Leaders in the Protestant Reformation to Which*

history in the Western tradition, going back to Aristotle's distinction between dialectic and rhetoric. Rhetoric, according to Aristotle, was defined as the ability to find, in each context, the appropriate "means of persuasion"—but had little to do with the discovery of content worth that persuasive effort.[35] Rhetoric, in other words, is contextual application, while dialectic deals with unchanging laws common to all.[36] This general attitude toward rhetoric was developed further in the work of Peter Ramus, who argued for a division between the five parts of ancient rhetoric, separating "invention and disposition"—the purview of dialectic and logic—from the lesser rhetorical arts of "style, delivery and memory."[37] The rationalism of the Enlightenment eclipsed linguistic ornamentation further.[38] But finally, this plain, theoretical style of argument was a "means of persuasion" in its own time and place. The goal of rhetoric—whether plain or ornate—was to persuade a particular audience of the validity of an asserted claim. Rhetoric was never understood to be truth itself, but it wielded the power to make truth convincing in the world. Whether in submissive silence or stylish ornamentation, rhetoric held the power to authenticate knowledge and transform hearts and minds.

In homiletics this separation between rhetoric and dialectic manifested itself in the confidence that one could extract the Word of God revealed in Scripture from one's own contextual communication and interpretation of that Word. Sermon preparation could be separated into two steps: (1) the extraction of the Word of God from its embeddedness in the rhetorical conventions of scriptural language and (2) the recontextu-

---

Is Prefixed a Biographical History of His Life (Philadelphia: Desilver, Thomas, 1834), 133–34.

35. Aristotle, *On Rhetoric: A Theory of Civic Discourse*, 2nd ed. (Oxford: Oxford University Press, 2006), 35.

36. McKeon traces this rigid border between rhetoric and dialectic through the thought of Boethius and forms of Scholasticism that made rhetoric a subordinate discipline to dialectic, since "unlike dialectic, grammar and rhetoric do not treat the nature of things, but . . . words significant by convention or context." See McKeon, "Rhetoric in the Middle Ages." McKeon, here, is quoting from Johannes Scotus Eriugena's *De divisione naturae*, Patrologia Latina 122, 4: 869–70.

37. François de Salignac de la Mothe-Fénelon, *Fenelon's Dialogues on Eloquence*, ed. and trans. Wilber Samuel Howell (Princeton: Princeton University Press, 1951), 10–11.

38. Francis Bacon, for example, developed a "scientific rhetoric." See James P. Zappen, "Francis Bacon and the Historiography of Scientific Rhetoric," *Rhetoric Review* 8, no. 1 (October 1989): 74–88.

alization of the derived core meaning of that Word. This way of thinking could result in a "restrained" approach to rhetorical speech, emphasizing the primacy of transcendent idea over contextual relevance.[39] But the opposite approach was as likely. In the American homiletic tradition, in particular, this division between rhetoric and theological revelation led to a handmaid that embodied Calvin's contradictory ambivalence toward rhetorical power. She was presented as submissively passive to the Word she served (in step one), but was responsible for giving "force," potency, and transformational appeal to that same Word (in step two).

One of the most significant homiletical tomes of nineteenth-century America—John Broadus's *Treatise on the Preparation and Delivery of Sermons*—serves as an example. Originally published in 1870, Broadus's work was influential enough in American homiletics that it went through four subsequent revisions—the latest, a significantly rewritten edition, published in 2004.[40] Written as a practical guide for preachers, the book, in more than five hundred pages, deals with issues of style, voice, and eloquence in the pulpit. It exemplifies a muscular pragmatism in American pulpit rhetoric in which eloquence is defined not by aesthetic rules but by the power it demonstrates in giving "impulse to the will."[41] In Ciceronian style, Broadus argues that true eloquence is power—and not simply power to move the emotions or delight the mind.[42] It causes people to act differently, to be different persons than before. Significantly,

---

39. Peter Adam describes Calvin's approach to emotional rhetorical appeals in this way in *Speaking God's Words: A Practical Theology of Preaching* (Vancouver: Regent College Publishing, 2004), 153. It is intriguing to note, however, how differently scholars like Michael Pasquarello characterize Calvin's rhetorical approach. Michael Pasquarello, *Sacred Rhetoric* (Grand Rapids: Eerdmans, 2005). Again, I think this points to unresolved tensions in Calvin's rhetorical practice—tensions that become increasingly polarized in the Protestant rhetorical tradition.

40. John A. Broadus, *On the Preparation and Delivery of Sermons*, 4th ed., ed. Vernon Stanfield (Vestavia Hills, AL: Solid Ground Christian Books, 2004). Stanfield adds and subtracts much from Broadus's original text, particularly amending the text's theological approach to rhetoric. To examine Broadus's original rhetorical approach, see *A Treatise on the Preparation and Delivery of Sermons, by John A. Broadus*, Michigan Historical Reprint Series (Ann Arbor: University of Michigan Library, 2006), a facsimile of the 1871 version.

41. Broadus, *Preparation and Delivery of Sermons*, 20.

42. Cicero, *On Oratory and Orators: With His Letters to Quintus and Brutus*, trans. J. S. Watson (Carbondale: Southern Illinois University Press, 1986), 69, argues that the goal of eloquent rhetorical performance is to "impel the audience whithersoever it inclines its force."

Broadus does not mention the power of the Holy Spirit anywhere in his opening discussion of rhetorical eloquence, nor indeed through the vast majority of the book.[43] Calvin believed that in sacramental practice, the believer experienced a spiritual ascension by the power of the Holy Spirit. Broadus describes a similar spiritual ascension during the sermon's proclamation. But in Broadus's description, the factors behind that ascension are the preacher's rhetorical gifts and the potency of the performative moment between preacher and congregation. He states that when a preacher "speaks to his fellow men, face to face, and electric sympathies flash to and fro between him and his hearers, . . . *they lift each other up*, higher and higher, into the intensest thought, and the most impassioned emotion—higher and higher, till they are borne as chariots of fire above the world."[44] According to Broadus, "There is [in preaching] a power to move men, to influence . . . life and destiny, such as no printed page can ever possess."[45] Broadus's preacher, though submissive to the "literal" truth of the Scriptures, is charged with a great task: making those ideas relevant, applicable, palatable, and transformative in his congregation. The responsibility is great, and the preacher must possess a number of innate and learned characteristics to meet the challenge. Broadus's preacher must possess "piety, natural gifts, knowledge, and skill."[46] Even his physical stamina is taken into account.[47] While the final paragraph of the book makes clear that the agency of the Holy Spirit has been assumed in Broadus's description of preacherly action, the preponderance of discussion on the preacher's virtues and vices makes his closing comments seem little more than an afterthought.

This separation between rhetoric and Word—representing in this case a demarcation between human and holy—raises the question of agency in the sermonic act. Who is mighty to save? Ironically, while the bracketing of rhetorical performance in deference to the revelation of the Word is meant to subjugate human gifts and context to transcendent

43. James Kay, *Slow of Speech and Unclean Lips: Contemporary Images of Preaching Identity*, ed. Robert Reid (Eugene, OR: Cascade, 2010), 15, notes that "the living God makes no appearance in Broadus's influential textbook until page 504."

44. Broadus, *Treatise*, 19, emphasis added. This image of the flying chariot is borrowed from an image in Plato's *Phaedrus*, trans. R. Hackforth (Cambridge: Cambridge University Press, 1952), 69.

45. Broadus, *Treatise*, 19.

46. Broadus, *Treatise*, 20.

47. Broadus, *Treatise*, 439. Broadus's preacher is, most certainly, a "he."

truth, in practice the human handmaid finds herself the agent of the congregation's spiritual ascent. That is, the congregation's spiritual transformation is dependent on the preacher's rhetorical action. Since the Word is absent and Other than the preacher's body, context, and voice, the preacher must face up to the challenge alone.

Though Broadus's classic demarcation between rhetoric and revelation has been eroded by the "rhetorical turn" of the twentieth century,[48] his division of labor between human and holy—and the polarities surrounding his understanding of preacherly agency—is alive and well. It can be seen in homiletic schools that have doubled down on the propositional perspicuity of Scripture's content. Peter Adam echoes Broadus's assumptions when he argues that it is possible to obediently teach a Scripture's singular meaning and, afterwards, in a second step "exhort" with persuasive passion.[49] But it is also seen in more subtle ways. David Buttrick's *Homiletic: Moves and Structures* is a postmodern attempt to equip the preacher with the skills of transformative persuasion through attention to how "sermons happen in consciousness."[50] Buttrick speaks from a startlingly different landscape than John Broadus, taking as his starting point the interconnection between subject and object, preacher and listener. The phenomenology of the sermon shapes not only his practice of preaching but his theology. For John Riggs, this creates a lack of clarity "as to what the sermon actually does."[51] For Buttrick, the moves and structures of preaching both create "a faith-world in human consciousness" and "mediate" God.[52] For Riggs, these are "theological 'apples and oranges.'" "If preaching tells a story in which Christians find their meaning in a faith-world," he explains, "then there need not be a transcendent reality related to and impinging on humanity."[53] And this is

48. Herbert Simons, *The Rhetorical Turn: Invention and Persuasion in the Conduct of Inquiry* (Chicago: University of Chicago Press, 1990), vii, discusses Richard Rorty's use of this term and its potential to move beyond "objectivist credos."

49. See Peter Adam's discomfort with Bullinger's formulation that "the preaching of the Word of God is the Word of God," in his *Speaking God's Words: A Practical Theology of Preaching* (Vancouver: Regent College Publishing, 2004), 118. See also his description of the preacher's surgeon-like skill (p. 142).

50. David Buttrick, *Homiletic: Moves and Structures* (Philadelphia: Fortress Press, 1987), xii.

51. John Riggs, review of *Homiletic: Moves and Structures*, by David Buttrick, *Journal of Religion* 69, no. 2 (April 1989): 271.

52. Buttrick, *Homiletic*, 20, 250.

53. Riggs, review of *Homiletic*, 271.

the challenge in Buttrick's work. Richard Lischer notes that given all that is "riding on the language of the sermon," Buttrick's "exhaustive guide to its right deployment" makes perfect sense.[54] But does the preacher's careful deploying of linguistic laws stand in for the work of the Spirit? Buttrick is a good Reformed preacher, so the Holy Spirit does arrive on the scene at the end of part one, but it is unclear how that Spirit relates to the power of language to create a new reality. In Buttrick's attempt to find universally applicable moves to shape a listener's consciousness, the border between the transformative performance of the preacher and the transformative performance of God collapses.

For homileticians like Lucy Atkinson Rose, ethical questions follow. In her book *Sharing the Word: Preaching in the Roundtable Pulpit*, she argues that placing the transformation of the congregation into the preacher's job description is "potentially dangerous," placing too much control in the preacher's hands.[55] The preacher cannot "evoke" the Word through her rhetorical mediation; she cannot "facilitate an experience, an event, a meeting, or a happening for the worshipers."[56] When a rigid boundary is maintained between the preacher's rhetoric and the revealed Word, the relational ontology at the heart of Protestant understandings of humanity is torn apart, and the implication arises that the human person has power to transform the congregation apart from the Word—taking on the role of the Spirit. Even when this power is understood as a product of sanctified obedience, as in the work of evangelical homileticians like Alex Montoya (or other Christian rhetoricians who stress the importance of *ethos*), *unction* is not understood as being "poured out on whomever [the Spirit] wills."[57] It can be "taken,"[58] and "learned."[59] The obedient

54. Richard Lischer, *The Company of Preachers* (Grand Rapids: Eerdmans, 2002), 337.

55. Lucy Atkinson Rose, *Sharing the Word: Preaching in the Roundtable Church* (Louisville: Westminster John Knox, 1997), 133.

56. Rose, *Sharing the Word*, 60.

57. Alex Montoya, *Preaching with Passion* (Grand Rapids: Kregel Academic & Professional, 2007), 34.

58. Ralph L. Lewis, *Speech for Persuasive Preaching* (Wilmore, KY: Asbury Theological Seminary, 1968). This speech text from a previous generation argues that one can "get unction" and speaks of the importance of "taking," as opposed to "receiving," the gift of the Holy Spirit (8). Despite its provocative language, the trajectory of this text is similar to Montoya's point that submissive holiness precedes—and engenders—spiritual power.

59. Montoya, *Preaching*, 18.

handmaid, insofar as she engenders a response from the congregation, becomes the measure and guarantee of revelation.

"Did your preaching fill the pews? Did people tune in? Did it *work*?" When rhetoric is imaged as a "powerful handmaid," such questions become the primary gauge of a preacher's success. When rhetoric's primary function becomes the exertion of power, performances that appease and entertain become a preacher's bread and butter. But the result can also be performances that manipulate and divide. Giving "impulse to the will" is an end that can justify any number of means.

Metaphor Two: Rhetoric as the Word Made Flesh

In his book *On Christian Doctrine*, Augustine describes the boundary between Word and words in the sermon through the metaphor of the incarnation. Taking for granted that thought can take on the body of speech but remain unchanged, Augustine draws this parallel: "In the same way, the word of God became flesh in order to live in us but was unchanged."[60] The "Word made flesh" would become one of the most commonly invoked metaphors for the preacher's performance. This language of incarnation would also dissolve the border between the Word's content and the preacher's experience. If the model of the powerful handmaid idealizes preacherly *agency*, asking the preacher to take over for God in transforming her people, this second model dissolves the borders of a preacher's *identity*, substituting the preacher's flesh for Christ's own.[61]

Give credit where credit is due. The benefits of the "Word made flesh" metaphor for pulpit rhetoric are many. First and foremost, the metaphor grounds rhetoric's justification in Christian soil, not in Greek

---

60. Augustine, *On Christian Teaching*, trans. R. P. H. Green (Oxford: Oxford University Press, 1997), 13. He relates this point explicitly to the work of preaching, quoting John 1:14 for good measure.

61. Paul Ricoeur's *Oneself as Another*, trans. Kathleen Blamey (Chicago: University of Chicago Press, 2002), 19, discusses the ways that agency and identity are interconnected, but not identical, and his argument has been helpful to the structure of my thinking. To do "practical philosophy"—to take account of performing bodies in the world—is to honor the "genuine polysemy inherent in the question" of the self, while at the same time, challenging the "disintegration of the self pursued by . . . deconstruction." This insistence on the uneasy but necessary borders between these categories resonates, in my mind, with a Protestant ontology grounded in relationship—though Ricoeur, of course, makes no reference to the action of the Spirit.

philosophy. Rhetoric is not necessary because Aristotle said so but because it is the nature of God's revelation to accommodate the Word to creation.[62] Second, using the metaphor of the incarnation to describe pulpit speech underscores a theological truth often overlooked by those who view rhetoric as persuasive skill alone. Christ is present in the sermon, mediated to the people of God as in the sacraments themselves. Finally, the "Word made Flesh" model maintains the agency of God as primary. Something miraculous occurs in the act of proclamation. As Karl Barth put it, the revelation of God is not made powerful by the "willing and doing" of humankind but is "primarily and decisively" God's own act.[63]

For his own part, Barth is careful, in laying out his understanding of the threefold form of the Word of God in his *Church Dogmatics*, not to collapse revelation, Scripture, and proclamation—despite his insistence that "in the event of God's Word" revelation, Scripture, and proclamation are "literally" one.[64] His model for their relation is sacramental, in the eventful Reformed sense of that word, rather than incarnational.[65] But over the course of the twentieth century, across a broad swath of theological perspectives, the model of the incarnation became theological shorthand for describing the miraculous nature of the sermon.[66] Rather than testifying powerfully to an absent Christ (i.e., rhetoric as persuasion), the sermon is understood to be the *embodiment* of the Word—or in more radically immanent versions, *as* the Word itself. The sermon's

62. This theme of accommodation also occurs in Calvin's understanding of sacramental signs. See Wright, "Calvin's Accommodating God."

63. Barth, *Church Dogmatics*, I/4.1, 93.

64. Barth, *Church Dogmatics*, I/4.3, 113.

65. See, for example, how Barth, *Church Dogmatics*, I/1.4, 94, distinguishes his perspective from Roman Catholic understandings of transubstantiation. Barth does dance this incarnational line in his use of Christ's "vulnerable" humanity as a metaphor for proclamation, but finally, his understanding of the boundary between preaching and revelation is not based on the hypostatic union but on God's promise to condescend to human performances of obedience. If there is transparency between preaching and revelation for Barth, it is the result of God's promise and the "true service" of God on the preacher's part (94).

66. I would distinguish here between projects that work with the incarnation as a *metaphor* for the sermon and those that use the incarnation as a *model* for the relationship between human and divine in the sermon. The former—as seen in projects like Charles Bartow's *God's Human Speech: A Practical Theology of Proclamation* (Grand Rapids: Eerdmans, 1997)—maintain an uneasiness between the categories of word and Words more indicative of Reformed sacramentology.

body—by the miraculous power of God and the potent characteristics of language—becomes contiguous with the flesh of Christ.

These twentieth-century formulations stem from many sources and overlap in complex ways. One stream grew from the New Hermeneutic, a theology of proclamation growing out of a Heideggerian understanding of linguistic power.[67] Another grew from a desire to find a middle ground from which to face the culture wars of the twentieth century and the increasingly entrenched debates about the primacy of revelation over and against the primacy of human experience.[68] Still others grew from a new attentiveness in the secular academy concerning the role of performance in mediating truth.[69] But whether in the work of Southern Baptists, evangelicals, or New Homiletic icons, rhetoric was given more than theological significance. Rhetoric became contiguous with the Word—or, more precisely, the Word revealed in flesh for us.

The homiletic theology of Fred Craddock serves as an example. Craddock goes further in his proposal for inductive preaching than pointing out the uneasy border between *method* and *message* in the sermon. In his discussion of whether or not the Word of God is *extra nos*, Craddock makes an analogy between the nature of human language generally and the Word that is Christ. Words are not meant to exist in isolation. They are meant to communicate. To describe Christ as *Word*, Craddock argues, means that it is in "sharing [the Word] that the Word has its existence."[70]

67. Gerhard Ebeling, *Theology and Proclamation: A Discussion with Rudolph Bultmann* (New York: HarperCollins, 1966). In stressing the form and content of Jesus's teaching for proclamation, Ebeling draws on the semiotic insights of Heidegger, arguing that proclamation has the character of a powerful "Word-event." For Ebeling, when a preacher teaches like Jesus, the Word takes on flesh and potency in the present—giving new meaning to Bultmann's claim that Christ is "resurrected into the sermon."

68. Clyde E. Fant, *Preaching for Today* (San Francisco: HarperOne, 1987), xiii, frames his "incarnational" approach as mediating between "Barth and Brunner," and between systematic and practical theology.

69. Jana Childers, *Performing the Word: Preaching as Theatre* (Nashville: Abingdon Press, 1998). In her discussion of the "echoes" between human and divine creativity, Childers draws on the work of secular performance studies scholar Alla Bozarth-Campbell, *The Word's Body: An Incarnational Aesthetic of Interpretation* (Tuscaloosa: University of Alabama Press, 1980), 23-24. Note also Jan Childers, "Seeing Jesus: Preaching as an Incarnational Act," in *Purposes of Preaching*, ed. Jana Childers (St. Louis: Chalice Press, 2004), 46.

70. Fred B. Craddock, *As One without Authority* (Enid, OK: Phillips University Press, 1971), 71.

Craddock affirms in a theoretical way that Christ is *extra nos*, but in practice the Word of God finds its identity in the communication between speaker and the hearer.[71] The Word for us, in Craddock's view, is contiguous with our own bodily communication of the gospel. In his book *Preaching Jesus*, Charles Campbell argues that Craddock, "despite his disclaimers, locates authority in individual human experience," and in so doing fuses the Word of God with "the presuppositions of modern, liberal American culture."[72] The Word of God becomes existential, interior, and dangerously malleable. It has little authority to challenge and critique the status quo. Equally dangerous, the particularity and limits of the preacher are ignored, leading to a kind of hegemony of experience.

Like the preaching of the powerful handmaid, this kind of incarnational preaching also has deep historical roots in the American homiletic landscape. John Broadus's pragmatic understanding of rhetoric as power represents one school of American thought. The romanticism of nineteenth-century preacher Phillips Brooks represents another. Best known for his influential definition of proclamation as "truth through personality" in the 1877 Beecher Lectures, Brooks argues that "truth has embodied itself in preaching."[73]

Those who heard Brooks speak attested to his power and passion in the pulpit. One characteristic comment explains, "He spoke less about truths of God and more as though he were speaking from God."[74] Jana Childers argues that Brooks's understanding of embodied truth is a powerful antidote to an understanding of rhetorical performance as "wrapping" or "presentation."[75] She points to Brooks's belief that there are only two kinds of preachers: "The gospel has come over one of them and reaches us tinged and flavored with his superficial characteristics, belittled by his littleness. The gospel comes through the other and we

71. This is quite different from saying that the Spirit mediates the Word in and through the communicative act.

72. Charles Campbell, *Preaching Jesus: New Directions for Homiletics in Hans Frei's Postliberal Theology* (Grand Rapids: Eerdmans, 1997), 130, 143.

73. Phillips Brooks, quoted in Charles W. Fuller, *The Trouble with "Truth through Personality": Phillips Brooks, Incarnation, and the Evangelical Boundaries of Preaching* (Eugene, OR: Wipf & Stock, 2010), 68.

74. Fuller, *Trouble with "Truth through Personality,"* 24.

75. Childers, "Seeing Jesus," 45.

receive it impressed and winged with all the earnestness and strength that there is in him."[76] When we see this preacher, we "see Jesus."[77]

In his critique of Brooks's theology, Charles Fuller acknowledges that a broad spectrum of American homileticians has built on this premise—from both evangelical and liberal traditions. In homiletic theology, Brooks's incarnational understanding of the preacher's body and character has been used to stress authenticity and integrity, contextual relevance, and the "sacramental" nature of proclamation.[78] Fuller, however, points to the romantic theology that undergirds Brooks's homiletic, his belief in the "essential goodness of the human soul" and his understanding of "nature and history as expressions of the Divine mind."[79] Brooks asserts that "the great truth of the Incarnation" is "that a perfectly pure, obedient, humanity might utter divinity, might be a transparent medium through which even God might show Himself [sic]."[80] In Fuller's view, this understanding leads to one of the prime deficiencies of Brooks's approach and the great danger of the incarnational model: "the preacher becomes the Word."[81] The flesh of the preacher is not held in Spirit-mediated relation with the Word made flesh. The flesh of the preacher *becomes* the Word's flesh, eclipsing the particularity of Jesus as well as the

76. Phillips Brooks, *Eight Lectures on Preaching* (London: SPCK, 1959), 8.

77. This, in fact, is the title of Childers's chapter, "Seeing Jesus," 39. To be fair, Childers stresses the "throughness" of the Word rather than the preacher's hypostatic union with the Word. Christ is revealed "through" us rather than "incarnated" by us. This is a helpful distinction in my view, though it suggests that the metaphor of the incarnation does not describe her understanding of the relationship between human and divine in the sermon most precisely. Tellingly, Childers often leans toward a metaphor suggesting pregnancy, as in her assertion that "the Word . . . impregnates us through the ear" (Childers, *Preaching as Theatre*, 26), or in her title *Birthing the Sermon: Women Preachers on the Creative Process* (St. Louis: Chalice Press, 2001).

78. Fuller lifts up homileticians as diverse as Stephen Olford, Leonora Tubbs-Tisdale, and Will Willimon as drawing on Brooks's incarnational premise. See Fuller, *Trouble with "Truth through Personality,"* 91-92. Again, each of these authors use Brook's incarnational model differently, some with greater caution and care than others. Fuller's larger project is to argue for the primacy of propositional truth in the sermon, and therefore he does not distinguish between "sacramental" and "incarnational" understandings of preaching—a distinction I find significant. The Reformed tradition, in particular, has conceived of the borders surrounding each quite differently.

79. Fuller, *Trouble with "Truth through Personality,"* 34, 14.

80. Fuller, *Trouble with "Truth through Personality,"* 52.

81. Fuller, *Trouble with "Truth through Personality,"* 96.

finite particularity of the preacher. The role of the Holy Spirit, which the Reformers found necessary in maintaining the uneasy borders of human and divine in the sacrament, is noticeably eclipsed.

The danger here is not solely theological. Like the imbalances of power that Lucy Atkinson Rose perceived in *transformational* approaches to pulpit rhetoric, ignoring the particularities and limits of human identity has ethical consequences—a danger not confined to the nineteenth century. Contemporary arguments concerning the hegemonic category of "experience" are a case in point. White feminism has struggled with its own romantic notions of *women's experience*, coming under fierce, justifiable critique from womanist and liberationist perspectives. Jacquelyn Grant gives a classic summary: "When theologians speak about women's experience as the source for doing feminist theology, it is necessary to specify which women's experience is being referred to, for the . . . experiences of White women and Black women have been far from the same."[82] Grant's request for specificity is part of the larger task of dismantling "the narrow frames" that norm and obscure the category of "woman."[83] Whenever the flesh of one person is collapsed into the flesh of another—when difference is not acknowledged—marginalization and erasure result. To make the flesh and bodily experience of the preacher coterminous with the Word of God is to suggest that the particularity of a preacher's experience is transcendently applicable across the uneasy borders of contextual identity. In erasing the particularity of Christ's flesh as Other, and in claiming that flesh as her own, the preacher steps outside her finite, human boundary and risks the erasure of the human diversity around her. She risks speaking for, naming, and prioritizing "experience" in ways that justify herself and her context.

The challenge that postmodernity and womanist thought have raised for feminism is how to deal with this uneasy border of testifying about another. How does one claim rhetorical testimony as a theological source but not collapse the boundaries of the self and other in ways that suggest a "God's-eye view?"[84] It is a question that confronts preachers in relation to their human brothers and sisters and in relation to God. More

---

82. Jacquelyn Grant, *White Women's Christ and Black Women's Jesus: Feminist Christology and Womanist Response* (Chico, CA: Scholars Press, 1989), 199.

83. Janell Hobson, ed., *Are All the Women Still White? Rethinking Race, Expanding Feminisms* (New York: SUNY Press, 2016), 2.

84. Mary McClintock Fulkerson, *Changing the Subject: Women's Discourses and Feminist Theology* (Minneapolis: Fortress Press, 1994), 384.

than this, ignoring difference in one sphere leads to ignoring difference in the other. Mary McClintock Fulkerson argues that as feminist theology has grappled with the limitations and necessity of "experience" as a category, it has found itself extending one of the basic tenets underlying Protestantism's *opus operantis* understanding: "God alone saves."[85] There is no easy union of fleshly things— not with humans and certainly not with God. There are uneasy cracks between our performing bodies, contexts, and discourses, which is part of what it means to have bodies in the first place.

Metaphor Three: Rhetoric as Cultural Mother Tongue

George Lindbeck's *The Nature of Doctrine: Religion and Theology in a Postliberal Age* was written to provide a responsible ethic for interreligious dialogue in a pluralistic world. It would become one of the late twentieth century's most influential theological responses to postmodernity. Mapping the shifting borders between religious practice and theological doctrine in his own field, Lindbeck points out that the cognitive-propositional mode of theology, a model of rigid boundaries between truth, context, and application, has been on the defensive ever since "Kant's revolutionary Copernican 'turn to the subject.'"[86] Lindbeck also notes the inadequacy of the "experiential-expressivist" model in ecumenical and interreligious conversation (i.e., the prioritizing of inner, individual experience). The powerful handmaid and Word made flesh metaphors I've described echo these propositional and experiential theological models respectively.

Lindbeck wants to try something different. He proposes a cultural-linguistic model of theological knowledge, which prioritizes the "external features of a religion" over and against one's internal experiences.[87] These external features are the "medium in which one moves, a set of skills that one employs in the living of one's life."[88] Drawing on the se-

---

85. Fulkerson, *Changing the Subject*, 370.

86. George A. Lindbeck, *The Nature of Doctrine: Religion and Theology in a Postliberal Age* (Louisville: Westminster John Knox, 1984), 21. Lindbeck's "turn to the subject" phrase is taken from Bernard Lonergan's *The Subject* (Milwaukee: Marquette University Press, 1968).

87. Lindbeck, *Nature of Doctrine*, 34.

88. Lindbeck, *Nature of Doctrine*, 35.

miotic work of Wittgenstein[89] and J. L. Austin,[90] as well as anthropologists like Clifford Geertz,[91] Lindbeck describes the "ontological truth of religious utterances" in terms of how they "function . . . in constituting a form of life" for a given community.[92] If religious practices and performances are the vocabulary of the community, doctrine serves as a kind of communal "grammar," offering the community an understanding of how their language works.[93] Meaning, in other words, is "immanent" within the linguistic system.[94]

In an attempt to mediate between the borders of propositional truth and human experience, Lindbeck prioritizes a different border: the borders of ecclesial practice. For Lindbeck, it is not the individual or the disembodied propositions of the community that carry theological meaning but the embodied performances of religious communities over time. It is the "cultural-linguistic" expression of the community that defines truth. This turn toward the community and its formative practices stresses the "performativity" of doctrine and the contextuality of knowledge, lifting up tradition as the mediator of the Word. But tradition is not sifted out of lived experience. It has an "aesthetic character" and can be found in the rhetoric of an individual native to that community—one who is "linguistically competent" in that communal world.[95] Tellingly, for Lindbeck, to be "Spirit-filled" is to be located "in the mainstream rather than in isolated backwaters" and is able to be "empirically recognizable" by "objective tests" of linguistic competence. The ideal, for Lindbeck, is to find "flexibly devout" practitioners who have "interiorized the grammar of

89. Lindbeck acknowledges the work of W. D. Hudson, *Wittgenstein and Religious Belief* (London: Macmillan, 1975), on his thought. Wittgenstein's "contention that private languages are logically impossible" is particularly useful for Lindbeck's argument. See Lindbeck, *Nature of Doctrine*, 38.

90. Lindbeck uses Austin's understanding of "performatory" language to make the point that "religious utterance . . . acquires the propositional truth of ontological correspondence only insofar as it is a performance . . . which helps create that correspondence." See Lindbeck, *Nature of Doctrine*, 65. In other words, language helps to create the truth of which it speaks. See John L. Austin, "Performative Utterances," in *Philosophical Papers*, 2nd ed. (Oxford: Clarendon Press, 1970), 232–52.

91. See Clifford Geertz, "Religion as a Cultural System," in *The Interpretation of Cultures* (New York: Basic Books, 1973), 87–125.

92. Lindbeck, *Nature of Doctrine*, 65

93. Lindbeck, *Nature of Doctrine*, 79.

94. Lindbeck, *Nature of Doctrine*, 114.

95. Lindbeck, *Nature of Doctrine*, 130.

their religion" to such an extent that they can apply that grammar to new situations and reliably judge the consequences on the basis of communal criteria.[96] They are adept speakers of an ecclesial mother tongue. It is a description of Spirit-filled persons that sounds very much like the main-stream communities that fill flexibly devout mainline churches, presumably similar to the congregations that shaped Lindbeck's heritage. One does wonder whether it adequately describes the spiritual importance of "peculiar speech" in minoritized Christian traditions or in thriving Pentecostal communions.[97]

Despite the performativity that grounds Lindbeck's understanding of truth, locating meaning within cultural-linguistic practice leads to problems. James Kay has pointed out that—despite its pushback against the experiential-expressive model—Lindbeck's cultural-linguistic approach collapses the borders between human and divine *identity* in a way similar to homiletic approaches that equate language or narrative with the identity of the "Word made flesh."[98] Instead of language being rooted in the poetic power of individual experience, of course, Lindbeck's understanding of language (and, therefore his understanding of the Word) is grounded in the linguistic practices of the church. For all practical purposes, Christ exists entirely within the borders of ecclesial life.[99]

The borders between human and divine *agency* also disintegrate. David Lose argues that from a postliberal perspective, faith is less about "trusting confidence" and is "closer to the Aristotelian notion of virtue or *habitus*."[100] The agency of the Spirit is outsourced to the agency of competent practitioners who have mastered the intricacies of being "flexibly devout." For preachers, these theological gaps have practical significance. They play out in the ongoing negotiation between one's self and one's expected *communal role*.

96. Lindbeck, *Nature of Doctrine*, 100.

97. Cheryl Bridges-Johns, "Epiphanies of Fire: Para-Modernist Preaching in a Postmodern World" (paper presented at the annual meeting of the North American Academy of Homiletics, Santa Fe, NM, 1996), 7.

98. See Hans W. Frei, *The Identity of Jesus Christ* (Eugene, OR: Wipf & Stock, 1997).

99. James Kay, *Slow of Speech and Unclean Lips: Contemporary Images of Preaching Identity*, ed. Robert Reid (Eugene, OR: Cascade, 2010), 118, specifically protests Frei's argument that the community's "story" of Christ—which Frei equates with the gospel narrative—is "equivalent to real presence."

100. David J. Lose, *Confessing Jesus Christ: Preaching in a Postmodern World* (Grand Rapids: Eerdmans, 2003), 121.

Charles Campbell's appropriation of postliberal theology for homiletics underscores one of the great insights of Lindbeck's framework—an insight embedded in the Reformers' sacramentology as well.[101] Materiality, community, and performance matter to the mediation of the Word. Careful reading of Scripture with believing brothers and sisters cannot be shortchanged. The text matters, just as the physical eating of the bread in Communion matters. But even Campbell points out that Lindbeck's model of Christian community "does not take sufficiently seriously the social, historical and material dimensions of culture."[102] While Lindbeck moves away from idealizations of propositional knowledge and individual experience, he replaces them with an idealization of the community of faith—and such idealizations are not only dangerous theologically, they are dangerous in the day-to-day negotiation of common life.

In her article "Exploring the Text-Practice Interface: Acquiring the Virtue of Hermeneutical Modesty," Sally A. Brown argues that there is an uneasy border between texts and communal interpretive practices that can never be "master[ed]."[103] Brown echoes William Placher's concern that in many proposals equating ecclesial rhetorical practice with truth, the nouns employed are "in the singular."[104] Terms like the *community*, *story*, and *tradition* work to exclude or erase difference within the community—including the difference between the preacher and community she serves. It is seen in preachers who speak with a "stained-glass" tenor—or with the self-conscious nervousness of one looking for one's voice. It is seen in the preacher who worries about the range of his register after being told by his parishioners that he sounds "too gay."[105] The definition of authenticity in the pulpit is a complex one—but when the vocation of proclaiming the Word is collapsed into the cultural-linguistic practice of a community, there is little space for the particularity of the preacher's body within the role. There is also

101. Campbell focuses his attention on the work of Hans Frei, in particular, but takes pains to underscore Lindbeck's influence on Frei's narrative understanding. See Campbell, *Preaching Jesus*, 63–82.

102. Campbell, *Preaching Jesus*, 80.

103. Sally A. Brown, "Exploring the Text-Practice Interface: Acquiring the Virtue of Hermeneutical Modesty," *Theology Today* 66, no. 3 (October 2009): 291.

104. Brown, "Exploring the Text-Practice Interface," 286–87.

105. This true story was shared by a recent student who had been given this unhelpful feedback by a congregant in his practical church.

little space for the prophetic Other of the Word to address the church from the outside and decenter practices that have lost their vulnerable, Spirit-mediated character.

The Missing Body (and Bodies)

Each of these metaphors struggles to image the role and function of the preacher's body in Protestant preaching, and each has influenced major schools of homiletic thought and practice. But each leaves a particular body underexplored in the preacher's act: the body of Christ. I'm not referring to Paul's ecclesial metaphor here (1 Cor. 12) but to Christ's risen person. The Reformers thought long and hard on the nature of Christ's resurrected body, and while they had distinct interpretations of that body's nature, all of them asserted its import. More significantly, none identified that body as coterminous with the church or the soul of the believer.[106] The body of Christ was particular, permeable, and provisional. It was actively performing in the world, which meant no human body could substitute. Humans could only mediate that body through Spirit-empowered acts of faith. And yet in the homiletic metaphors described, Christ's body is collapsed into the preacher's experience, displaced by ecclesial tradition, or left in safe quarantine as preachers do the dirty work of rhetoric alone. The borders between earth and heaven are not opened by the Spirit but torn apart by a powerful handmaid, dissolved in immaculate flesh, or bridged by the tradition and tongue of a Mother Church.

This language, of course, intentionally evokes the idealized traditions surrounding the person of Mary mentioned at the start of this chapter. I do not use the language to belabor a critique of Catholic mariology. Those critiques are most effectively raised by Catholic feminists themselves. Instead, I use the language to alert Protestant homiletics to idealizations in our own rhetorical traditions. I use the language to underscore the resonances between descriptors of the church's *perfect woman*

---

106. Thomas Davis, *This Is My Body: The Presence of Christ in Reformation Thought* (Grand Rapids: Baker Academic, 2008), 158, argues that Zwingli's perspective is more complicated than it is often made out to be, discussing a kind of "functional" rather than "substantial" presence of Christ's natural body—brought about through the action of faith-filled contemplation. The gathered community does not substitute for Christ, nor are they abandoned by him.

and the church's *perfect preachers*. The connection may seem strange at first. Homiletics has a long history of excluding women from the pulpit. But the connection is part of Western philosophy's DNA.

In her article on the deep connections in Western thought between rhetoric's persuasive power and the female body, Jane Sutton traces the metaphor of "proper rhetoric" and "proper woman" from ancient Greece through the Enlightenment. She compares the tradition's fear and fascination with rhetorical persuasion to its fierce control and categorization of the gendered body. Despite the ubiquity of this "proper woman" metaphor, women themselves were not deemed properly persuasive or virtuous enough to be appropriate rhetorical instruments. If appropriate rhetoric was idealized and imaged as the silent, submissive woman, women who dared to speak had already failed.[107] Such contradictions and exclusionary tendencies are embedded in any rhetorical model that standardizes performative practice, and feminists have worked hard to distance themselves from such idealizations.[108]

Finally, more than Christ's body has gone missing in these idealizations. The diverse bodies of fully human preachers are missing as well. To *idealize* and to *ignore* are two ways of saying the same thing. It was not so long ago that one teacher of pulpit performance argued that to be sufficiently "persuasive," rhetoric must be reclaimed from the "distortions of old maids and effeminate men."[109] It is still argued, in various traditions, that women cannot act *in persona Christi capitis* because their female flesh cannot embody the Word.[110] And, as scholars like Musa Dube insist, the hegemonic influence of the Western missionary project

107. Jane Sutton, "The Taming of the Polos/Polis: Rhetoric as an Achievement without Woman," in *Contemporary Rhetorical Theory: A Reader*, ed. John Louis Lucaites, Celeste Michelle Condit, and Sally Caudill (New York: Guilford Press, 1998), 101–21.

108. Andrea A. Lunsford and Cheryl Glenn, "On Rhetoric and Feminism: Forging Alliances," in *Landmark Essays on Rhetoric and Feminism 1973–2000*, ed. Cheryl Glenn and Andrea A. Lunsford (New York: Routledge, 2015), 13, describe the attempts of feminist rhetoricians to build an "alternative to agonistic rhetoric through strategic use of speech, silence and resistance guided by nonviolent principles."

109. Lewis, *Speech for Persuasive Preaching*, 8. Lewis's book was published in 1968 and can still be found in seminary libraries.

110. Scott P. Richert, "Can a Woman Be a Priest in the Catholic Church?," *Learn Religions,* updated August 7, 2018, https://www.learnreligions.com/woman-as-priest-in-catholic-church-542111.

continues in the priority given to so-called first-world perspectives and practices in theological institutions.[111]

When I teach these metaphors in my classes, I never know what to focus on first: how these metaphors have been used to exclude and marginalize human bodies within and outside of Christian communities, or how these metaphors fail theologically to communicate the richness of the Reformers' sacramental vision. The two are intimately related. When the particular, permeable, provisional body of the risen Christ is marginalized in our theological metaphors for preaching, bodies within Christ's church and bodies of Christian preachers are also silenced.

What Is Your False Shadow?

Jane Sutton concludes her article on rhetoric's complicated history by expressing her nervousness about working within the rhetorical tradition at all, even as her work as a scholar demands it. "It asks," she states, "that I write with an eraser."[112] Sutton's dilemma is shared by women preachers who claim a vocational call long denied them—or homileticians who want to "start with the body" in the teaching of preaching. Preachers soon discover that the shadow of a "proper woman" is waiting for them in the pulpit, "an idealization that is the other side of tyranny."[113] The first step in being overshadowed by the Spirit is leaving these false shadows behind.

Here's the question I give my students: *What is your false shadow?*

What is the shadow of what you "should be" that holds you back from vulnerable, risky relation with the risen Christ? What is your dependence of choice when the Spirit's shadow seems too costly or unreliable? Is it the metaphor of the *powerfully passive handmaid*—the perfect exegete whose performance is the Word's "special sauce"? Are you the preacher who would never dream of saying that your body matters when interpreting Holy Scripture—but blames herself when that Word doesn't transform? You brush off praise with self-deprecating speed, but your rhetorical backpack is full of tricks and tips—ways to be just a little more powerful, a little more relevant, a little more in control of the congregation's

111. Musa Dube, "Curriculum Transformation: Dreaming of Decolonization," in *Border Crossings: Cross-Cultural Hermeneutics*, ed. D. N. Premnath (Maryknoll, NY: Orbis, 2007).

112. Sutton, "The Taming of the Polos/Polis," 121.

113. Mary Gordon, quoted in Johnson, *Truly Our Sister*, 12.

response. You are a handmaid carrying the weight of eternity on your shoulders. The Word has spoken, and your impossible job is to convince the world that it's true. Even on the weeks you deliver the goods, how do you keep living up to the hype?

Or perhaps your shadow is the looming self-authorization of your own experience: your own *immaculate flesh*. It is not that you are more powerful than your congregation, but your experience is a little more . . . divinely transparent. Your narrative, body, and voice have the power to transcend divides and to heal. If you can just be authentic enough. If you can just be virtuous enough. If you can just be holy enough. Let me be clear. I have known Christian preachers who live as self-sacrificial witnesses to Christian faithfulness. They believe their bodily witness matters, and I do too. But their bodily witness does not have salvific power, and that witness does not authorize or justify their preaching. Preachers are not called because they are purer than the rest of their congregations, just as preachers are not called because their prayers are more powerful than those from the pew. The cost of believing otherwise is dear. Preachers who base their callings on their purity spend their ministries in self-justification, hiding, and denial. Or they simply walk away.

There is one final shadow, of course. This one is particularly strong for students in the middle of their theological education, but it can linger for years into a preacher's ministry. Perhaps your temptation is not to be more powerful or purer than your congregation. Perhaps it is simply to please your congregation. Perhaps your shadow is the embodiment of tradition—the *protector of the mother tongue*. It is your job to guard the community's language, fulfill their expectations, and uphold their cultural-religious practices. Your job is to be the example that doesn't make anyone who matters nervous. And part of the job is knowing who matters. It is not your job to rock the boat or push the envelope. It is your job to be fluent—to speak the language, share the stories, follow the rules, and pass those rules along. It is your job to embody your expected role.

What is your false shadow? I ask. *What keeps you from being, first and foremost, yourself?*[114]

And remarkable conversation follows. My students don't need coaxing. They know the shadows that make them jump.

What would it mean to step out from under these shadows, I continue, *and be overshadowed by the Spirit instead?*

114. A paraphrase of Johnson's hope for Mary.

It's as hard a question as the question about "starting with the body."
And the room grows quickly silent.

Starting with the Body of the Word

I know where I would start.

I would start with the body.

But because of rhetoric's dangerous deliveries and false shadows,
for me, "starting with the body" means *starting with the body of Christ*.
More precisely, starting with the body in the teaching of preaching means
starting with the inaccessible and necessary body of the Word, a body
that is absent in text and sermon, and yet present through the power of
the Spirit of God. It means starting with one's corresponding limitations,
one's weakness rather than one's strength. It means recognizing that one
is not only separated from Christ because of his divinity. One is also separated from Christ by his humanity (i.e., his localized, bordered, human
flesh). There is no unmediated access to Christ's body, just as, finally,
there is no unmediated access to the human bodies that surround us.
To start from the vulnerability of this place points one toward the messy
work of interpretation and performances without guarantees.[115] But to
do otherwise risks standing in shadows of essentialized, idealized bodies
that resemble neither Word, nor preacher, nor community of faith. They
are shadows as dangerous to Protestant understandings of grace as they
are to feminist iconoclasm.

To faithfully proclaim the Word, a Shadow of a different order is
required.

115. *Vulnerability* is Barth's word. See his *Church Dogmatics*, I/1, 94.

CHAPTER 3

....

Starting with the Body—the Resurrected Body

We should be asking ourselves the same sorts of questions when we write our texts . . . as we do in living our lives. How to dismantle the world that is built to accommodate only some bodies?

Sarah Ahmed, *Living a Feminist Life*

So, what does "starting with the body of Christ" mean?

It sounds pious enough but also rife with theological speculation. The entire question seems above our pay grade. Whose version of "Christ's body" are we talking about? The Reformers never reached a consensus. There is some *particular, permeable, provisional* common ground in Protestant understandings of Christ's risen person, but anyone who's compared *ubiquity* with *real presence* knows there are also wide differences.[1] Describing the nature of Christ's resurrected flesh has been the subject of extensive, esoteric debate, and it has significant christological implications. Those debates are not unimportant—but grounding a theology of pulpit performance in the crosshairs of those distinctions seems circular at best and divisive at worst. It also seems disconnected from the work of preaching. As a homiletic instructor, I'd like a method with more descriptive grit. James Kay argues, "Performance needs a theological compass and theology needs a performative

---

1. For a concise account of these differences, see David Steinmetz, "The Eucharist and the Identity of Jesus in the Early Reformation," in *Seeking the Identity of Jesus,* ed. Beverly Roberts Gaventa and Richard B. Hays (Grand Rapids: Eerdmans, 2008).

55

lens."[2] It's not a bad summary. Christ's body present and absent through the power of the Spirit is a good direction to head. But one cannot really see the compass needle without human performances that bring that resurrected body's action into focus.

Feminist theologians like Pamela Young agree. Young argues that since Christ's person is grounded in context and lived relation, christology must start with the "earliest witnesses of faith."[3] Rather than understanding Christ through his relation to God or the relation of the believer to the church, Young argues for a christology that flows from the "relation of the earliest believers to Jesus," a witness that "gave rise eventually to both the biblical texts and the continuing community that came to be the Church." It's a fancy way of saying that the Bible should guide our discussion since embodied "context is crucial to [Jesus's] significance."[4] More provocatively, it asserts a relationship between theology's attentiveness to Christ's body and its attentiveness to human bodies. Critically, for Young this relationship is not based on philosophical essences or theological ideals. It is based on lived, interactive events that leave traces of evidence behind. To ignore human witnesses of faith is to ignore evidence of Christ's living impact in the world: his interactive, performing body. And when Jesus's bodily presence is denied, human marginalization flourishes. The diverse bodies of preachers get ignored—yes. But more than this, diverse bodies in the congregation and world get ignored.

In the summer of 2018, the world held its breath as a heroic rescue attempt saved the lives of twelve trapped Boy Scouts in a Thai cave. With countless others, I rejoiced over their safe return to their parents' arms. Over those same tense weeks, Europe's decision to prevent vital rescue operations in the Mediterranean meant that 483 refugees, many of whom were children, drowned.[5] The refugee story barely registered. A book

2. James Kay, *Preaching and Theology* (St. Louis: Chalice Press, 2007), 3.

3. Pamela D. Young, "Encountering Jesus through the Earliest Witnesses," *Theological Studies* 57 (1996): 513.

4. Young, "Encountering Jesus," 515. Young readily acknowledges the importance of "present context" in relating to Christ and the Spirit but stresses the importance of the mediating structure of Scripture. She states, "However important present context is for understanding him, we have no access to him at all except through the earliest witnesses of faith." See Young, "Encountering Jesus," 513–21.

5. "483 Drown in the Mediterranean While Rescue Ships Are Trapped in Port," *CARE4CALAIS*, July 8, 2018, https://care4calais.org/news/483-drown-mediterranean -rescue-ships-trapped-port.

about the pulpit performances of preachers might seem far removed from such tragedy. What is at stake seems much less dire: the silencing of a voice, the burnout of a call, the recapitulation of a conviction, the twisting of a conscience. But pulpit performances are woven together with dicey histories of racism, colonialism, and patriarchy. Similar to these idolatries, replacing the body of Christ with the body of the preacher, the body of the church, or a body of cultural knowledge requires that rigid borders of authorization be preserved. All too often, cultural, spiritual, and physical violence follow. To dismantle this world, a world that Sarah Ahmed describes as "built to accommodate only some bodies," one must locate Christ elsewhere.[6] One must start with a resurrected body that stands outside of fixed histories and constructed jurisdictions—but testify to this body's active disruption and remaking of both. And this *is* the witness of the earliest believers—not simply in the content of their proclamation but in their homiletic performances.

This book is headed toward Luke's Nativity texts and his account of Mary's "overshadowed" labor in particular. But before we can assess that text's usefulness as a metaphor for preaching, we need descriptions of what Spirit-empowered preaching looks like postresurrection. We need *biblical*, descriptive grit. By examining three sermons in Acts (Acts 7; 20:17-38; 10:34-48)—a book authored by Luke—we will see that after the resurrection, Spirit-empowered preaching testifies to the *particular, permeable, provisional* body of the living Jesus. It is a body that cannot be replaced by or dissolved into ecclesial communions or apostolic charisms. And yet it marks those bodies with a relational vulnerability quite different from the idealizations I described in chapter two. In Acts, a preacher's identity, agency, and role show evidence of a living dependence, and as such they become sites of grace.

There is a church chorus that promises: "Turn your eyes upon Jesus . . . And the things of earth will grow strangely dim."[7] This chapter suggests something different. It argues that when we turn our eyes to Jesus, the things of earth gain clarity and perspective. Through the Spirit's witness, the things of earth become *particular, permeable, provisional* signs of a risen Savior. And in so doing, they disrupt the taken-for-granted certainties of a broken world.

---

6. Sarah Ahmed, *Living a Feminist Life* (Durham, NC: Duke University Press, 2017), 14.

7. Helen Lemmel, "Turn Your Eyes upon Jesus," 1922.

The Strange World of Acts

There used to be a story about Acts told by giant-sized New Testament scholars. Acts shows how the church continued its mission in Jesus's absence.[8] It is the story of how the church's body became Christ's risen body in the world—Christ's hands and feet.[9] It is the story of the power of *story* itself, particularly Jesus's story. Mirroring that story, reliving that story, retelling that story in word and deed was the church's new mission.[10] Scholars like Ernst Käsemann would argue that, in contrast to the Pauline Epistles, the ascended body of Christ does not "penetrate the body [of the church] pneumatologically" in Acts. Instead, it provides a far-off example for imitation.[11] The church has an "unmistakable independence" in relation to its divine Head.[12] Reframing Hans Conzelmann's reading, Käsemann argues that Acts's ecclesiology makes the church "the center of time" and "the content of theology."[13] Christ may reign by the power of the Spirit, but he has left the building.

This story was reinforced by those who found a cruciform arc in Acts's narrative. While the church grows in strength and numbers in Acts's early chapters, resistance and conflict grow as well, so that by the end of the narrative, Paul is under house arrest: preaching boldly, but

---

8. Hans Conzelmann's influential *Die Mitte der Zeit* [The Theology of St. Luke], trans. Geoffrey Buswell (London: Faber, 1960), was significant in shaping this understanding. Human history, in Conzelmann's reading of Luke, is divided into three epochs that build on the insights of the others: the age of the prophets, the age of Jesus, and the age of the Spirit and church.

9. Scholars like Ernst Käsemann would argue that, in Acts, the church became the "earthly body of the exalted Lord." See Ernst Käsemann's "Ephesians and Acts," in *Studies in Luke-Acts*, ed. Leander Keck and J. Louis Martyn (Nashville: Abingdon Press, 1966), 290.

10. Robert Tannehill, *The Narrative Unity of Luke-Acts: A Literary Interpretation* (Philadelphia: Fortress Press, 1986), 288–89, describes the "sacred pattern that hallows and reassures" Acts's readers by providing a "pattern of prophetic suffering to which Jesus and his followers must submit."

11. Käsemann's point is well taken. There is indeed a difference in the way that Paul talks about Christ living "in" the body of the believer (2 Cor. 4:10) or the believer living "in" Christ (1 Cor. 1:30) and Acts's more removed descriptions of having "belief in" Christ (Acts 11:17) or being baptized "in the name of" (Acts 2:38) Jesus.

12. Käsemann, "Ephesians and Acts," 290.

13. Käsemann, "Ephesians and Acts," 290. For Conzelmann, the time of Jesus was the *Mitte der Zeit*. Despite this difference, both scholars stress the ecclesial impact of Christ's absence.

with no simple evidence to prove his proclamation. The text simply says, "Some were convinced by what he had said, while others refused to believe" (Acts 28:24). In the opinion of Charles Talbert, Acts's narrative shape—away from triumphalism and toward sacrifice—parallels Luke's Gospel.[14] Once again, it is not the church's job to interact with a Savior. It is the church's job to imitate him in a kind of "succession narrative."[15] "Who God is and what God does" is of less concern than emulating the role models and values of the narrative world.[16] The church has been given a script to follow, and their performance is an "eschatological phenomenon" legitimated by how closely they follow that script.[17]

It is a "What Would Jesus Do?" sort of story, and there is much to recommend it ethically. Imitating Jesus is a good bet. But it leaves a significant question unanswered. *By what power is this cruciform narrative accomplished?* Is there any relationship between this narrative arc and the actual, ascended Person that it mirrors? Are the histories of Christ and the church running parallel to each other, or do they intersect?

Käsemann is clear. His description of Acts depends on a crisp delineation, an "unmistakable independence" between the realms of heaven and earth. The only problem is that this description does not adequately account for the interaction that regularly occurs between these realms in Acts. This is a book in which the heavens "open" (7:56; 10:11) and "flash" with blinding, revelatory light (9:3). The Spirit is "poured out" in Acts (2:33) and "falls" to earth (10:44). Persons, in turn, are "filled" (4:8; 4:31; 6:3; 7:55; 9:17; 13:9; 13:52; 19:6) with this Spirit's power. These are apocalyptic disruptions that point to the present agency of God breaking into the human plane.

Beverly Gaventa agrees, underscoring the in-breaking, "unpredictable" power of God's Spirit in Acts.[18] She argues that God's action is the book's primary catalyst, pointing out the strangeness of the book's name in relation to the book's content. Despite its traditional title, *The Acts of*

14. Charles H. Talbert, *Reading Acts: A Literary and Theological Commentary on the Acts of the Apostles*, Reading the New Testament (Macon, GA: Smyth & Helwys, 2001), xxiv.
15. Talbert, *Reading Acts*, xix.
16. This is Robert Brawley's critique of Robert Tannehill's work in *Theology Today* 47, no. 4 (1990): 455.
17. Käsemann, "Ephesians and Acts," 290.
18. Beverly Gaventa, *The Acts of the Apostles* (Nashville: Abingdon Press, 2003), 76.

the Apostles, "Luke's second volume concerns neither the apostles' action, nor those of the church as a whole, for behind everything stands God's plan." For all of its careful narration of the community's remembered history and its mirroring of Christ's cruciform character, human action is finally not the point. "God is the prime agent in what happens."[19] Rather than reading Acts as a hagiographic account of human heroes, she suggests that "it is almost as if [the apostles] wander around Asia Minor until God grants them a direction."[20] In the words of Willie Jennings, Acts is "God's drama, God's complete exposure . . . and God acts plainly . . . in ways that are irrevocable."[21]

But it's not just that God's power is generally present; *Christ is present—and this is perhaps the strangest thing about the book.* To be clear, Acts repeatedly insists that Christ's ascended absence is real. Acts is firm in its conviction that Jesus has been "lifted up," out of the earthly realm (1:9). Peter asserts the specificity of Jesus's location "at the right hand of God" in his Pentecost sermon, distinguishing Jesus from David, who "did not ascend into the heavens" (2:34). Indeed, Peter insists that Jesus "must remain in heaven until the time of universal restoration" (3:21).

And yet Jesus's power in the narrative is palpable. The apostles clearly resist taking any credit for the miraculous acts they perform. It is the "name of Jesus" (4:10), not any human efficacy, that is responsible for their extraordinary actions of healing the lame or enduring persecution (5:41). In case this name is misunderstood as a magic talisman, the story of the sons of Sceva serves as a warning (19:11-16). It is not the name itself that has power; it is the Person who grants the authority to use the name that is strong to save. Despite the echoes of Jesus's authority seen in Peter's raising of Dorcas (9:40) or in the healing properties of the apostolic touch (5:15; 19:11, 15), the disciples' witness is consistent. Neither their teaching nor their charisma effects salvation. They are but "witnesses" (3:15) to a greater power. In the case of Paul, Jesus's ascended presence actually breaks onto the scene, resulting in his Damascus road conversion (9:5). In the case of Stephen, by the power of the Spirit, Christ is visible, "standing at the right hand of God" (7:56). When Peter heals Aeneas, he speaks directly of Christ's presence: "Aeneas, Jesus Christ heals you;

---

19. Gaventa, *Acts of the Apostles*, 66.

20. Gaventa, *Acts of the Apostles*, 235. Paul and Silas's travels, thwarted by "the Spirit of Jesus" (Acts 16:7) and redirected by a vision of a man from Macedonia, serve as but one example.

21. Willie Jennings, *Acts* (Louisville: Westminster John Knox, 2017), 2.

get up and make your bed!" (9:34). Despite his absence, Christ's present power resonates throughout. He is still active on the scene.

I've belabored this point because we've gotten used to the oddness of Jesus's presence and absence in the narrative—and in Christian doctrine. We have working practical theologies that give us a shorthand for living into the mystery. We encourage youth to be "Jesus's hands and feet" on their summer mission trip, and we sing "Precious Lord, Take My Hand" at a funeral. It's natural to emphasize the piece of the paradox that fits our present need. But none of these shorthands really describe the strangeness of Acts's relationship between heaven and earth—human and divine.

Imagine, for example, if one were to stage Acts as a play. What characters would need casting? Would Jesus be seen on stage after his ascension, or would his role be taken over by an actress playing the Holy Spirit?[22] Perhaps Jesus would swoop in from the rafters or look down from a balcony. Perhaps the play wouldn't need someone in the part of the Spirit at all. Just Jesus shining down a flashlight or pouring down buckets of holy glitter that stick to apostolic skin. Is Jesus shouting them directions? Is he moving them like puppets on a string? How would one visualize Peter's claim that "Jesus Christ heals you" (9:34) or Paul's even stranger assertion that Christ "proclaimed light" to Jews and gentiles alike (26:23) after the resurrection? Pause there for a moment. Paul is saying that Christ has continued to preach—even in his absence. Not just that Christ *was* preached. But that Christ *did* preach. How exactly? And what does that mean for the performances of human preachers? Bodies make things complicated.

All of which to say, the text of Acts paints a complex picture of the church's performative job description. The church is doing more than imitating a tragic hero or improvising his story in a new context. Their Spirit-filled bodies and their apostolic authority do not replace the activity of a divine agent—no matter how closely they live into a given script. It was Aristotle who named the cathartic power in mimetic imitation.[23] Entire schools of homiletic thought have been based on mirroring his model of

22. This might be Conzelmann's take on the challenge. He suggested that the Spirit might be a partial substitute for Christ's presence. See Conzelmann, *Theology of St. Luke*, 97.

23. Aristotle, *Poetics*, trans. Ingram Bywater, in *Introduction to Aristotle*, ed. Richard McKeon (Chicago: University of Chicago Press, 1973), 670.

narrative structure.[24] But finally, Aristotle and Acts describe different worlds. Susan Garrett describes Acts as "strikingly apocalyptic,"[25] a designation that draws on the broad definition found in *The Encyclopedia of Apocalypticism*: "the belief that God has revealed the imminent end of the ongoing struggle between good and evil in history."[26] But Garret's description of God's apocalyptic action in Luke-Acts underscores that God has not only revealed an event to be accomplished at a future date. God is actively at work bringing that end to pass on the visual human plane.[27]

And yet. Human agency, differentiation, and difference remain.

Secular performance theorists like Richard Schechner have described the abnegation of the self that accompanies religious rituals of possession. Human agency may exist in ritual, he argues, but it is inversely related to the participants' experience of transcendent power.[28] Leland Roloff, an oral interpretation theorist, parses the problem differently. Roloff describes the "mysterium tremendum" evoked by an expansion of the performer's self. For Roloff, the successful artist constitutes the world of both the text and the audience, creating a transcendent "oneness" between listener, text, and performer.[29] For these theorists, oneness is the key characteristic of transcendent performance, whether that transcendence is channeled through a performer's passivity or evoked through her mystic power. The mark of spiritual presence is the collapse of borders between audience and performer, performer and script—and between performer and *mystery*.

How unlike Acts this seems.

Neither "evocation" nor "trance" provides an adequate description

24. See Eugene L. Lowry, *The Homiletical Plot: The Sermon as Narrative Art Form*, exp. ed. (Louisville: Westminster John Knox, 2001). Lowry's narrative loop sketches an Aristotelian understanding of a tragic-comedy, imitating the shape of the gospel and the history of Jesus.

25. Susan Garrett, *The Demise of the Devil: Magic and the Demonic in Luke's Writings* (Minneapolis: Fortress Press, 1989), 59.

26. *The Origins of Apocalypticism in Judaism and Christianity*, ed. John J. Collins; *Encyclopedia of Apocalypticism* 1 (New York: Continuum, 1998), vii.

27. Acts 19:11–12 provides an example. While the healing power carried through handkerchiefs that had touched Paul's skin suggests a kind of power intrinsic to Paul's person, Luke "explicitly states that God was responsible."

28. Richard Schechner, *Performance Theory*, 2nd ed. (New York: Routledge, 1988), 36.

29. Leland Roloff, *The Perception and Evocation of Literature* (Glenview, IL: Scott, Foresman, 1973), 5, 158.

of the Spirit-empowered performances of the apostles. Acts takes pains, in fact, to distance God's power from the power of the magician or the power of the possessed—suggesting that a different model of the relationship between divine and human is needed. When Simon the magician (Acts 8:9–25) is rebuked for trying to purchase the apostle's spiritual potency, part of what is at stake is the freedom and initiative of God's Spirit. The Spirit is no commodity controlled by human means and manipulation. What is also at stake, however, is the aforementioned tension between the presence and absence of Christ on the scene. Simon's request to buy the apostles' spiritual power shows a misunderstanding of that power as "impersonal and free-floating."[30] He speaks as if it were a spiritual authority carried within the bodies of the apostles themselves and able to be transferred to others at will. In his view, the apostles do not simply mirror an absent Christ, they substitute and stand in for him. Acts, however, repeatedly points to the distinction between Christ and his followers, stressing Christ's Otherness.[31] In the language of Acts, the apostles are not *successors* of Christ but *witnesses* to Christ.[32] More significantly, in Acts's plot, Christ is not an absent force to be evoked but a present Actor to whom one relates.[33] Jesus and the apostles have distinct bodily histories in Acts. They are separate characters in the narrative, which is part of why Paul's language in asserting Christ's proclamation to the gentiles gives one pause.

But this tension between Christ's presence and absence underscores more than divine freedom. It also complicates trance-like interpretations of Paul's claim. If magic manipulation is anathema to Acts's understanding of the relationship between human performance and the divine, so is the transparency of human performance that dissolves the actor into a

---

30. Garrett, *Demise of the Devil*, 66. Garrett notes that even as Acts works hard to distance God's power from magic, their distinction is not readily apparent to all (Acts 4:7). For Luke, it was the "source of instrumental power" that made the difference (98–99).

31. One notable exception is Jesus's identification with the persecuted members of the Way (Acts 9:4).

32. Gaventa, *Acts of the Apostles*, 42.

33. See Steve Walton, "Jesus: Present and/or Absent? The Presence and Presentation of Jesus as a Character in the Book of Acts," in *Characters and Characterization in Luke-Acts*, ed. Frank Dicken and Julia Snyder (London: T&T Clark, 2016), 124, on this tension between Jesus's physical absence and his characterization as "active from heaven."

mere *accident*—in the sacramental use of the term.[34] Christ is not made present through the abnegation of human personhood. Neither is he localized within, nor his action identical with, human action on the ground. There is something decidedly different between Acts's accounts of the apostolic action and its description of demon possession that cause persons to cry out "with loud shrieks" (Acts 8:7) irrespective of their will. The apostles deliberate (Acts 15:1–21), they disagree (Acts 15:36–40), and become "convinced" (Acts 16:10) through processes of discernment.[35] When they preach, they speak in first person and as themselves, not in the voice or persona of Christ. Even in Acts's description of the ecstatic events surrounding Pentecost—the "speak[ing] in other languages" (2:4) attributed by some in the crowd to "new wine" (2:13)—Peter retains an ability to stand and reflect on the experience in a way that differentiates between the *I* of his experience and the Lord to whom he gives witness (2:14, 29).

And finally, this is because Acts *starts with Christ's resurrected body* in its theological understanding of apostolic power. Acts starts with a resurrected body that neither disappears in the heavens nor dissolves in earthly history. If Christ's active presence in the narrative pushes back against an understanding of the disciples as possessing a godlike power of their own, Christ's absence maintains Christ's freedom and Otherness from human action—even acts of trance-like passivity. In contrast to Schechner's and Roloff's understanding of "oneness" between "Absent Other" and human performer, or Aristotle's understanding of mimetic analogy between the two, Acts insists on the *particularity*, *permeability*, and *provisionality* of each. It insists on an *embodied relation* that Jennings calls the "intimacy intrinsic to this new spatial dynamic of faith in Jesus."[36] It is a relationship necessitated by the belief that the resurrected Jesus has both a physical reality and relevance. More to the point, it is

---

34. The analogy here is with a transubstantiative understanding of sacramental elements in which Christ's presence "required the reduction of bread and wine to their accidents," a view that Luther in particular criticized. Christ's presence in the sacraments was miracle enough; a second miracle that negated the essence of the elements was not required. See Steinmetz, "Eucharist and the Identity of Jesus," 277.

35. Luke Timothy Johnson, *Scripture and Discernment: Decision Making in the Church* (Nashville: Abingdon Press, 1983). Johnson describes the communal discernment surrounding Peter's vision in Acts 10 in detail.

36. Willie Jennings, *The Christian Imagination: Theology and the Origins of Race* (New Haven: Yale University Press, 2010), 270.

necessitated by Acts's repeated assertion that the resurrection was an embodied event (2:24; 3:15; 10:40; 26:23).[37]

This is Acts's true priority: to testify to the power and presence of the resurrected Jesus in his absence through the Spirit's power. It knows what is at stake. It refuses to replace a Savior with a script—whether it be a script of Roman decree, of communal identity, or of religious tradition. Not even the script of Jesus's own story will suffice. His body is necessary. Through the Spirit, he touches down and works within all the scripts of life—but is determined and replaced by none.

In the world of Acts, preachers are not sorcerers or ciphers. They are signs—witnessing to an embodied Presence that is real if unseen. Preachers' performances bear traces of this embodied Person because preachers have bodies themselves. They are also particular, permeable, and provisional. Christ's body, when present by the Spirit, leaves a mark. Three sermons (Acts 7; 10:34-48; and 20:17-38) serve as examples. In each case, it is not the excellence of the preacher's mimetic performance that is Acts's primary concern, nor is it the preacher's ability to stand in for a Savior. The text is interested in the preacher's transformation, their dependence, and their vulnerability. The text "turns our eyes upon Jesus" *through the things of earth*—through the basic building blocks of performance. Through the Spirit's unsettling of a preacher's (1) identity, (2) agency, and (3) communal role, Jesus's living relation with the preacher comes into view, challenging a world in which human idealizations of authority and power are the final arbiters of value—a world where "only some bodies matter."

Signs of the Spirit in Things of Earth: Traces of Embodied Relation

Stephen's sermon in Acts 7 can be a mystery for teachers of preaching. It is the longest sermon recorded in Acts and can seem the least helpful for homiletic instruction. Imagine Stephen's intro class feedback: "Clearer focus needed. Where is the good news? Don't insult congregation." And then there is the whole issue of stoning. Luke has already made it clear that Spirit-filled sermons can get one killed (Luke 4:14-30), but one might

---

37. Luke is the Gospel that mentions Christ's eating of broiled fish to prove he is no ghost (Luke 24:42).

reasonably prefer three thousand conversions (Acts 2:41)! The text makes clear, however, that Stephen's sermonic defense to the Jewish council is as Spirit-inspired as Peter's Pentecost witness. It is this "wisdom of the Spirit" that provokes and silences his opponents, leading to their secret instigation of heresy charges (Acts 6:10–11).

Stephen's Acts 7 Sermon and the Spirit's Unsettling of Identity

Stephen is accused of speaking against the temple and the "customs" of Moses (6:13–14). In Stephen's sermon responding to these charges, the unsettling of his listeners' identity is his primary focus. He reassigns the roles they occupy in their shared narrative history and in relation to the identities of their ancestors. More than this, he calls into question the benefit of imitating those ancestors in the first place. It is a strange defense for one who has been accused of heresy. Wouldn't it make more sense for Stephen to explain his actions within a framework of faithfulness to the tradition? Indeed, Stephen's sermon draws heavily on the narratives that shape that tradition and lifts up heroes within it, specifically dwelling on Abraham, Joseph, and Moses (7:2, 9, 20). More than this, scholars of Hellenistic Judaism see traditions of Jewish scholarship shaping Stephen's exegetical descriptions.[38] But finally, Stephen's sermon is not about those heroes. It is about the tension between those heroes and their communities.[39] Stephen identifies his listeners with those elements of tension. In Stephen's words, "You stiff-necked people, uncircumcised in heart and ears, you are forever opposing the Holy Spirit, just as your ancestors used to do" (v. 51).

Don't miss the radical underbelly of this claim.

Stephen does not simply make the counter charge that his accusers are the tradition's real opponents; he argues that they are actually reenacting a kind of unfaithfulness already present in the ancestral tradition itself. In other words, Stephen does more than argue for the faithfulness of his own behavior in relation to a traditional norm or implicate his op-

---

38. Michael Whitenton, "Rewriting Abraham and Joseph: Stephen's Speech (Acts 7:2–16) and Jewish Exegetical Traditions," *Novum Testamentum* 54, no. 2 (2012): 165, notes how Luke draws on "'Jewish' exegetical techniques" to shape Stephen's argument.

39. Particularly in his discussion of Abraham's descendants as "resident aliens" (Acts 7:6), Joseph's brothers (7:9), and his account of the repeated rejection of Moses's leadership (7:27, 35).

ponents for their failure. *He complicates the assumption that conformity to tradition, in itself, is a simple, uniform good.* Stephen maintains that, at times, the ancestors themselves acted in opposition to the Spirit of God. The unsettling of the audience's identity in Stephen's sermon, then, is not just a matter of recasting them in unflattering roles in their narrative history. It is a matter of unsettling that history as a dependable and faithful ground of identity.

Idolatry is a recurring theme in Stephen's argument. He mentions Israel's request that Aaron "make gods" for them (v. 40), specifically mentioning the gods of other nations by name (v. 43). Even his discussion of the temple (vv. 47–50) suggests that "houses made with human hands" (v. 48) can succumb to a kind of materialism akin to idolatry. The worship of idols seems a far cry from the construction of a temple, but Stephen's sermon suggests a similar misunderstanding of God's character can underlie both. The throne of the Most High is in "heaven" (v. 49), and God cannot be encapsulated within or overly identified with any human structure. Stephen suggests that the temple itself, if overly identified with God's presence and power, localizes God within an earthly, material plane in a way unfaithful to God's nature.

Significantly, Stephen does not reject tradition as a source of guidance out of hand. He draws on Israel's foundational narratives to make his point. He explains Christ's identity in terms of God's promises to the Israelites over time. In lifting up Moses's promise that "God will raise up a prophet for you from your own people as he raised me up" (v. 37; Deut. 18:15), Stephen lays the groundwork for his argument that Jesus is that prophet. Furthermore, in killing Jesus, the religious establishment has reenacted the killing of "those who foretold the coming of the Righteous One" (v. 52). Stephen unsettles the symbols, structures, and narratives of the tradition by way of the tradition itself, refusing either to essentialize or dissolve its influence.[40] For Stephen, then, faithfulness requires something more complicated: a present-tense discernment of tradition. One has to know the part one is playing in the narrative and the ways in which the tradition itself has supported or opposed God's action—insights gained through the Spirit's wisdom (Acts 6:10).

40. This balancing act complicates Shelly Matthews's argument that Luke's rhetorical aim is to establish "radical discontinuity" between Christian and Jewish identity through Stephen's sermon. Ancestral tradition is muddied, yet simultaneously engaged. See Shelly Matthews, *Perfect Martyr: The Stoning of Stephen and the Construction of Christian Identity* (Oxford: Oxford University Press, 2010), 100.

This Spirit-endowed insight confronts the self-understanding that the religious authorities have constructed, their core beliefs about who they are and their relationship with the past. Stephen closes his increasingly feverish account with the words, "You are the ones that received the law as ordained by angels, and yet you have not kept it" (Acts 7:53), a claim that results in their significant anger (v. 54). It does not, however, precipitate Stephen's death. Finally, it is the Spirit's action in the closing verses of chapter 7 that leads to Stephen's demise. The Spirit destabilizes more than the narrative identities of Stephen's listeners. The Spirit destabilizes Stephen's identity, marking his performance with Christ's own.

Stephen, "full of the Holy Spirit," gazes into heaven and sees "Jesus standing at the right hand of God" (v. 55), saying as much. *This* claim causes the crowd to "cover their ears, and with a loud shout all rush together against him" (v. 57). There is something about the vision of Christ's risen, ascended place at God's right hand that takes Stephen's argument from the merely heretical to blasphemous in the eyes of his accusers. It is reminiscent of Jesus's own claim that he would "be seated at the right hand of the power of God" (Luke 22:69), a claim that implied to those listening that Jesus was God's Son. "What further testimony do we need?" Jesus's accusers ask (Luke 22:71).

Note that the dangerous offense of Stephen's Spirit-empowered vision is not the identification of Christ within the traditions of the community, but rather the claim that Christ's true identity transcends that tradition, even as it touches down within it. Similar to Stephen's allusion to Isaiah 66:1–2 in describing the Most High, it would appear that Jesus also transcends any "house" built by human hands. His physical location suggests that "heaven is [his] throne and earth [his] footstool" (Acts 7:49).

But Acts's account does more than affirm Christ's transcendence. The vision echoes Acts's broader claim of Christ's simultaneous *presence and absence* in relation to human history. Stephen's person and actions, at this point, are instructive. There is strange reflexivity in this Spirit-inspired vision, for just as Stephen looks at Christ, there is something of Christ reflected in the behavior of Stephen. There is, in this bloody account of Stephen's death, a similarity between the person of Christ and the person of the disciple.[41] There is a loss of life at the hands of religious officials, and there are words that harken back to Jesus's own words on

---

41. Many scholars have noted these similarities. See, for example, David Moess-

the cross: "Receive my Spirit" and "do not hold this sin against them" (Acts 7:59–60; see Luke 23:34, 46).

To be clear, *Stephen is still himself.* Jesus's visual presence at God's right hand precludes the possibility that Stephen's identity has been collapsed into Christ's. Neither is Stephen's performance solely an imitation of a cruciform narrative script penned in the past. Stephen is not alone on the stage. Acts emphasizes that there are two bodies—two actors—on the scene, and it is *in Christ's person* that Stephen finds his hope and peace in the face of violent destruction. Stephen does not take comfort in the redemptive power of his own performance, and Acts does not describe Stephen's performance as a substitute for Christ's presence. And yet, for all of that, there is a way in which Stephen is also no longer himself; at least, he is no longer himself alone. There is a kind of reflected glory—a participation that results from Stephen's turning his eyes on his ascended, crucified Lord.[42] Stephen, to say it simply, does not simply bear witness; he bears a *resemblance.* Those around Stephen may not see his vision of Jesus, but through Acts's narration of his words and martyrdom, the reader sees Jesus's life and witness *in* Stephen. More accurately, we see Jesus reflected through Stephen's faithful *particular, permeable, provisional* performance. This is no mimetic imitation performed in Christ's absence. Like the reflection of a mirror, Stephen's action flows from Christ's bodily presence on the scene. Christ does not simply provide a narrative script for Stephen's action; Christ's presence makes Stephen's faithful mirroring possible.[43]

Stephen's vision of the ascended Christ works as both a turning point and interpretive key in Stephen's sermon, informing what comes before and instigating what comes after. If Stephen's sermon unsettles the identities of his listeners, Stephen's words in death, prompted by a Spirit-filled vision of Christ's ascended body, unsettle his own identity, suggesting relational, performative participation between his person and the Savior to whom he bears witness. It is a destabilization that suggests the complicated relationship Paul alludes to in his sermon to Agrippa

---

ner, "'The Christ Must Suffer': New Light on the Jesus-Peter, Stephen, Paul Parallels in Luke-Acts," *Novum Testamentum* 28 (1986): 220–56.

42. *Reflected glory*, referencing Paul's language in 2 Cor. 3:18.

43. This point is crucial given Shelly Matthews's careful description of how the "extreme mercy" of Jesus's forgiveness prayer was "constructed upon a scaffolding of Jew vilification." Nonviolent rhetoric, similar to any human script, can be used for violent ends. Discernment is needed. See Matthews, *Perfect Martyr*, 130.

(Acts 26:23) between the risen Christ and preacher. It also resonates with the affirmation of Galatians: "It is no longer I who live, but it is Christ who lives in me" (Gal. 2:20). One thing is clear. It is an unsettling that ultimately costs Stephen his life.

Paul's Acts 20 Sermon and the Spirit's Unsettling of Agency

If Stephen's sermon provides an example of the unsettling work of the Spirit within with the category of *identity* (i.e., who one *is*)—Paul's sermon to the Ephesian elders in Acts 20:17-38 provides an example of a similar unsettling of human *agency* (i.e., what one is able to *do*). Again, this destabilization is associated with the Spirit. The sermon points to the mystery of double agency in the human-divine encounter—but more than this, it complicates the border that separates "who one is" from "what one does." This uneasy border suggests an actively passive dependence, linking the paradox of Christian freedom and captivity (Acts 20:22) to a living relationship between the believer and Christ. It is a relationship that impacts human action even as it is impacted by the same.

Paul's sermon to the Ephesian elders in Acts 20:17-38 is significant in Acts for a variety of reasons. Not only is it Paul's final sermon before his imprisonment, it is also a sermon that is directed toward the church, dealing with issues that face the community of faith rather than the conversion of those who have yet to make a commitment to Christ. It stresses the "importance of the life of the believing community" in a book where evangelistic outreach is the more common context.[44] In so doing, it addresses the problem of the staying power of the church during a time of uncertainty and persecution.[45] The sermon comes at a time when the church faces the impending absence of another body—the body of Paul— and his exhortation to the Ephesian church leadership assumes that there is work to be accomplished and choices to be made.

The speech begins with Paul's own account of his ministry among

44. Gaventa, *Acts of the Apostles*, 282, notes that "it is by no means obvious that Luke would have recognized a distinction" between the two. The passage belies attempts to characterize Paul's mission as unconcerned with the church's interior life.

45. The perceived tension between the staying power of the church and the apocalyptic stress on the gospel's interruption and destabilization of history is discussed at length in Susan Eastman, *Recovering Paul's Mother Tongue: Language and Theology in Galatians* (Grand Rapids: Eerdmans, 2007), 11.

the Ephesians, displaying in miniature the mystery of divine and human agency that runs throughout Acts. While Paul focuses on *his* actions, *his* proclamation and teaching, and *his* narrative (i.e., Paul "lived" [v. 18], "serving . . . with all humility" [v. 19], "did not shrink" [v. 20], "testified" [v. 21]), Paul's story takes place within the context of his "captiv[ity] to the Spirit" (v. 22). This captive status is underscored by Paul's assertion that he is going to Jerusalem by the Spirit's direction, knowing that "imprisonment and persecutions are waiting for me" and that none of his listeners "will ever see [his] face again" (vv. 23, 25). As Gaventa stresses, Paul speaks "not as a free human being whose capture is imminent, but as one already captive of the Lord."[46] Paul describes his labor not merely as "service" but as the service of a slave [*douleuōn*] (v. 19)—a designation that "has been present in Luke-Acts since the opening lines" (Luke 1:38; Acts 2:18; 4:29; 16:17).[47]

Paul's description of his own status as a captive, in this case, serves to emphasize the freedom of the Spirit he serves. In Acts, God's Spirit is a free and active Agent. It cannot be bribed, bought, or summoned. The verbs associated with the Spirit are telling. The Spirit appoints (Acts 13:4), testifies (Acts 20:23), and forbids (Acts 16:6-7). It is not only Christ who indicates divine action in Acts's landscape. As William Shepherd points out, the Spirit is a fully realized character in the narrative, speaking "through scripture (Acts 1:16; 4:25; 28:25) and independently (Acts 8:29; 10:19-20; 11:12; 13:2; 21:11),"[48] acting in explicit and extraordinary ways. This is a world where the Spirit can whisk Philip away at will (Acts 8:39-40) and fall on human communities independent of ritual practices such as baptism (Acts 10:44-48). This last point underlines the extent of the Spirit's freedom. The unclear relation between water and Spirit baptism in Acts means that even faithful practices do not guarantee or isolate the Spirit's power.[49] There is an independence and assertiveness to the Spirit's work that emphasizes the gracious authority and leadership of God at every point.

46. Gaventa, *Acts of the Apostles*, 290.
47. Gaventa, *Acts of the Apostles*, 285. Gaventa refers here to Mary's declaration that she is the Lord's "slave"—language obscured in the NRSV.
48. William Henry Shepherd, *The Narrative Function of the Holy Spirit as a Character in Luke-Acts* (Atlanta: Scholars Press, 1994), 91.
49. Roger Stronstad, *The Charismatic Theology of St. Luke* (Grand Rapids: Baker Academic, 1990), 70, concludes that the "complex record of the gift of the Holy Spirit in Luke-Acts rebukes all attempts to formulate a monolithic doctrine of the means by which the Holy Spirit is conferred." In Acts, the freedom of the Spirit is primary.

This makes Paul's exhortation to the Ephesian leaders to faithfully shepherd their community more confusing. If human action has so little impact on the Spirit's intervention in the world, what is the point? And yet the captivity to the Spirit that Paul describes does not result in passivity. When Paul declares that he is "no longer responsible" for the Ephesians in his absence (Acts 20:26), the comment only underscores his prior responsibility in declaring to them "the whole purpose of God" (v. 27). The Spirit's leading is not equated with the human leadership of the church, and it cannot be taken for granted. The leadership is told to "keep watch" (v. 28), as "savage wolves" will come to disrupt the flock, some originating from within the boundaries of the community (vv. 29–30).

This is the mystery of the uneasy border between divine and human agency in Acts. The Spirit is the One who directs the mission, leads the apostles, and elects the overseers (v. 28). And yet this direction is not separated from the human agency and responsibility of the believers themselves. It is a mystery at the core of this new community's identity. *Are they "who they are" because of their faithful, active performance of Paul's instructions—or because of God's claiming of them, passive and helpless, through the power of the gospel?*

Verse 28 answers the conundrum decisively with a bodily, even bloody, image: the image of the crucified Jesus. Finally, according to Paul, the blood of Christ makes the church who they are.[50] And they have been "obtained" through the blood of Christ. The verb, in this case, is in the past tense and apparently alludes to Jesus's death—in a manner unique for Acts.[51] But this foundational appeal to God's past action does not seem to indicate a settled and complete state of affairs. In the very same sentence, Paul links this past-tense event to a present-tense urgency in relation to human faithfulness and a lived dependency on the Spirit—a combination that indicates that God is still presently active

---

50. Technically, the phrase can be translated "the blood of his own" or "his own blood," an ambiguity that has caused much theological discussion, particularly regarding the attribution of Christ's human characteristics and experiences to God. See Gaventa, *Acts of the Apostles*, 288. See also Bruce McCormack's discussion of Calvin on this point in "Union with Christ in Calvin's Theology: Grounds for a Divinization Theory," *Tributes to John Calvin: A Celebration of His Quincentenary*, ed. David Hall (Phillipsburg, NJ: P&R, 2010).

51. Gaventa points out, "Nowhere else does Luke directly connect the death of Jesus with the church's own existence." See Gaventa, *Acts of the Apostles*, 288.

in sustaining the church's identity and witness.[52] The same holds true for the body and blood of Christ themselves. If Paul's accounts of his own ministry and Christ's resurrection power are to be believed, Christ's blood has not simply been spilled in the past but is currently coursing through a resurrected body, a present reality, removed as it may be from the earthly realm (Acts 20:24).

This, then, is why Acts's uneasy border between divine and human agency matters so much. The point of Paul's sermon is not to strike some carefully conceived balance between the two (i.e., the church labors and God labors, and when the right balance is struck, they continue Christ's ministry together). Rather, Paul's sermon emphasizes human and divine agency in such a way that it makes the church dependent on the blood of Jesus Christ, the love of God, and power of the Holy Spirit in its present, daily life. The church's relational identity with Christ comes into focus through the Spirit's unsettling of agency in lived experience.[53] It is a relationship performed in time through the Spirit's present and active intervention.

In this way, Paul's sermon destabilizes the relationship between basic grammatical categories, between subject and predicate, between *church* and *practice*. Paul's pneumatology will not allow the church to think that their behavior does not matter—that they are who they are *regardless* of what they do. Neither will it allow the church to identify their behavior as the ground of their identity—that they are who they are *because* of what they do. Instead, Paul's sermon describes a performed ecclesial identity that grows out of and arcs toward a constant dependence on the blood of Christ and the Spirit's power.

52. This lived dependency is also suggested by Luke's unusual vocabulary at this point. While *obtained* is translated as "purchased" or "bought" in the NASB and NIV, Luke does not use his more common word for "purchase" or "buy" (*agorazō*) in this case. Instead, the NRSV's translation of "obtained" comes from the verb *peripoieō*—which implies a "reserving for oneself with deep personal interest" or "preserving alive." "4046. peripoieō," *New Strong's Exhaustive Concordance of the Bible* (Nashville: Thomas Nelson, 2003). It is used in Luke's writings only at one other point—to describe the attempt to preserve one's life in Luke 17:33. In the LXX, it appears in Isaiah 43:21, which the NRSV translates as "formed for myself." Luke's usage implies a past action that has a present, ongoing impact and more personal engagement than a monetary transaction might imply.

53. *Unsettling* does not indicate deconstruction. It is a mediating term that makes space for human agency even as it refuses to essentialize it as an autonomous category.

The issue at stake is similar to what was at stake for the Reformers in their *opus operantis* understanding of the sacrament's efficacy. Luther and Calvin's insistence on the uneasy border between action and passivity in the sacrament grew from their firm belief that the sacrament is an act of God—not an act of humankind. And yet to separate God's work from our own response in lived history is to take God's action for granted, locating God's presence within human structures and rituals rather than in God's free expression of love. It is, in essence, to trap God within materiality and institutions themselves. For these Reformers, just as the Holy Spirit made possible the affirmation of Christ's presence and absence in the sacrament, the Holy Spirit made possible this *actio mere passiva*.[54] The Spirit's work results in a relational nexus between identity and action, where *who we are is impacted by what we do—and what we do is impacted by who we are*.[55] We are saved "by grace . . . through faith" (Eph. 2:8).

Paul's sermon does not discuss sacramentology, attempt systematic pneumatology, or use language of participation in relation to the person of Christ. And yet the sermon indicates a kind of lived dependency. Paul's sermon describes an uneasy border between the church's performance and its identity, a relational agency that results in a loss of familiar certainties. Rather than reaffirm the church's status or freedom from sin on the basis of Christ's past action alone—*ex opere operato*—Paul reminds his listeners that the church's identity requires a moment-by-moment dependence on the Spirit's power and the person of Christ. The Spirit's unsettling of human agency allows the church's relationship to Jesus to be experienced as a daily gift of grace.

Peter's Acts 10 Sermon and the Spirit's Unsettling of Communal Role

If *identity* deals with the question of who we are and *agency* deals with the question of what we are able to do, *communal role* asks, To whom and for what are we responsible in the work of performance? It deals, most simply, with the issue of *why* we perform. One's understanding of a role is impacted by questions of identity and agency, of course, but highlighting the question of role brings the relationship between performer and com-

54. John Calvin, *Institutes of the Christian Religion*, Library of Christian Classics (Philadelphia: Westminster, 1960), 2:1303
55. Brian Gerrish, *Grace and Gratitude* (Minneapolis: Fortress Press, 1993), 74.

munity into focus. For Schechner and Roloff, an "absent Other" mutes differences between performer and audience, as well as differences within the audience. In contrast, the embodied relation between Christ and his followers in Acts—a relationship mediated by the Spirit—leads to human relationships that honor difference. Peter's sermon at Cornelius's house (Acts 10) provides an example of the Spirit's unsettling of a communal role through the disruption of social boundaries. The resulting vulnerability does not result in the negation of ethnic difference, nor does it negate the community's relationships with texts, traditions, and practices. Yet again, in destabilizing Peter's relationship to the gathered community, the Spirit creates a dynamic role discerned through relation to a living Lord.

Peter's sermon at Cornelius's house is the culmination of a series of stories in which outsiders are welcomed into the new Christian community. Acts 8 recounts the conversions of Samaritans (vv. 5–8) and the Ethiopian eunuch (vv. 26–38), and chapter 9 describes the conversion of Saul. The arc of the narrative mirrors Christ's promise to the disciples that they will be "my witnesses in Jerusalem, in all Judea and Samaria, and to the ends of the earth" (Acts 1:8). As Aaron Kuecker points out, Acts does not simply highlight the significance of the disciples' *witness* in this evangelistic expansion. It underscores the *my* that precedes it. The qualifier, "'my witnesses,' implies both witnesses *to* and witnesses *belonging to* Jesus."[56] The disciples are not autonomous actors defined by their obedient, successful action. They are linked to Christ, and Christ's action, as well as the action of the Spirit, directs their human performances.

In Acts's description of Peter and Cornelius's encounter, divine action is once again primary. Both Peter and Cornelius receive visions that instigate their meeting (Acts 10:3, 11), and the Spirit speaks directly to Peter, telling him to go with Cornelius's servants "without hesitation" (vv. 19–20). Spatial reminders of the ascension are also present. As with Stephen, Peter sees "the heavens opened," although instead of seeing the face of Christ, he sees a vision of clean and unclean animals "coming down" on a sheet—animals he is told to kill and eat (vv. 11, 13). Likewise, when the Holy Spirit interrupts Peter's sermon later in the narrative, it falls (v. 44)—reinforcing Peter's claim that it is Christ who "pours out" the Spirit from above (Acts 2:33). The location of God's presence above and

---

56. Aaron Kuecker, *The Spirit and the "Other": Social Identity, Ethnicity and Intergroup Reconciliation in Luke-Acts* (New York: T&T Clark, 2011), 104.

outside the expected ways of the world underscores the central theme of the passage: Peter's affirmation of Jesus Christ's universal lordship.[57] Rather than encasing Christ's presence and ministry within accepted narratives, practices, and borders of the community, Peter's experience of the Spirit leads to his assertion that Christ "is Lord of all" (Acts 10:36), including the very narratives and practices that define the community.

This affirmation of Christ's lordship has practical implications for Peter, most specifically in the provisionality of the categories of clean and unclean. As the voice in his vision clearly states, "What God has made clean, you must not call profane" (Acts 10:15). The vision, combined with the Spirit's directive to go to Cornelius's home, leads Peter to apply this insight to his understanding of Jewish-gentile relationships. Peter tells Cornelius, in explanation of his "unlawful" visit to this gentile home, "God has shown me that I should not call anyone profane or unclean" (v. 28).

Kuecker makes the point that this unlawful designation is misleading as "there is no Levitical law prohibiting social intercourse . . . with non-Israelites"—preferring the translation "forbidden" or even "disgusting."[58] His point is that in Peter's initial vision, God's present action is understood to destabilize a *ritual* boundary, but in Peter's encounter with Cornelius, a different boundary comes into view: the *ethnic* boundary of the self and other.[59] When the Holy Spirit interrupts Peter's sermon, however, it is clear that there are ritual consequences for this ethnic disruption. It calls Peter to rethink his apostolic role in relation to this gentile gathering. Baptism, previously understood to be a gift for the circumcised alone, is reenvisioned as a gift for all over whom Christ is Lord. As Peter states, "Can anyone withhold the water for baptizing these people who have received the Holy Spirit just as we have?" (Acts 10:47).

Significantly, the baptism of Cornelius's household does not result in the abnegation of their gentile status (v. 45). When Peter says, in his report to the church in Jerusalem, that "the Spirit told me to go with them and not to make a distinction between them and us" (Acts 11:12), he does not mean that "they" are now to be considered Israelites or that they must become circumcised. The miracle of the event is that the Spirit and

57. Matthew Sleeman explores the possibility that the voice from heaven in Acts 10 is, in fact, the voice of Christ, *Geography and the Ascension Narrative in Acts* (Cambridge: Cambridge University Press, 2009), 226-27.

58. Kueker, *The Spirit and the "Other,"* 190-91.

59. Kueker, *The Spirit and the "Other,"* 190-91.

the "repentance that leads to life" has been given "even to the Gentiles" (11:18). The miracle is that difference is neither dissolved in relationship nor communal relation disintegrated by difference.

One can imagine that Peter would have an easier time in his role as preacher if he had a stable set of marching orders. He would have known his task: either remake gentiles into the likeness of his tradition or leave behind tradition in light of the difference he encounters. But, as with other preachers in Acts, Peter stands on uneasy borders. His understanding of himself, his community, and God undergo transformation even as he preaches his sermon (Acts 10:44). The Spirit falls, and the community he has been called to serve changes around him. Indeed, *his* thinking is changed through their Spirit-filled praise. The community does not disintegrate into individual, isolated units disconnected from Peter's use of the Jewish narrative tradition (vv. 42-43).[60] But neither is it monolithic, demanding hegemonic conformity. There is, instead, a *participatory unity . . . while maintaining difference*. The community is defined by a God who chooses the witnesses, regardless of ethnic boundaries. The church's role as a witness is still primary—as it is for the preacher—but the Spirit destabilizes how that role looks, and once again, the church's dependence on Christ comes into view. Finally, *Christ's* ownership (i.e., "*my* witnesses") distinguishes the church, and because of that, what witness looks like on the ground shifts and changes in response to those whom God chooses to include. Communal roles, identities, and practices are renegotiated and reformed in light of God's action.

There is, then, in Acts's account of Peter's sermon to Cornelius, a relinquishment of the "superintendence of the communities' social boundary to the Holy Spirit" and a corresponding loss of homogeny in expected norms.[61] Communal rituals, significant in providing group cohesion and marking identity, become sites of both participation *and* difference, provisional in authority and able to be redefined by the Spirit's presence. As with my discussion of identity and agency, such unsettling suggests a living dependence on the action of the risen, ascended Christ: the Lord of "all" (Acts 10:36).

60. Robert Tannehill, *The Shape of Luke's Story: Essays on Luke-Acts* (Eugene, OR: Cascade, 2005), 183, in fact, stresses Peter's attentiveness to "the Jewish context of Jesus' ministry" in his sermon.
61. Kuecker, *Spirit and the "Other,"* 183.

The Resurrected Body and an Unsettled Practical Theology

Acts exhibits a dogged naivete when it comes to Christ's bodily resurrection. Its descriptions of character and plot pointedly refuse any narrative method that might domesticate the extraordinary claim at the center of its proclamation. Jesus is no ghost; he is alive, embodied, and located at God's right hand. And yet he is actively present through the Spirit, who somehow brings Christ into living relationship with the performing bodies of believers. Acts shows us this through the Spirit-empowered marks left behind on these faithful human performances. The unsettling of preacherly identity, agency, and communal role point to a Christ who is *both bodily absent and yet actively present*, who *transforms who we are by empowering what we do and empowers what we do by transforming who we are*, and finally, who brings about *participatory unity while maintaining difference*.

The political and social consequences of this witness to Christ's resurrected person should not be underestimated. One might dismiss a project that starts with the resurrected body of Jesus as being parochial or pietistic in its concerns and influence. There might seem little practical relevance in Acts's insistence that Jesus's resurrected body continues to have particular, permeable, provisional life. Isn't focus on Christ's body an evasion from the work of attending to the human bodies excluded, appropriated, or abused by this world's empires? What does starting with Jesus's resurrected body have to do with dismantling such a world? It seems beside the point.

And yet, in the narrative of Acts, Jesus's resurrected body actively disrupts the false constructions of autonomy, power, and authority on which these idolatries rest. Willie Jennings traces the impact of Acts's Spirit-empowered "joining" between the disciple and Christ on both kinship identity and political allegiance. For Jennings, this impact is more than spiritual; it creates new space for relating to the world God loves in ways that are, finally, not defined by that world. When "the body of the disciple . . . has joined her or his body to the risen Savior, Jesus," identity and history lose their stranglehold on that disciple's destiny, Jennings insists, and "the imperial project dies."[62]

In their book *Preaching Fools: The Gospel as a Rhetoric of Folly*, Charles Campbell and Johan Cilliers connect the destabilizing work of the Spirit

---

62. Jennings, *Acts*, 9.

in proclamation to God's apocalyptic work on the cross. Drawing on the language of "liminality" to describe "that in-between space where the movement of the Spirit occurs," Campbell and Cilliers describe the Spirit's work in experiences of "presence and absence" and on "borders that remain porous" to change.[63] At every point, they connect this liminal work to the "folly of the cross," which "interrupts all dominant notions of power and success, turns human visions of grandeur on their head and inverts 'old age' value systems."[64]

In one way, this understanding of the cross's power is foreign to Acts's sermons. When Acts speaks of the cross, it speaks in terms of the sinfulness of those who crucified Jesus, rather than as a key to understanding God's salvation (2:23; 3:15; 4:10; 7:52-53). In Acts, Jesus's resurrection is the ultimate demonstration of God's power and authority (2:24; 10:40; 26:23). And yet the two are related. In Peter's Pentecost sermon, the pouring out of the Spirit immediately precedes his claim that God's righteous, risen Messiah and the crucified Jesus of Nazareth are one and the same (Acts 2:36).

Peter's focus on Christ's person illuminates Acts's distinctive emphasis. In Acts it is not the cross that has power. It is the crucified One who now reigns in glory. In Acts it is the person of Christ that matters, the embodied Jesus, crucified, raised, and reigning. *The Spirit in Acts does not bring about "destabilization" or "liminality" in order to mirror Christ's work on the cross; instead, it destabilizes human practices and communities through a present-tense relationship with a crucified and living Lord.* The Spirit's work is characterized by this lived dependence.[65] Christ's body is not colonized, homogenized, or objectified. It is not substituted with a body of our own design, culture, or history. Neither is it replaced by narrative memory. It intersects, transforms, and interprets each of these categories, making them the gracious means and prophetic witness of divine encounter. The body of Christ remains Other, accessible through the Spirit's gift and mediated through the vulnerability of lived relation.

A number of New Testament scholars have explored the significance

63. Charles Campbell and Johan Cilliers, *Preaching Fools: The Gospel as a Rhetoric of Folly* (Waco, TX: Baylor University Press, 2012), 37, 42.

64. Campbell and Cilliers, *Preaching Fools*, 53.

65. Note that the goal here is not to recreate or embody Christ's form but to live in relation and bear witness to Christ. One's relationship to Christ does affect the human participant but does not make this primary relationship superfluous. The *lived dependence* is the point.

of this embodied christology for ethics, politics, and communal life. Kavin Rowe reflects on the affirmation of Jesus's lordship in the context of the Roman Empire.[66] Brittany Wilson examines the impact of Jesus's body on masculine constructions of gender.[67] Aaron Kuecker examines the significance of Jesus's person on sociological categories of the ethnic "Other."[68] I speak to its unsettling of my own practical theological discipline and its implications for working preachers. If Jesus's body can be neither dismissed from nor dissolved into the church's scripts, purity, and practices, then the beautiful Pauline affirmation that we "are the body of Christ" (1 Cor. 12:27) is not an *ex opere operato* reality. It has the same Spirit-empowered, performed-in-time provisionality as the sacraments themselves. The church bears Christ, proclaims Christ, even mediates Christ. But it never replaces Christ.

And this insight is critical for preachers who discover that the church, as it is currently constructed, is not built to accommodate their bodies. It matters to women whose communions deny them access to the pulpit. It matters to those whose affirmation of God's presence in queer bodies bars them from ordination. It matters to bodies around the world who are invisible or expendable in the West's theological discourse. Christ is present in and through the church by the power of the Spirit, thanks be to God. But Christ always transcends the church, destabilizing totalizing assumptions about human autonomy, power, and authority. Resonating with God's prophets throughout history, Christ calls the church to replace these familiar certainties and false shadows with a Spirit that cannot be evoked, managed, or guaranteed (Isa. 40:13; 61:1; Joel 2:28-29).

This is why *starting with the body of Jesus* is so crucial for our theology of the Spirit and our practices of pulpit performance. The cart cannot be placed before the horse. Our job as teachers of preaching is not to affirm the self-authenticating power, purity, and practices of the church. It is not our job to create ecclesiologies that conflate Christ's action with the church's action, or worse, the outworking of human history itself. It is not even our job to create rigid models of Christian practice. The narrative theology of Acts refuses to play this game. At every point, the unsettling of the Spirit makes the building blocks of human performance—the

66. Kavin Rowe, *World Upside Down: Reading Acts in the Graeco-Roman Age* (Oxford: Oxford University Press, 2009), 151–52.

67. Brittany E. Wilson, *Unmanly Men: Reconfigurations of Masculinity in Luke-Acts* (Oxford: Oxford University Press, 2015).

68. Kuecker, *Spirit and the "Other."*

identity of the characters, the agency of the actors, the expectations of communal role—dependent on embodied relation with Christ. And this destabilization, flowing from Christ's absent and present person, creates a cruciform "interrupt[ion]" of dominant notions of authorization and success.[69]

And this is the rub. Given all that unsettling, what is a practical theologian to do?

If the narrative of Acts is meant to point preachers toward dependence on Christ's person rather than provide a road map for behavior, the prescriptive work of the homiletician seems counterproductive at best. Even *unsettling* or *liminality* can become false guarantees of divine presence. Rowe echoes the dilemma in his mining of Acts for a practical theology of mission. For all of the theological significance surrounding communal practices in Acts, if these become the ground for a "general definition of mission," the beating heart of Acts's witness is ignored.[70] The resurrection of Jesus by God is no "explanatory scheme"; it is the "fount from which mission springs."[71] And this is practical theology's catch-22. Attempts to describe Christ's impact on believing bodies through the Spirit can create new scripts that bypass the necessity of Jesus as effectively and exclusively as those of empire. It is embodied relation that matters. But how is that taught? How is that even described?

When a teacher attempts to explain the concept of color to a small child, she or he is faced with a dilemma. How does one isolate the blue of a bowl from its other characteristics or show that *blue* is not a word for the bowl itself? The solution is often straightforward. Give the child multiple examples of blue—preferably markedly different examples. *How are these things different—and how are they similar?*

My move to Mary is such an attempt. Using Mary's Spirit-empowered pregnancy to describe the Spirit-filled labor of a preacher may seem like comparing apples and oranges. But in Luke-Acts, the two share striking similarities, even in their difference. They share a similar Spirit-instigated unsettling of identity, agency, and communal role, growing from a similar theological commitment to an embodied God. In their comparison, a metaphor emerges that describes what embodied relation to Christ looks like in practice. In my view, Mary's bearing body is useful in describing

---

69. Campbell and Cilliers, *Preaching Fools*, 53.
70. Rowe, *World Upside Down*, 152.
71. Rowe, *World Upside Down*, 152.

the relation between preacher and embodied Word precisely because of its difference. As a metaphor, the comparison requires contextual interpretation, inviting the kind of dependent, dynamic discernment it describes.

When Peter quotes the prophet Joel in his Acts 2:16–21 Pentecost sermon, he makes a significant "modification" to the text.[72] When Joel speaks of God's Spirit falling on "male and female slaves," he does so after a litany of second-person possessives (i.e., "your" sons and daughters, "your" old and young men [Joel 2:28–29]). Peter shifts the identity of these slaves by adding the possessive pronoun *mou* (my) to their description (Acts 2:18). These are no longer *douloi* and *doulai* (i.e., slaves) in an economic sense, "but rather . . . slaves *belonging to God*."[73] Peter extends the meaning of Joel's text to include himself and his public act of prophesy.

Self-designation as God's *doulos* occurs at several key moments in Acts (2:18; 4:29; 16:17; 20:19), but its first usage is found in Luke's Gospel. Gaventa notes that Mary is the first in Luke's narrative to describe herself in this way.[74] When Mary responds to the angel Gabriel, she says of herself, "Here am I, the servant [*doulē*] of the Lord" (Luke 1:38).[75] The outpourings of the Spirit that occur at the start of both books suggest that the resonance is more than coincidental.[76]

When Luke and Acts are read with an eye to their narrative unity, Mary's designation of herself as God's handmaid foreshadows Peter's

---

72. Kuecker indicates that there are, in fact, five "modifications" of the LXX text. It is, of course, difficult to speak of the New Testament modifications of texts to which we do not have direct access—thus, I adopt Kuecker's use of quotation marks. See Kuecker, *Spirit and the "Other,"* 120.

73. Kuecker, *Spirit and the "Other,"* 121.

74. Gaventa, *Acts of the Apostles*, 285.

75. Gaventa summarizes the significance of this vocational description in Luke-Acts in "Standing Near the Cross," in *Blessed One: Protestant Perspectives on Mary*, ed. Beverly Roberts Gaventa and Cynthia L. Rigby (Louisville: Westminster John Knox, 2002), 54.

76. Paul Minear, "Luke's Use of the Birth Stories," in *Studies in Luke-Acts*, ed. Leander Keck and J. Louis Martyn (Nashville: Abingdon Press, 1966), 129–30, argues that Acts's account of Pentecost "plays an analogous thematic role" as the Nativity texts of Luke, emphasizing how both Mary's birth of Christ and Acts's account of Pentecost set the "tone and temper of the stories and speeches that follow"—specifically through their common emphasis on the Spirit.

sermon.[77] For his part, Peter's language does more than simply link himself and his listeners to Joel's description of the *douloi* and *doulai* who prophesy in God's name. It also links them to the experience of the first person in Luke's narrative to claim her Spirit-empowered status as a *doulē* of God. Luke creates a pneumatological, vocational link between Mary, Peter, and all those who prophesy through the Spirit's power.

Chapter four will explore this connection, asking whether the handmaid who delivered Jesus in a stable might illumine the lived dependency between Spirit, Christ, and "handmaids" who prophesy—and whether, through Mary's ordinary witness, a world "built to accommodate only some bodies" trembles.[78]

77. Robert Tannehill, *The Narrative Unity of Luke-Acts* (Minneapolis: Fortress Press, 1989), 2:3, argues that reading Luke-Acts as a narrative unit illuminates the meaning of the books individually.

78. Ahmed, *Living a Feminist Life*, 14.

CHAPTER 4

The Spirit-Filled Handmaid

If there is anyone who is treated less like a person than a pastor—
it's a pregnant woman.

A pregnant pastor

In chapter two we saw that when the body of Christ is not given its particular, permeable, provisional due in theologies of performance, human bodies are marginalized. Practical theologies and working preachers become dangerous. My discussion of Acts flips that argument on its head. When Christ's resurrected body *is* discerned in human performances, the theological significance of bodies comes into view. Through the Spirit, they become relational sites of christological revelation, marked by this crucified Other. More than this, as diverse witnesses to Christ's resurrected person, they dismantle a world built only for some. Christ is revealed as present and absent, beyond the grasp of institution and authorization, even as he participates in the lives of his people. All this dismantling raises a different practical theological question. How is this human labor of embodied relation described—particularly when caused by a Spirit beholden to no one but God? How does the preacher's sacramental relationship with Christ come into view but not replace Christ as the point?

Though the start of Luke's Gospel is separated from the start of Acts by the world-altering events of Easter, Luke's description of Mary's pregnancy shares Acts's commitment to Christ's *particular, permeable,* and *provisional* body. Christ is hidden by a womb in Luke's Nativity and by the heavens in postascension Acts, but a similar christological logic undergirds the narratives of each. And a similar dependence on the Holy Spirit is required for embodied relation with Christ to occur. Mary's pregnancy is surprisingly helpful in describing the theological promise of preaching's Spirit-empowered vocation.

Mary's pregnancy also helps preachers visualize the uneasy, performative borders of embodied relation with the living God. At its most basic level, pregnancy provides a picture of a relationship in which difference and otherness are maintained, a relationship where *who one is*, is affected by *what one does*, and vice versa. Motherhood is a dynamic role shaped by a generative tension between individual and community. Mary's pregnancy, however, is also instigated by the Spirit, providing a picture of divine and human participation performed over time. In this way, Mary's body becomes theologically meaningful, a reflexive sign of Christ's work in her. As a flawed and faithful disciple, Mary's ordinary labor becomes a site of revelation. Jesus comes into view through the ways that Mary's identity, agency, and communal role are changed—which is why Luke doesn't waste time fixating on Mary's purity, power, or perfection. For Luke, the particularity and vulnerability of bodies allow them to bear witness to Christ's own.

This is an encouraging word for women and preachers both since purity, power, and perfection are hard to come by. But if Mary's particularity is what makes her relation with Christ theologically meaningful, then this chapter is swimming upstream. We are not used to thinking of Mary's particularity. We're used to her looming larger than life or fading away. Not only have idealizations of Mary's body eclipsed her relation to Christ, they have also eclipsed the diverse, bodily experiences of women themselves. Mary's body has been used to silence and norm that diversity—*especially through the tradition's treatment of her pregnancy*. Before we can discuss ways that Mary's body might be theologically revelatory, then, we must name the ways her body has been used as an agent of theological, sociological, and existential harm. And so, we begin with the dangerous subject of Mary's bearing body.

The Dangerous Body of Mary

I've never had a child, and I won't have a child. I had a parishioner who once told me that I would never fully understand the love of God because of this. It made me so angry—until a friend turned the comment on its head. "You may understand the love of God better," she said, "because you'll never equate a human, parental version of God's love for the real thing."[1]

In the Protevangelium of James, Salome—an understandably doubting midwife—scoffs at the prospect that Mary has given birth in a manner that leaves her body unscarred and unopened. She states, "Unless I put [forward] my finger and test her condition, I will not believe."[2] The midwife's hand "falls away" as if "by fire" in attempting her examination, and though her hand is restored by the Christ child, the lesson is clear. Curiosity about the particulars of Mary's bearing body is dangerous business. Salome is certainly not the last woman to have suffered pain in attempting to make Mary's bearing body the subject of historical or theological reflection.

Mary's Pregnancy as Ideal or Norm

For many women, this entire inquiry is dangerous territory. Given centuries of ecclesial fascination with Mary's pregnant body and Luke's lack of details, describing Mary's pregnancy in hopes of illuminating the relation between Spirit and body in preaching is a bit like walking into a minefield. The romantic idealisms of rhetoric that this project has sought to complicate are dwarfed by the archetypes surrounding Marian motherhood. These mariological ideals haunt the borders of our discussion, for they have been used to marginalize the bodily experience of women who have borne children—as well as those who have not.[3] Mary Hines

1. Conversation with a female pastor, September 25, 2012.
2. Scholars date the Protevangelium from the mid to late second-century. See Beverly Gaventa's helpful excerpt of Oscar Cullman's translation of Papyrus Bodmer 5 in the appendix of *Mary: Glimpses of the Mother of Jesus* (Minneapolis: Fortress Press, 1999), 142.
3. Jennifer Glancy, *Corporal Knowledge* (Oxford: Oxford University Press, 2007), 82, carefully catalogs a number of early church meditations on Mary's pregnancy and experience of childbirth that stress the "extraordinary" nature of her birthing experience (i.e., lack of pain, blood, afterbirth, or opened body). Glancy argues that these depictions are part of broader theological and cultural discourses surrounding childbirth and have contemporary implications for "the ways that childbearing bodies are socially read" (90). On the other hand, John Van den Hengel, "Miriam of Nazareth: Between Symbol and History," in *The Feminist Companion to Mariology*, ed. Amy-Jill

notes that, in one of her recent courses on the theology of Mary, all of the registered students were young men. The women avoided the course because, in their words, "There was just too much baggage for them to summon up interest in studying Mary."[4] Mary's bearing body has been a tool by which a patriarchal tradition has used the glorification of "the Feminine" to make up for the absence of actual females.[5] In lifting up the Virgin Mother as the standard for women everywhere, many women found themselves with a troublesome model, regardless of whether the narrative gaps surrounding Mary's childbirth were filled with extraordinary miracle—or ordinary mess.[6]

In the traditions that assert the unnaturalness of Mary's pregnancy, traditions that deny shows of blood, pain, or even an opening of the birth canal,[7] Mary's childbirth has overshadowed and denigrated the natural, generative ruptures and uneasy labors of birthing women.[8] As Jennifer Glancy states, "Mary's body is exceptional in ways that imply

---

Levine (Cleveland: Pilgrim Press, 2005), 136–37, catalogs and critiques depictions of Mary's labor that romanticize and universalize the "natural" experience of childbirth, "reducing the 'feminine' to the role of motherhood."

4. Elizabeth Johnson, *Truly Our Sister: A Theology of Mary in the Communion of Saints* (New York: Continuum, 2003), 9.

5. Sarah Coakley's chapter "Mariology and 'Romantic Feminism,'" in *Women's Voices: Essays in Contemporary Feminist Theology*, ed. Teresa Elwes (New York: Marshall Pickering, 1992), 106–10, addresses the romantic feminism of Leonardo Boff, arguing that the "feminine 'other'" that he lauds is a "male construct" and a "thinly-disguised reorientation of traditional gender stereotypes."

6. Tertullian—unlike many others who give early accounts of Mary's birth—stresses the ordinariness of the occasion. For him, it is precisely the "torture" and "uncleanness" of Mary's "sewer of a body" that foreshadows the cross. See Tertullian, *Against Marcion* 4.21, in Glancy, *Corporal Knowledge*, 124.

7. The aforementioned and highly influential Protevangelium of James is a case in point. As Glancy describes, "in the *Protevangelium*, Mary is protected not only from sexual activity but also from the stain of menarche. Mary's body is tightly bounded, neither tacky with menses and lochia nor stretched by her child's emergence into the world." See Glancy, *Corporal Knowledge*, 108. For two more examples of early Christian reflections on the uniqueness of Mary's birth, see Jonathan Knight, *The Ascension of Isaiah* (Sheffield: Sheffield Academic Press, 1995); and Susan A. Harvey, "Odes of Solomon," in *Searching the Scriptures: A Feminist Commentary*, ed. Elisabeth Schüssler Fiorenza et al. (New York: Crossroad, 1994), 86–98.

8. For Ignatius of Loyola, a Moor's assertion that Mary gave birth in a way similar to other women—even though she had conceived as a virgin—was enough to make Ignatius consider "strik[ing] him with a dagger." Glancy, *Corporal Knowledge*, 134.

other women's bodies are intrinsically shameful."[9] Mary's clean, closed, quiet labor has also underscored her submissive, silent characterization by the church. By extension, it has informed the silent, submissive service of mothers who aspire to imitate her. This ideal has been a burden for mothers who, like Susan Griffin, see their own experiences waiting "blind and dumb, unspoken" in the face of the "unstained" Virgin.[10] For women artists, writers, and preachers who are mothers as well, the ideal leads to vocational questions about the incompatibility of motherhood with creative work that requires mess, space alone, vocalization, and self-expression.[11]

On the other hand, traditions that exult in the natural quality of Mary's bodily history, conflating her experience with contemporary experiences of pregnancy, ignore both the particularity of Luke's account of Mary and the particularity of every woman's labor. They do so, of course, to fill in the details of a historical person about whom we know virtually nothing. But as Jorunn Økland cautions, "If research into the historical Jesus, the main character in the Gospels, has not after 150 years resulted in an image that can be either defined or agreed upon, it is even more difficult to try to reach any historical conclusions about a secondary figure such as Mary."[12] The difficulty is not only the lack of information available but the consistent allure of reading one's own experience onto another—creating the Mary one wishes to see. Glancy notes that even among contemporary obstetricians and midwives, there are "competing discourses and practices" around the definition of natural childbirth.[13] One cannot assume a normative account of natural pregnancy without privileging the natural experience of some as the experience of the whole.

This issue is even more acute for women who have, as Serene Jones

9. Glancy, *Corporal Knowledge*, 108.

10. Susan Griffin, "Feminism and Motherhood," in *Mother Reader: Essential Writings on Motherhood*, ed. Moyra Davey (New York: Seven Stories, 2001), 35.

11. Susan Rubin Suleiman, "Writing and Motherhood," in *Mother Reader: Essential Writings on Motherhood* (New York: Seven Stories, 2001), 134, discusses the tension between production and reproduction that she sees in many mother/artists—tying this tension to Julia Kristeva's critique of the Virgin Mary's veneration in Western culture. There is, Suleiman argues, the fear that a writing mother will be a "failed mother."

12. Jorunn Økland, "'The Historical Mary' and Dea Creatrix: A Historical-Critical Contribution to Feminist Theological Reflection," in *A Feminist Companion to Mariology*, ed. Amy-Jill Levine (Cleveland: Pilgrim Press, 2005), 150.

13. Glancy, *Corporal Knowledge*, 87-90.

discusses in *Trauma and Grace: Theology for a Ruptured World*, suffered "reproductive loss," particularly through miscarriage or an inability to conceive. Jones notes that certain feminist accounts of Mary can alienate women grieving such losses by conflating Mary's story into the natural female experience.[14] Such accounts also leave unaddressed the relationship between Mary's bearing body and the bodies of women who have chosen not to have children. Mary's maternal visibility—and, more particularly, her use within the tradition to evoke women generally—can silence the natural bodies of women who have never experienced pregnancy or birth. These definitions quickly become barbed. In an Advent Bible study, a first-time mother-to-be beams, round and heavy. "I have never felt closer to Mary than I do this Christmas." The group leader winces, wondering how to name and honor the experience of another woman across the room undergoing IVF treatments. But the other woman names the experience herself: "I have never felt farther away."[15]

The deeper question, of course, is what is at stake in constructing a narrative of Mary's bodily history in the first place. If the early church's stress on Mary's extraordinary birth is meant to set her apart from women, even as women are encouraged to imitate her, a stress on Mary's natural experience of motherhood can be used to provide a natural model for female legitimacy and transgression. Either in its uniqueness or its naturalness, Mary's body has become a norm for female experience, undermining the diversity of women's bodily testimonies. It is no wonder that women, post-Salome, have been wary of touching the subject.[16]

Mary's Pregnancy as Metaphor: A Humble Alternative

The difficulty echoes the problematic relationship that Adrienne Rich describes between feminism and "the body." Rich comments on her

14. Serene Jones, *Trauma and Grace: Theology in a Ruptured World* (Louisville: Westminster John Knox, 2009), 144.

15. True story told by a pastor in my introductory preaching course, 2018.

16. Birgitta of Sweden, a medieval mystic unique in her birthing of eight children, does provide a fourteenth-century vision of Mary's birth of Christ. Tellingly, the moment of birth is described as a miraculous materialization. Mary's bodily shape changes when her son appears outside of her—but her body has nothing to do with his sudden presence beside her on the clean straw. See Birgitta of Sweden, *Revelaciones*, ed. Birger Bergh (Uppsala: Almqvist & Wiksells Boktryckeri, 1967), 7:21–22.

own desire to attend to her bodily connection with other women and yet her struggle to relate to that physicality as "a resource rather than a destiny."[17] She fiercely claims her particularity but concedes that part of her "authentic life" was uncovered when she "shed her uniqueness" and embraced the descriptive category of gender—all while refusing to let that category define her.[18] In *Eros for the Other*, Wendy Farley echoes and politically extends Rich's point by arguing for the need "to find some conceptuality [of women] that will make criticisms of patriarchy intelligible without requiring an a-historical sameness, an 'essential' woman."[19] Kwok Pui-Lan notes a similar challenge in "linking the local with the global" in social analyses of female identity that respond to transnational economic power. We are markedly different, and yet our lives are linked. How do the identities of other women shape our understandings of ourselves?[20]

This negotiation of uneasy overlaps and divergences articulates, I think, a part of the challenge at hand. For Rich, relationships between the female bodies of others and her own body are real and significant, but also particular, performative acts of interpretation. They assume an active inquiry: *In what way does another's experience of being a woman intersect my own—and in what way does it not?*

The question describes the interpretive work required of metaphor, where "figurative meaning emerges in the interplay of identity and difference."[21] In Paul Ricoeur's understanding, its key characteristic is this "interplay" between the "is" and "is/not" of metaphor.[22] Metaphor, for Ricoeur, is movement that finds concreteness through its performance in time. Such performance points beyond itself. It is provisional and plurivocal. It does not mediate a singular, unified truth. Instead, it "writes with

17. Adrienne Rich, "Of Woman Born: Motherhood as Experience and Institution," in Davey, ed., *Mother Reader*, 96.

18. Rich, "Of Woman Born," 97.

19. Wendy Farley, *Eros for the Other: Retaining Truth in a Pluralistic World* (University Park: Pennsylvania State University Press, 1996), 177.

20. Kwok Pui-Lan, "Feminist Theology as Intercultural Discourse," in *The Cambridge Companion to Feminist Theology*, ed. Susan Frank Parsons (Cambridge: Cambridge University Press, 2002), 34.

21. Paul Ricoeur, *The Rule of Metaphor: Multi-Disciplinary Studies in the Creation of Meaning in Language*, trans. Robert Czerny (Toronto: University of Toronto Press, 1977), 199.

22. I draw here from Ricoeur's understanding of the "is/is not" tension as the eventful dialectic that comprises metaphor. See Ricoeur, *The Rule of Metaphor*, 248.

an eraser," to use Sutton's turn of phrase. It points to a truth it cannot quite name.[23] Its meaning depends on one's performative engagement, even as it resists the limits of that performance. Metaphors depend on participants having skin in the game.

Relating to the bodies of women as a "resource rather than a destiny" through performed acts of interpretation suggests a way forward for this project's attempt to relate the narrative of Mary's pregnancy to the labor of contemporary mothers—and the labor of preaching. What is at stake is not the assertion of a norm but the engagement of a metaphor. As Økland states, "It is the metaphorical in . . . historical events that has the potential to mean something to us," though such an engagement is always "fortunately . . . ambiguous."[24] Such an engagement assumes the provisionality of the performance even as it assumes its necessity. It asks the reader to stand on the uneasy border of interpretation, moving between the particularity of the text and one's own lived experiences— between "Protestant-like"[25] and "feminist-like"[26] ways of engaging the text. Luke's narrative description of Mary's pregnancy invites readers to bring their own bodies to the text as resources of meaning. However, like all metaphors, it resists those shapes. Mary has a context and story that is particular, a narrative body that is distinct. This narrative body must be given its due, for it is, finally, the only body of Mary to which we have access.

Indeed, the world of Luke's Nativity requires that the reader ask not

23. Not all linguistic philosophers would characterize metaphor in this way. Janet Soskice, *Metaphor and Religious Language* (Oxford: Clarendon Press, 1989), 93, for example, does attribute an untranslatable, "irreducible" quality to metaphors used in particular contexts. Soskice's larger project argues for the validity of religious metaphors as truth claims, rejecting what she calls a "split referent" theory of metaphor for a unified, immediacy of meaning "effected by the speaker's employment of the whole utterance in its context" (53). I suggest that Soskice's attention to the borders of difference that intersect contexts, as well as the listener's performed engagement with metaphor, is underdeveloped.

24. Økland, "'Historical Mary' and Dea Creatrix," 163.

25. Beverly Gaventa, "All Generations Will Call Me Blessed," in *A Feminist Companion to Mariology*, ed. Amy-Jill Levine (Cleveland: Pilgrim Press, 2005), 124. Gaventa emphasizes the significance of the text itself—independent of the reader's personal or ecclesial interpretive lens.

26. Bonnie Miller-McLemore, "Pondering All These Things," in *Blessed One: Protestant Perspectives on Mary*, ed. Beverly Gaventa and Cynthia Rigby (Louisville: Westminster John Knox, 2002), 105. Miller-McLemore references Gaventa's language in arguing for a feminist prioritization of a reader's "experience" in interpretation.

only how one's bodily experience intersects with the story being told but how it doesn't. This approach is no univocal, reader-response conflation, any more than Rich suggests that one woman's experience can be read with ease onto another's.[27] Allowing Mary to "appear" as an embodied character in Luke's text requires the acknowledgment that there are limits to our understanding; we cannot *be* who she *is*.

Luke insists, in fact, that Mary's experience *is* particular.

In emphasizing the Spirit's role in initiating Mary's pregnancy, Luke asserts that women are not only separated from Mary by the specificity of their own experiences, but they are separated from Mary by an act of God lived out in ordinary time and space, even as it calls the natural order into question. Luke's description of Mary's pregnancy intentionally holds the natural and unnatural in tension. To categorize it as one or the other, or to collapse the two, is to miss Luke's point. It is, in fact, on this uneasy border where resonances between the world of Luke's Nativity and the world of Acts come into view. Rather than fetishizing motherhood, Mary's Spirit-empowered pregnancy provides a resource for describing bodily participation of another sort: the Spirit-empowered, embodied relationship between Jesus and Acts's preachers.[28]

The Strange World of Luke's Nativity

At first glance, Luke and Acts seem decidedly different.

The disruption of ethnic and ritual boundaries in Acts 10:45-47 seems far removed from the opening of Luke's Gospel, which is pregnant with

27. By "reader response," I refer not to a general notion of a reader's participation in the creation of textual meaning but to a more narrow definition summarized by Reed Way Dasenbrock, "Do We Write the Text We Read?," in *Falling into Theory: Conflicting Views on Reading Literature*, ed. David Richter (Boston: Bedford Books, 1994), 247-48, as a "hermeneutics of identity." Such a view, often associated with theorists like Stanley Fish, understands readers as "writing the text" as they engage it, or in Dasenbrock's words, "understanding a text by making it like us."

28. Suleiman expresses her concern over certain feminist writers' "fetishization" of motherhood and the female body in their theories of language—particularly dealing with the work of Chantal Chawaf and Luce Irigaray. Suleiman sees this fetishizing as leading to "codification of style" that stresses "'liquid' syntax, lyricism at all costs, receptivity, union, nonaggression"—and the assertion that there is "only one genuine mode of feminine writing." See Suleiman, "Writing and Motherhood," 129.

Jewish religious devotion.[29] The narrative begins in the temple (Luke 1:8–9) and speaks glowingly of Zechariah and Elizabeth's blameless living "according to the statutes and regulations of the Lord" (1:6). Mary and Joseph circumcise Jesus and present him in the temple, "according to the law of Moses" (2:21–22). The Abrahamic covenant is referenced repeatedly (1:55, 73), as is Jesus's connection to David (1:32; 2:4).[30] Luke takes pains to emphasize God's "conservative" faithfulness to "ancient promises" and the continuity of religious practices and traditions.[31]

Indeed, there are enough differences between the opening of Luke's Gospel and the rest of his writings that historical-critical biblical scholars have questioned the authenticity of these first two chapters and have "not taken into consideration statements that are peculiar to them" when describing Luke's theological worldview.[32] Given that Luke himself admits to using many sources to create his account (Luke 1:1–3), Paul Minear agrees that a unique source is a probable explanation.[33] But in Minear's view, the existence of such a source does not diminish the texts' importance in understanding Luke's larger project. Minear points to significant similarities between the narrative landscapes of Luke 1–3 and the rest of Luke-Acts. On the basis of both linguistic evidence and thematic content, Minear insists that the birth stories are "fully congenial in mood and motivation" to the theological arc of Luke-Acts as a whole, suggesting, minimally, significant redaction on Luke's part.[34] Luke's fingerprints are evident in the birth stories, and in Minear's view, they "set the stage" for "all subsequent speeches and actions" in the book.[35]

29. Roger Stronstad, *The Charismatic Theology of St. Luke* (Peabody, MA: Hendrickson, 1988), 36.

30. R. L. Brawley, "Abrahamic Covenant Traditions and the Characterization of God in Luke-Acts," in *The Unity of Luke-Acts*, ed. J. Verheyden (Lueven: Leuven University Press, 1999), 131.

31. Robert C. Tannehill, *Luke* (Nashville: Abingdon Press, 1996), 57.

32. Hans Conzelmann, *The Theology of St. Luke*, trans. Geoffrey Buswell (New York: Harper & Row, 1960). Conzelmann serves as an example (118). Among other difficulties, Luke's emphasis on the Spirit's activity in the birth stories disrupts Conzelmann's progression of epochs—making his exclusion of these texts a significant precursor to his argument.

33. Paul Minear, "Luke's Use of the Birth Stories," in *Studies in Luke-Acts*, ed. Leander Keck and J. Louis Martyn (Nashville: Abingdon Press, 1966), 124.

34. Minear, "Luke's Use of the Birth Stories," 112.

35. Minear, "Luke's Use of the Birth Stories," 129. Minear's point is echoed by Tannehill and others who argue that the "infancy narrative provides much of the

For Minear, this stage does not simply affirm the continuity of religious tradition. It is a stage on which the "marvelous response of God" to the prayers and needs of God's people is made known.[36] The infancy stories are a "tightly knit cloth" where miraculous and nonmiraculous threads intersect, making it difficult to separate the one from the other.[37] In Luke, as in Acts, the intersection of divine encounter and human action is a recurring textual feature. Elizabeth, long barren, becomes pregnant (Luke 1:36-37). Zechariah, temporarily dumb, breaks forth in prophetic speech (v. 67). Divine messengers abound (vv. 11, 26; 2:9). And then, of course, there is Simeon's claim that God's salvation has come to Israel as a poor, unknown, and seemingly ordinary baby (2:29-32). For Minear, these examples of divine action give Luke's opening chapters a "perversely eschatological" character.[38] I. Howard Marshall agrees, noting that it is "not salvation history, but salvation itself" that is the central theme of Luke.[39] And this salvation is no abstract theological concept. It is embodied in a concrete, historical figure. "Jesus Himself," in embodied form, is regarded as the fulfillment of God's prophesy.[40] Despite the infancy stories' clear emphasis on God's faithfulness in and through time, they make clear that a decisive, divine intervention has taken place in Jesus's birth. The infancy stories do more than announce the continuing unfolding of God's salvific plan; they announce, in the words of the angel, "to you is born this day . . . a Savior" (2:11).

This eschatological tone is underscored by the text's attentiveness to the Spirit. The Spirit is mentioned repeatedly in Luke's opening chapters, initiating the canticles of Zechariah (1:67) and Simeon (2:27), as well as the blessing of Elizabeth that precedes Mary's song of praise (1:41). The Spirit also "fills" the baby John (1:15). This collection of Spirit-filled characters resonates with Peter's citation of Joel in Acts 2. Joel's list of those who will prophesy in the "last days" (Acts 2:17-18) reads remarkably well as a description of the diverse persons who are Spirit-filled in Luke 1-2 (i.e., Zecha-

theological context for understanding Jesus' ministry in the rest of the gospel." See Tannehill, *Luke*, 40.

36. Minear, "Luke's Use of the Birth Stories," 129.
37. Minear, "Luke's Use of the Birth Stories," 129.
38. Minear, "Luke's Use of the Birth Stories," 125.
39. I. Howard Marshall, *Luke: Historian and Theologian* (Exeter: Paternoster, 1970), 92.
40. Marshall, *Luke*, 125.

riah, Elizabeth, John, Mary, Simeon).[41] While it has become ecclesial short-hand to describe Acts's account of Pentecost as the inaugurating moment of the Spirit's outpouring on God's people, Luke makes clear that the Spirit has been actively present since the Gospel's beginning. Raymond Brown notes that "the outpouring of the prophetic spirit which moves people to act and speak [in Luke], resembles very closely the . . . outpouring of the prophetic spirit in Acts." Brown even suggests that "the infancy narrative is closer in spirit to the stories of Acts than to the Gospel material."[42] For Joseph Fitzmyer, these resonances are significant in pointing to a similar theology of the Spirit in both texts. In Fitzmyer's words, the Spirit that "falls" at Pentecost is the "*same* Spirit . . . active in the infancy narratives."[43]

All well and good. But this leaves practical theologians in the same bewildering territory where we found ourselves at the end of chapter three. Given the "perversely eschatological" landscape of Luke and Acts, how is faithful, Spirit-empowered action described? And more to the point, how is faithful preaching described?

One tempting road suggests itself: comparing Luke's Nativity canticles with Acts's sermons. There is an "observable kinship" between these songs and the sermons of Acts, underscoring God's salvific action on behalf of those in need.[44] An enterprising homiletician could mine these similarities for rhetorical characteristics of Spirit-inspired speech. More tempting still, the homiletician might conflate these characteristics with the presence of the Spirit itself. The characteristics could then be used

41. While there is no one-to-one correspondence in this regard, the range of Spirit-filled characters in Luke shares Acts's breadth. It includes, for example, "old" and "young" men, and "daughters" and "sons" of the tradition (Acts 2:17). There is, of course, a female *doulē*, as well (2:18).

42. Raymond Brown, *The Birth of the Messiah: A Commentary on the Infancy Narratives in Matthew and Luke* (Garden City, NY: Image Books, 1979), 243.

43. Joseph Fitzmyer, "The Role of the Spirit in Luke-Acts," in Verheyden, *Unity of Luke-Acts*, 181.

44. Minear, *Studies in Luke-Acts*, 116. Minear notes the similar themes in the hymns of Luke 1–2 and summaries of the kerygma found in Acts, referencing C. H. Dodd's basic study *The Apostolic Preaching and Its Developments* (New York: Harper, 1936). For more contemporary examples of comparisons between the canticles and Acts's sermons, see Aaron Kuecker's *The Spirit and the "Other"* (New York: T&T Clark, 2011), 51, 68–69, for a discussion of Simeon's claim that Jesus is a "light for the Gentiles" (Luke 2:32) as a precursor to the "expanding . . . ethnic horizon" of Acts's sermons. See also Loveday Alexander's comparison of Simeon's speech and Paul's final prophesy (Acts 28:26–28) in her "Reading Luke-Acts from Back to Front," in Verheyden, *Unity of Luke-Acts*, 434.

as proof of the Spirit's presence, or worse, the human means by which one instigates or evokes the Spirit's action. But by now, the conundrum is clear. Such an approach misses the forest for the trees. It would attend to the words of Luke-Acts's speeches in isolation from the divine, pneumatological Agent who instigates them. It would make salvation history, rather than *God's salvation*, the point.[45] If Luke is clear about anything with regard to God's agency in and through faithful, human performances, it is that God is free. In the Gospel account, as in Acts, the surprise of God's announcement of good news is not orchestrated or expected. It is experienced as interruptive, discomfiting grace. Human responses to this good news look less like a road map and more like an embodied response to a living relationship.

All of which suggests a less expected Lukan conversation partner for Acts's depictions of Spirit-empowered preaching.

There is a pivotal act of the Spirit in Luke's Nativity account that has, thus far, gone unmentioned. It is, on its surface, an event that seems to have little relevance to the act of preaching: the "overshadow[ing]" of the Spirit used to explain the impossible fact of Mary's pregnancy (1:35, 37). But this act shares important characteristics with Acts's understanding of the living relationship between Christ and preacher made possible by the Spirit.[46] Luke's description of Mary's virgin birth makes clear that Christ's mediation is not the result of natural, human processes. Neither is it the result of Mary's purity or power. And yet Mary's body undergoes a pregnancy ordinary enough to look like scandal. Her body bears the marks of the Savior she carries. Her labor matters. At this intersection of

45. One way of understanding the potential pitfalls of this approach is through Calvin's nervousness about adhering to "signs" that are overly identified with the material reality they are meant to represent. See Brian Gerrish, *Grace and Gratitude: The Eucharistic Theology of John Calvin* (Minneapolis: Fortress Press, 1993), 137. In Calvin's thought, when a sign mirrors the signified to excess, there is a danger that the one will be mistaken for the other and the mediating role of the Holy Spirit will be eclipsed. For example, when a homiletician uses an apostle's sermon rhetoric as the rhetorical model for the contemporary preacher, it is possible for the material proximity of the subject matter to be misleading—attributing efficacy to the apostle's rhetoric itself, rather than the Spirit's work through the words. The signifying "words" and the salvific "Word," in this case, can be conflated.

46. Again, the point is not that characteristics of faithful, Christian practice are not useful for the practical theologian. The point is that, for Acts, these characteristics flow from—and further necessitate—a living dependency on Christ. They do not substitute for him.

the natural and extraordinary, Mary's body witnesses to the necessary role of the Spirit in making this relation with Christ possible, and the Spirit in turn confirms Mary's full humanity. In Luke's description, Mary's bearing body is no transcendent symbol, transparent substitute, or natural essence. It does not dissolve into abstraction. Neither is it, in and of itself, Luke's point. And yet because of the Spirit, Mary's particular, permeable, provisional body testifies to the "apocalyptic event of Christ ... in all of its living potency."[47]

Not by Purity, Power, or Passivity

It's important to clarify some things at the start. In Luke's account, the Spirit does not overshadow Mary because of some innate purity of character. Or at least Luke doesn't try to convince us of the fact. In her influential study on Mary in the Gospels, Beverly Gaventa points to Luke's "lean description" of Mary as a "virgin, engaged to a man whose name was Joseph" (1:27).[48] While Elizabeth and Zechariah's descriptions note their "righteous" status before God (1:5-7), Mary's description tells us nothing that would distinguish her as particularly worthy of the calling she will receive. When the angel of God tells Mary that she has "found favor with God" (1:30), no explanation as to how Mary obtained this favor is given. The text does not attribute particular holiness or spiritual potency to Mary apart from the fact that, in Elizabeth's words, "she ... believed that there would be a fulfillment of what was spoken to her by the Lord" (1:45). Mary makes a point, in fact, of stressing the "lowliness" of her status, which makes God's gracious favor all the more cause for rejoicing (1:47-48). In the words of Karl Barth, what sets Mary apart is not her sinlessness or her ability to serve as an ideal in and of herself, but rather the fact that she has been "received and blessed" by God.[49]

There is, of course, a specific aspect of Mary's bodily experience that

47. David Congdon, "Eschatologizing Apocalyptic: An Assessment of the Present Conversation on Pauline Apocalyptic," in *Apocalyptic and the Future of Theology: With and Beyond J. Louis Martyn*, ed. Joshua Davis and Douglas Harink (Eugene, OR: Cascade, 2012), 133.

48. Beverly Gaventa, *Mary: Glimpses of the Mother of Jesus* (Minneapolis: Fortress Press, 1999), 52.

49. Karl Barth, *Church Dogmatics*, I/2, ed. Geoffrey W. Bromiley and T. F. Torrance, trans. Geoffrey W. Bromiley (Edinburgh: T&T Clark, 1978), 140.

Luke does find significant—the fact she is an unmarried virgin. Luke takes care to emphasize the miraculous, fatherless nature of the event, particularly through Mary's response to Gabriel's announcement that she will be with child. Mary herself raises the question of her virginity, asking, "How can this be?" (1:34).[50] In response, Gabriel tells Mary that "the Holy Spirit will come upon you, and the power of the Most High will overshadow you" (v. 35). Because of the Spirit's creative, overshadowing work, "the child to be born . . . will be called the Son of God" (v. 35). Such language, in Raymond Brown's view, is not meant to suggest a kind of "quasi-sexual" union but instead stresses the power and presence of God through whom "nothing will be impossible" (v. 37).[51] Nancy Duff agrees. "The virgin birth," she argues, "proclaims that God makes a way out of no way and brings into existence that which was not there before."[52] The Spirit's active involvement in making Mary's pregnancy possible emphasizes that Christ's entrance into the world is an act of God, a "miraculous event, tantamount to a new creation."[53] This is not an event brought about by Mary's natural capacity or power.

But neither is it brought about by any unnatural capacity on Mary's part. Mary's virginity, for example, does not hold a special spiritual potency. This has been an ambiguous point within the tradition and in certain readings of Luke's Gospel itself. Among Luke's seven depictions of women who speak prophetically, each is "either a virgin, a widow (Lk. 2:36–38), or a woman well advanced in age (1:18)," leaving open the possibility that the Spirit's interaction with women is "predicated on the

50. Mary Foskett, *A Virgin Conceived* (Bloomington: Indiana University Press, 2002), 16, points out that the term *parthenos* in Luke 1:27 can be translated as either "virgin" or "young woman" but that "Mary's question tips the interpretive scale" toward the former. Scholars like Jane Schaberg, *The Illegitimacy of Jesus: A Feminist Theological Interpretation of the Infancy Narratives*, 20th anniv. ed. (Sheffield: Sheffield Phoenix Press, 2006), are not convinced, arguing famously and controversially that Jesus was conceived illegitimately, mostly likely through rape.

51. Brown, *Birth of the Messiah*, 290. Examining Luke's vocabulary, Brown argues that the phrase "will come upon you" is "not sexual" in this case—pointing to its use in Acts 1:8 to describe the "coming upon the disciples at Pentecost." Similarly, "overshadow" is used "to describe God's presence in the sanctuary and . . . at the transfiguration" (Luke 9:34).

52. Nancy Duff, "Mary, Servant of the Lord: Christian Vocation at the Manger and the Cross," in *Blessed One: Protestant Perspectives on Mary*, ed. Beverly Gaventa and Cynthia Rigby (Louisville: Westminster John Knox, 2002), 62.

53. Gaventa, *Mary*, 57.

absence of female erotic activity."[54] Such connections between virginity and spiritual power are seen in theological interpretations of Mary's virginity as "a physical virtue in and of itself,"[55] whether these stem from the ongoing battle between spirit and flesh in the Christian tradition or from the use of virginity as a symbol of autonomy and power associated with goddess worship.[56] Such interpretations are inconsistent with Luke's larger emphasis on the Spirit poured out on "all flesh" (Acts 2:17), and more importantly, with Luke's consistent stress on God's agency, freedom, and gracious action. Mary's virginity is not Luke's emphasis.[57] The Spirit's miraculous ability to bring Christ's saving body into relationship with the world is at the Annunciation's heart.

That bears repeating. Mary's body is not Luke's focus—not as a norm or archetype or prescriptive script. Her purity is unrecounted, and her spiritual power unregaled. But her fully human body does matter. It is important to Luke that she is not passive or transparent, just as it is important that her humanity does not dissolve in her Spirit-empowered encounter. She is not, for example, divinized—which may bring a sigh of relief to women who are tired of measuring up to her. Gaventa notes that even after Jesus's birth, Luke narrates Mary's human limitations. While she "understands some things, . . . much about her son and his future remain unclear and perhaps even troublesome."[58] While she is twice referenced as the mother of Jesus later in Luke's Gospel (Luke 8:19-21; 11:27-28), both verses stress that her familial tie does not give her special status. Those who "hear the word of God and obey it" (v. 28) are the ones who are "blessed."

Given his ambivalence about her role as mother, it is remarkable that Luke notes Mary's pregnancy at all. After all, he doesn't use it to underscore Jesus's miraculous origins, nor does he say enough about it to make it a useful description of faithful motherhood. The description

54. Foskett, *Virgin Conceived*, 138. In Acts 21:9, Philip's daughters are also virgins with the gift of prophesy. Foskett and others argue that Luke's connection between virginity and prophesy reflect larger cultural assumptions.

55. Johnson, *Truly Our Sister*, 29. Johnson points to Ambrose and Jerome as examples—as well as Pope Siricius, who said that "Jesus would have rejected his mother if she had conceived other children" (28).

56. Johnson, *Truly Our Sister*, 31.

57. Though Mary's virginity does seem more theologically generative for Luke than Matthew, who highlights the potential shame of her situation.

58. Gaventa, *Mary*, 62.

of the birth is "utterly ordinary."[59] *What purpose does it serve?* Elizabeth Johnson notes that "later apocryphal gospels will present a picture of an effortless delivery with Jesus arriving as a ray of light or passing through Mary's womb the way the risen Christ passed marvelously through walls and locked doors. . . . But Luke knows nothing of this idea."[60] Luke begins the story of Jesus's birth with the pedestrian details of a Roman census (Luke 1:3) and the daily dangers and discomforts of an occupied homeland. The birth itself is told in two verses (2:6–7), saying simply that Mary "gave birth," "wrapped him in bands of cloth," and "laid him in a manger" (v. 7). This is not an author who shies away from describing the miraculous intervention of God in human affairs (1:36, 64; 2:13), but Mary's birth of Christ is described as nothing unusual, with the exception of Mary and Joseph's "insignificance" and vulnerability in a setting far from home.[61]

What matters most for Luke about Mary's body, it would seem, is what it says about Christ's own.

Once Again, Starting with the Body of Christ

In Acts, the Spirit-filled bodies of believers testify to the reality and relevance of the risen Jesus—his *particular, permeable, provisional* flesh. The Spirit's mediation of Christ in faithful human performances points to Christ's lordship over death and lived history (Acts 10:36). Luke's description of Mary's pregnancy maintains a similar claim, though expressed in the gentler words of angelic greeting: "The Lord is with you" (Luke 1:28). For Duff, the greeting becomes a summary of the doctrine of the incarnation. God "chooses to be present" to a "sinful and unworthy world" through the person of Jesus.[62] Similar to Acts, Luke's account of the Na-

---

59. Gaventa, *Mary*, 60.

60. Johnson, *Truly Our Sister*, 277. I note here that the more the limitations of Mary's humanness are dissolved, the more rigid and closed her bodily borders are seen by the tradition. When she is understood as sinless co-redemptrix (i.e., when the distinctions between Mary and Christ are downplayed), Mary's body is increasingly unaffected by Christ's birth—and vice versa. There is a way, in the church's readings of Mary, that the dissolving of her human identity and an essentializing of her physical body work as two sides of the same coin.

61. Gaventa, *Mary*, 61

62. Duff, "Mary, Servant of the Lord," 64.

tivity shifts our vision. Luke's combination of natural and unnatural elements in Mary's pregnancy keep readers from conflating her body into some universal norm or some singular, exclusionary ideal. They turn our attention instead to Mary's participation in the body of the Word made flesh—a living participation, performed in time and made possible by God's Spirit. What matters to Luke is Mary's participation in the bearing of *Christ's* body.

More to the point, it is Christ's *body* that is at stake.

For Christ to be "with" the world, Christ must be Other than the world. His body cannot be dissolved into the identity of the mother to whom he relates.[63] The angel tells Mary, "The Lord is *with* you"—not "The Lord *is* you." And yet because he is born in time, Christ's body is a *performing body*, a body that is in active relation to humankind. His bodily borders participate fully in time and space. They are *particular*, *permeable*, and *provisional*, and they cannot be dismissed, for this relation is no natural affair. It is a pneumatological gift. The Spirit is the means by which Mary and Christ experience participation, making clear that "the *Lord*" is with Mary.[64] Christ is not bound by the linearity, scarcities, and prejudices of the human plane in which he participates. He disrupts its foundational assumptions. As Marshall insists, Christ is "with" us in order to "save."[65]

Finally, Mary's bodily details are of little interest to Luke.[66] But here

63. This is an obvious point when Christ is visible as a distinct, unique person in the Gospel narrative—but apparently, given Marian tradition, it has been less obvious in relation to his existence *in utero*, when his body is hidden within another's. Interestingly, the issue is raised again postascension when Christ's body is "hidden" from sight, in heaven.

64. The christology of Luke and Acts is a notoriously thorny problem—described by C. M. Tuckett as a "mini-storm center" in recent research. Scholars like C. F. D. Moule have argued that an understanding of Jesus as "Lord" is peculiar to Acts and strangely absent from Luke's Gospel. In Tuckett's view, Moule carries his point too far. See C. F. D. Moule, "The Christology of Luke-Acts," in *Studies in Luke-Acts*, ed. L. E. Keck and J. L. Martyn (Nashville: Abingdon Press, 1968), 160–61; and C. M. Tuckett, "The Christology of Luke-Acts," in Verheyden, *Unity of Luke-Acts*, 133. C. Kavin Rowe, *Early Narrative Christology: The Lord in the Gospel of Luke* (Grand Rapids: Baker Academic, 2009), influentially notes that Jesus is named Lord while still in the womb (Luke 1:43) by a Spirit-filled Elizabeth. And this christology carries over into Acts. See C. Kavin Rowe, "Acts 2:36 and the Continuity of Lukan Christology," *New Testament Studies* 53 (2007): 37–56.

65. Marshall, *Luke*, 92.

66. Foskett notes that, unlike other ancient novels that describe the divine im-

is the irony. When Luke "starts with the body of Jesus" in describing God's saving work, a fully human Mary appears. *Christ's body—mediated by the Spirit—allows Mary to remain fully herself.* At the base of the feminist critiques surrounding Mary's idealization is a distrust of embodied experience that transcends human limits. According to philosopher Alison Weir, this is a familiar burden for women. In Western myth, women are regularly forced to "*be* mediation, to unify human and divine law, individual and community, the male self with himself and the universal."[67] We are the keepers of the "Feminine" (with a capital *F*). In the case of Mary, this philosophical mediation is further complicated by theological speculation: how does Spirit-inspired participation in Christ's body affect a person? In certain traditions, Mary can become a woman in-between, romanticized, co-opted, and unseen—a disappearing act that clergypersons (and particularly clergywomen) know something about. A pregnant preacher laughs, "If there is anyone who is treated less like a person than a pastor—it's a pregnant woman."[68] There's a smile on her lips, but her eyes are rueful.

Christ's bodily presence keeps Mary from fading away into a symbolic substitution. It is Jesus, not Mary, who is born to save. His body articulates the particularity, limits, and significance of Mary's own. The point is key. *Because of the action of the Spirit and the embodied presence of Christ, Mary is free to stop "standing in" for God or "standing in" for women in general.* She is free to be a resource rather than a norm.

And as a resource, new connections between Mary's experience and the experiences of others blossom. After rejecting the link between Protestantism's erasure of Mary and its "idealization of modern motherhood," Bonnie Miller-McLemore "ponders" again how her real-life experiences of motherhood might reappear in her interpretation of Mary and illumine Luke's text. She notes, for example, Mary's pondering attentiveness, anguish, and awe.[69] Queer theologians like Marcella Althaus-Reid

---

pregnation of a human woman, Luke includes no details of Mary's physical appearance. In contrast "to the novels that focus on the *dynamis* of a virgin's beauty and desire, the only *dynamis* identified in this scene is that of the Most High." See Foskett, *Virgin Conceived*, 123.

67. Allison Weir, *Sacrificial Logics: Feminist Theory and the Critique of Identity* (London: Routledge, 1996), 97.

68. From an interview with a pregnant pastor, January 2013.

69. Bonnie Miller-McLemore, "Pondering All These Things," *Blessed One* (Louisville: Westminster John Knox, 2002), 105–10.

find in Mary a resource for disrupting "heterosexual conceptions of womanhood," rejecting conceptions based on "God the Father's heterosexuality."[70] Preachers who see God embracing infertility reframe Mary as a surrogate mother "carrying a baby that God Herself cannot."[71] The Spirit's overshadowing places Mary's experience in conversation with mothers and fathers whose parenthood transgresses traditional norms and natural processes, even as the Spirit's overshadowing results in what seems an ordinary pregnancy. When Mary is allowed her particular, holy labor of testifying to and mediating Christ, she invites a range of bodies into relationship. And in that messy, human work of interpretation, she invites *our* bodies to appear.

How is Mary's experience like my own—and how is it different?

If Acts is any indication, preachers like Stephen, Paul, and Peter have a lot to say on the question. Similarities between the Spirit's filling of these male preachers and the Spirit's overshadowing of Mary are not found in simple conflations of behavior. Pregnancy and preaching are different things. But in Acts and Luke, they are affected by a similar Spirit-empowered, embodied relation with Jesus—a relation where human personhood does not disappear even as it changed in the encounter. Such a relation has visible effects. In Acts, the Spirit unsettles the performative building blocks of *identity*, *agency*, and *communal role*, marking Acts's preachers with a cruciform loss of autonomy, power, and authority that flow from a lived dependency on Christ. The Spirit brings about a similar cruciform disruption to Mary's *identity*, *agency*, and *communal role*. In this way, the Spirit's overshadowing of Mary does more than allow her to "appear." Through the Spirit, as with the sermonic performances of Acts, her pregnancy testifies to the One she carries. Mary bears witness to Christ in her body as she bears him into the world.

Once Again, Signs of the Spirit

Queerness remains at the heart of the stories about Mary.[72]

70. Marcella Althaus-Reid, *Indecent Theology* (New York: Routledge, 2000), 67.

71. Kelli Hitchman-Craig, "God Seeking Surrogate (Luke 1:39–55)" (sermon, Duke Divinity School, Durham, NC, October 19, 2016).

72. Robert E. Goss, "Luke," *The Queer Bible Commentary*, ed. Deryn Guest, Robert Goss, and Mona West (London: SCM Press, 2015), 527.

In my opening chapter, I shared a hunch that theology's "bodily forget-ting"—be it a forgetting of Christ's body, Mary's body, or the diverse bod-ies of preachers and interpreters—is tied to a *pneumatological* forgetting. In Luke and Acts, the Spirit allows the bodies of diverse persons to enter into a living relation with an embodied Savior. It is the Spirit that marks their bodies as witnesses to Christ's own. The Spirit destabilizes the *iden-tity*, *agency*, and *communal roles* of human performance so that God's saving work in Jesus becomes visible. When we pay attention to the work of the Spirit in Mary's pregnancy, we discover a fully human, scandalous witness to the revealed God.

Mary's Pregnancy and the Spirit's Unsettling of Identity

It would have been much easier for Mary if Jesus had arrived in an ordi-nary or at least a culturally acceptable way. The Hebrew Bible is full of examples of divinely instigated pregnancies that occur after marital re-lations have begun (Gen. 21:1–2; Judg. 13; 1 Sam. 1:19–20). Certainly, God might have waited until Mary and Joseph were married to bring Jesus into the world. If demonstrating God's dynamic, creative power was the point, God could have waited until Mary was old and "barren," as is the case with Elizabeth or Sarah. Why would the Spirit "overshadow" Mary when she is young, engaged, and a virgin?

The angel tells Mary that because of the Holy Spirit's overshadowing power, "therefore" the child to be born to Mary will be "holy; he will be called the Son of God" (Luke 1:35). And this presents itself as the most obvious answer.[73] While biblical characters like John, Samson, and Sam-uel are set apart for God's work, or even filled with the Spirit (Luke 1:15), prior to birth, none of them are described as God's Son. Mary's virginity, in this case, points to a relationship of a different order between Jesus and God. Mary's body testifies to the mystery of Jesus's identity.

But there is a certain irony in the angel's prediction. "Son of God" is a designation that Acts uses sparingly (interestingly, only in the voice of

73. Such a response by the angel lends itself to readings that highlight a "male-constructed deity"—with the Spirit standing in for the paternal agent. But such an application is carefully avoided by Luke in his oblique description of the interaction between Mary and the Spirit. Indeed, Acts uses similar language to describe the power (*dynamis*) the apostles received when the Holy Spirit comes upon (*eperchomai*) them (Acts 1:8). See Foskett, *Virgin Conceived*, 119, 122.

Paul [Acts 9:20; 13:33]). And in Luke, it is the devil or those possessed by demons who use the term most frequently (4:3, 41; 8:28). The accusation that Jesus might illegitimately consider himself God's Son, an accusation he answers ambiguously, is the deciding factor in the council's condemnation of Jesus to death (Luke 22:70). If the angel is concerned about testifying to Jesus's identity through Mary's body, the attempt appears to have limited success. Certainly, an unnaturally closed birth canal would have been a better place to start, with a ready midwife to make an examination! Outside witnesses to the Annunciation or a faint halo around Mary's head would have helped. A more ordinary pregnancy is not the only thing that would have made life easier for Mary. A less ordinary pregnancy would have helped as well.

The tension in Luke's account between the "unnatural" and "natural" aspects of Mary's pregnancy creates a dilemma for Mary—an unexpected, untraceable pregnancy for one who is engaged. Luke's repeated acknowledgment of Mary's engagement (1:27; 2:5) surrounds Mary's story with an element of scandal. Mary Foskett reminds her readers that "biblical law rendered betrothed virgins . . . culpable in cases of illicit sexual encounter."[74] And yet Mary chooses this difficulty. In accepting an "exceedingly difficult call . . . like the greatest of the prophets, Mary allows socially derived honor to be supplanted by divine vocation."[75] She believes (Luke 1:45) the word of the Lord, though she has no physical evidence to prove either the veracity of that vocation or her experience of the Spirit's shadow.

Perhaps this is a second reason why the Spirit works through a young, engaged virgin: to make Jesus's identity as God's Son vulnerable to scandalous misinterpretation. It is a suggestion reinforced by Simeon's Spirit-filled prophesy in the temple. When Simeon prophesies over the baby, through the Spirit's power, he tells Mary that the child is a "sign that will be opposed, so that the inner thoughts of many will be revealed" (Luke 2:34–35). While Jesus has a physical body that can be touched and observed, Jesus's identity must be spiritually discerned—often through explicit divine intervention (1:41-43; 2:10-12, 27-32). This is a recurring Lukan theme. Gaventa points out that the "giving and withholding of sight" is a common motif in Luke,[76] as are characters whose identities

---

74. Foskett, *Virgin Conceived*, 123.
75. Foskett, *Virgin Conceived*, 124.
76. Beverly Gaventa, "Learning and Relearning the Identity of Jesus from Luke-

shift and change over the narrative's course (13:16; 19:9; also Acts 9; 13:9). For Gaventa, both motifs reinforce the view that the perception of Jesus's identity in Luke "comes to human beings only as a result of God's gift," an idea especially evident in the Emmaus account.[77] In the case of Elizabeth and Simeon, such discernment is explicitly linked to the work of the Spirit (Luke 1:41; 2:27). Neither Jesus's body nor Mary's reveals the truth of Christ's identity when read according to the patterns of the world.

It is strange, perhaps, to think about Jesus as being both *present* and *absent* in Luke's Gospel. Christ's ascension at the beginning of Acts appears to separate Luke and Acts into strikingly different historical moments, one in which Jesus is bodily immanent and accessible, and one in which he is transcendent and absent. But Acts's account complicates such a view. In Acts, Christ is present, despite his absence. The Nativity account reveals a similar tension. At the vulnerable intersection of an unnatural pregnancy that appears natural and scandalous, Christ is "absent" even in his presence. More particularly, his body requires an act of God to be perceived. Just as Stephen required the Spirit's opening of the heavens to perceive Christ's body "standing at the right hand of God" (Acts 7:55), the Spirit gives Simeon and Elizabeth the eyes to interpret the "sign" before them.

For Sarah Coakley, Jesus "is no less personally mysterious and elusive in his earthly life than in his risen existence."[78] This is her starting place for deconstructing old dichotomies between "the historical Jesus and the risen Christ" and discerning Christ's risen reality "*now*" in the Spirit's "rupture of expectation."[79] For Beverly Gaventa, the constant "relearning" of Christ's identity in Luke—his opacity even in his presence—provides a theological challenge to the "chilling" ethical conflation of Jesus's lordship with contemporary political power and any other attempt to arrive at the identity of Jesus through "human intellect and volition."[80] Finally, it is the mystery at the heart of the cross and resurrection. And, tellingly, this theological theme is obscured when Mary's

Acts," in *Seeking the Identity of Jesus: A Pilgrimage*, ed. Beverly Roberts Gaventa and Richard B. Hays (Grand Rapids: Eerdmans, 2008), 164.

77. Gaventa, "Identity of Jesus from Luke-Acts," 164.

78. Sarah Coakley, "The Identity of the Risen Jesus," in *Seeking the Identity of Jesus: A Pilgrimage*, ed. Beverly Roberts Gaventa and Richard B. Hays (Grand Rapids: Eerdmans, 2008), 308.

79. Coakley, "Identity of the Risen Jesus," 316.

80. Gaventa, "Learning and Relearning," 155.

bearing body, its vulnerabilities, doubts, and lack of "proof," is idealized or ignored.

Pregnancy has at times been conceived as an experience in which an embryonic child is fully present, immanent, and identified with the mother.[81] But Luke's description of Mary's natural-unnatural pregnancy takes care to maintain Christ's Otherness from Mary, both as "Son of God" and as embodied, human baby. The bodily testimonies of pregnant women in this case are instructive. For many women, natural pregnancy is not only an experience of immanence but also of mystery, opacity, and Otherness. In her reflections on pregnant experience, Iris Marion Young describes pregnancy as an "experience of my insides as the space of another, yet my own body."[82] Amy McCullough's interviews with pregnant clergywomen affirm Young's description. For these women, pregnancy is a "profound time of Othering."[83] Women describe their child *in utero* as a "fun, loveable alien" who has "staked its own bodily claim."[84] Bodily boundaries intersect but are maintained. One is intimately connected to a child whose face and form are hidden from view. Arguably, a child conceived by the unnatural circumstances Luke describes would seem more "Other" still.

This ambiguous border between Christ's presence and absence connects Mary's body to the "sign that will be opposed" (Luke 2:34), marking her pregnancy with that sign's vulnerability. The Spirit's unnatural action in bringing about Mary's natural pregnancy foreshadows the scandal of the cross. Through the Spirit, Mary's identity is linked to the history of Christ. Simeon follows up his challenging words about Christ with a particular word for Mary: "and a sword will pierce your own soul too" (Luke 2:35). Simeon makes clear that the child Mary has carried has

81. Julia Kristeva, "Toward a Theory of Self and Social Identity," in Weir, *Sacrificial Logics*, 174-75, traces, for example, an idealization of maternity through the medieval and modern "cult of the Virgin Mary" that "consecrates" all mothers as a place of "immediate fusion, pure gratification—a dream of wholeness, prior to the separation of language from the body."

82. See Iris Marion Young's "Pregnant Embodiment," in *On Female Body Experience: "Throwing Like a Girl" and Other Essays* (Oxford: Oxford University Press, 2005), 49, for a discussion of transcendence and immanence in relation to Merleau-Ponty's phenomenology.

83. Amy McCullough, "Preaching Pregnant: Insights into Embodiment in Preaching" (paper presented, Academy of Homiletics, Chicago, IL, November 15-17, 2012), 185.

84. McCullough, "Preaching Pregnant," 178, 176.

lasting implications for her person. There is more implied here than the intimate bonds of motherhood and the foreshadowed grief of a mother who will lose her son. The text points broadly to the joys and challenges of living in embodied relation with a sign opposed to the ways of the world. In Luke, such a relation is made possible by the *Spirit's* distinctive work, and it is marked by that work. Because of the Spirit, Mary's body reflects the One she bears. Mary, in other words, is not only pained by Jesus's death; through the Spirit-empowered scandal of her pregnancy, she testifies to it.[85] In this case, the bodily testimonies of those who have laid aside security and honor to embrace God's call, persons like Stephen (Acts 7:54–60), seem more insightful than natural mothers in describing the "sword" that pierces Mary's heart.[86]

Or perhaps a more contemporary example of the risks involved in embracing God's call is relevant. A lifelong Methodist and queer Christian sits in my office and tells me she has postponed her ordination process for a time—at least until her Conference has determined its position on ordaining LGBTQ clergy. She has been advised that at present her Conference will affirm a "don't ask, don't tell" policy. There is just one problem. Her identity as queer and her testimony as Christian are all tied together, and she cannot sit before the Board of Ordained Ministry describing one without the other. For her to testify to the ways Jesus has marked her life with his own, she has to reveal who she really is. "I won't lie," she says. She will wait until the Conference makes up its mind, and everyone in the room knows what is at stake. Then she will speak truth. She will witness to the Christ who has marked her identity with the scandal of God's call and let the chips fall where they may.[87]

---

85. As Raymond Brown suggests—she is also judged by it. Brown connects Simeon's reference to a "sword" with the sword of Ezekiel 14:17 that "passes through the land" selecting some for salvation and some for judgment. See Brown, *Birth of the Messiah*, 463.

86. There are many potential examples. For Johnson, Moses serves as a conversation partner for Mary's experience. Johnson notes the similarities between the annunciation and the literary form of "prophetic call" texts such as Moses's commissioning at the burning bush (Exod. 3:1–14). See Johnson, *Truly Our Sister*, 249.

87. Conversation used with permission, December 2018.

Mary's Pregnancy and the Spirit's Unsettling of Agency

The Spirit's impact on Mary's pregnancy not only unsettles her "identity," bringing her body into vulnerable relation with Jesus. It also unsettles Mary's agency, requiring an active dependence that includes consent. In a manner unusual for the many texts of the time that describe the impregnation of a woman by a god, Luke makes clear that Mary agrees to God's "overshadowing" presence.[88] This dual affirmation of Mary's assent and God's action has led to widely divergent interpretations of Mary's agency in Luke's text. The tradition has emphasized either her passive submission or her powerful faith. Indeed, these are often conflated, suggesting that there is a spiritual potency in submission that can evoke spiritual power.[89] In this understanding, Mary's faithful passivity to God is understood as a sort of exchange whereby she earns the honor of bearing Christ through her obedient "perfect co-operation."[90] But such views give salvific emphasis to Mary's action (or nonaction). God initiates contact with Mary, and God's faithfulness to God's promise (Luke 1:35, 37) enables Mary's familiar response, "Let it be with me according to your word" (v. 38). Note that these words do not come after the angel's opening greeting, but *after* a promise of God's sovereignty and action—(i.e., "Nothing will be impossible with God" [v. 37]). Her response is no barter for the glory of mothering the Messiah. It is inspired by *God's* character and action in the world.

But it is a response, all the same.

Luke gives Mary's action significant attention. Foskett notes that despite Luke's emphasis on divine intervention, Mary is the subject of

88. Foskett, *Virgin Conceived*, 124.

89. Such an understanding is descriptive of nineteenth-century Holiness preachers like Phoebe Palmer and Sarah Cooke, who understood a "holiness of heart" to bring with it an "enduement of power." See Susie C. Stanley, *Holy Boldness: Women Preachers' Autobiographies and the Sanctified Self* (Knoxville: University of Tennessee Press, 2002), 91. Tellingly, Cooke's autobiography is titled *The Handmaiden of the Lord* (Chicago: T. B. Arnold, 1896).

90. "Perfect co-operation with the grace of God" and "perfect openness to the action of the Holy Spirit" is the orthodox Catholic opinion, as explained by Pope John Paul II in "Our Lady Intended to Remain a Virgin," General Audience, July 24, 1996. See Duff, "Mary, Servant of the Lord," 69. Alternately, the idea of an exchange of obedience for power is fleshed out by Julia Kristeva through an analysis of artistic traditions surrounding the Virgin Mary in her important chapter "Stabat Mater," in *Tales of Love*, trans. Leon Roudiez (New York: Columbia University Press, 1987), 257–58.

three significant verbs: "*She* will conceive, *she* will bear a son, and *she* will name [her child]."[91] Rowan Williams agrees that the "miracle" of the incarnation is not primarily a "break in the natural order" but this mystery of an "interweaving of the sovereign freedom of God, the contingent freedom of Mary in relation to God, and the freedom of Jesus, shaped by . . . the changes and chances of the history into which he comes."[92] The fact that Luke narrates Mary's response at all, a response "unparalleled in biblical birth narratives, serves to convey a sense of agency that counters the representation of Mary as vulnerable object."[93] For Luke, Mary's response matters.

Mary says, "Here am I, the servant [*doulē*] of the Lord" (v. 38).

Not all have interpreted those words positively. For René Laurentin, the words perpetuate the passive "psychological model of a perpetual minor."[94] Feminists have questioned Mary's capacity to say no to God in the first place, a dangerous extrapolation when coupled with an image of God "as a male authority figure."[95] And then there is the violent, oppressive history surrounding those designated as "slaves," the literal translation of *doulē*. For many womanist scholars, Mary's response is deeply problematic in light of slave women in the American South who were required to "serve the physical requirements of the males of the household, not only feeding and cleaning them but servicing them sexually."[96] Mary's response can be read as compliance in the face of abuse, a caricature of Christian virtue used by Christian slaveholders to "bind slaves to their condition."[97]

And yet in Luke and Acts, the "slave" of God does not only describe a virgin teenager. It describes prophets (Acts 2:18), an ecclesial community (4:29), and apostles (20:19). This complicates interpretation of the term.

---

91. Foskett, *Virgin Conceived*, 118.

92. Rowan Williams, "'The Seal of Orthodoxy': Mary and the Heart of Christian Doctrine," in *Say Yes to God: Mary and the Revealing of the Word Made Flesh*, ed. Martin Warner (London: Tufton Books, 1999), 22.

93. Foskett, *Virgin Conceived*, 124.

94. René Laurentin, "Mary and Womanhood in the Renewal of Christian Anthropology," *Marian Library Studies* 1 (1969): 78.

95. Johnson, *Truly Our Sister*, 26.

96. Johnson, *Truly Our Sister*, 27. See Delores Williams, *Sisters in the Wilderness: The Challenge of Womanist God-Talk* (Maryknoll, NY: Orbis, 1993).

97. Shawn Copeland, "Wading through Many Sorrows: Toward a Theology of Suffering in Womanist Perspective," in *A Troubling in My Soul: Womanist Perspectives on Evil and Suffering*, ed. Emilie Townes (Maryknoll, NY: Orbis, 1993), 122.

When Paul describes his service to God as that of a slave (*douleuō* [Acts 20:19]), he describes captivity to the Holy Spirit (v. 22) in which he takes responsibility for his behavior and charges the Ephesian elders to do the same. There is an active passivity in this description, a connection between *who one is* and *what one does* in daily Spirit-empowered relationship with Christ. In the words of Renita Weems, "Mary was not as helpless or inexperienced as she's been made out to be. Nor was she quite as passive."[98] Her claimed identity is an act of self-definition.

Once again, there is an analogy in the natural experience of pregnancy that illuminates the mystery. Pregnancy intersects a human woman at both the level of identity and agency. It changes who one *is* in ways that seem outside of one's autonomous control, but it is also something that one performs in time.[99] Often, the active agency of the pregnant woman has been overlooked in descriptions of pregnancy and childbirth. In *The Woman in the Body*, Emily Martin discusses the ways in which women's bodies have been constructed as either passive, dangerous, or unimportant in the process of bearing a child.[100] Given this reluctance to speak of a woman's pregnancy as an active process, it is no surprise that *passivity* and *submission* have become the primary ways to talk about Mary's interaction with the child in her womb. But while it is true that the miracle of life growing inside a mother happens in spite of her day-to-day activity, bearing a baby is work—or, to put a finer point on it, *labor*. And this labor does not simply begin at the moment of delivery; it begins the moment that one's blood and body come into a lived relation with an other. Young notes, for example, the way this physical relation brings with it a new sense of one's own body and agency through "the material weight that I am in movement."[101] In a concrete, embodied

---

98. Renita Weems, *Showing Mary* (New York: Warner Books, 2002), 75.

99. Young describes the "temporality" of pregnancy and its impact on one's understanding of identity in relation. "The pregnant subject," she states, "is not simply a splitting in which the two halves lie open and still, but a dialectic. . . . Though she does not plan and direct it, neither does it merely wash over her; rather, she *is* the process." See Young, *Female Body Experience*, 54.

100. Emily Martin, *The Woman in the Body: A Cultural Analysis of Reproduction* (Boston: Beacon Press, 1987). Young agrees, particularly discussing the ways that the "normal procedures of the American hospital birthing setting" increase the "passivity" of women in the birth process. See Young, *Female Body Experience*, 58. These are procedures, of course, to which Mary would not have been privy.

101. Young states, "I am an actor transcending through each moment to further projects, but the solid inertia and demands of my body call me to my limits, not as

way, pregnancy describes the passively active border between "being and becoming."[102]

For Mary, to live as a *doulē* of God is to live in embodied relation with Jesus, a relation that requires her active participation. It is a relationship that changes *who she is* through *what she does*. However, by the Spirit's power, it also affects *what she does* by changing *who she is*. And this is where the analogy to natural pregnancy falls short of Mary's experience, even as it suggests it. For Mary, bearing Christ to the world does not only transform her in the way that mothers are transformed by their children. She is transformed in the way that a disciple is transformed by a Spirit-empowered relation with Jesus.[103]

When Luke describes the way that the church has been "obtained" through the "blood of [God's] own Son" (Acts 20:28) in Paul's Ephesus sermon, he uses an unusual verb to describe the transaction. Rather than use the more common word for "purchase" or "buy" (*agorazō*), Luke uses the verb *peripoieō*, implying an ongoing act of "preserving alive."[104] In the LXX, it appears in Isaiah 43:21, which the NRSV translates as "formed for myself."[105] Luke's usage implies a past action that has a present, ongoing impact and personal engagement. He describes a relation to Christ's blood that is formational, rather than transactional. The material connections of pregnancy and placental blood, blood that "preserves alive" and "forms" over time, suggest themselves.[106] It is a

---

an obstacle to action, but as a fleshly relation to earth." See Young, *Female Body Experience*, 52.

102. Charles Campbell and Johan Cilliers, *Preaching Fools: The Gospel as a Rhetoric of Folly* (Waco, TX: Baylor University Press, 2012), 51.

103. Gaventa makes a point of honoring of the distinctiveness of the roles of "disciple" and "mother" in Mary's experience. See Gaventa, *Mary*, 73. For Gaventa, Mary's self-designation as *doulē*, confirmed by its use in the rest of Luke-Acts, is a description of discipleship. While I have underscored the way that the embodied experience of pregnancy illuminates the experience of a disciple, I affirm this distinction. To put a finer point on it, Mary is not—to use the language of 1 Timothy 2:15—"saved through childbearing" even though the child she bears is Jesus. She is saved through her discipleship to Christ—*in a way descriptive of childbearing*. She is a saved in a way that affects both *what she does* and *who she is*.

104. "περιποιέω," *The Greek-English Lexicon of the New Testament*, ed. F. Wilbur Gingrich and Frederick Danker (Chicago: University of Chicago Press, 1979), 650. See also, "4046. peripoieō," *New Strong's Exhaustive Concordance of the Bible* (Nashville: Thomas Nelson, 2003).

105. "περιποιέω," *Greek-English Lexicon*.

106. In the one other time the verb is used by Luke (Luke 17:33), it is in parallel

description of lived relation to Christ that implies a larger "womb" at work in the world.

When Mary bears a son to the world, she discovers a new identity in the process, and not only the identity of mother. In embracing the labor of her pregnancy and the work of the Spirit in that labor, she allows her body to be transformed by a lived dependence on a Savior (Luke 2:11)—and she receives a new name: the *doulē* of the Lord (1:38).[107] To submit one's agency to this kind of formative relation does require a certain death to one's own autonomy and power, but it is a far cry from an abnegation of the self. Indeed, as Mary's song of praise reveals, her experience of being God's *doulē* is one of joy and blessing (1:47–48). Through her embodied relation with Christ, Mary does not simply give birth; she is born again.

And she is not alone. Claiming one's identity as a pastor and preacher can require a similar submission and can call forth a similar song. Yolanda Correa is an ordained Puerto Rican pastor. The stole she received at ordination is important to Correra, symbolizing "a yoke, a covenant made between Christ and us." Just before entering the sanctuary, she pulls one side of the stole so that it hangs unevenly around her neck. "In my particular case, I always have the right side be longer than the left, understanding [that when wearing a yoke] . . . the oldest animal, who is stronger and more experienced, always carries the heavier weight in the journey of plowing the soil." She is used to parishioners trying to pull it straight until she explains to them the theological significance. She does not bear this yoke alone. In the labor of ministry, there is One who bears the yoke with her, and her uneven vestment testifies to this Presence. "I believe the stole symbolizes the arms of my Lord that arc around me, . . . telling me, 'you can because I am with you.'" Through the Spirit's unsettling work, she bears Christ's burden and Christ bears her.[108]

---

construction with the verb *zōogoneō*, which literally means to "bring to birth." See "2225. zōogoneō," *New Strong's*. See also "ζωογονέω," *Greek-English Lexicon*, 341.

107. It would be more obvious, of course, for her to say, "Here am I, the *mother* of the Lord." Mary uses, instead, a self-designation that Luke will later use to describe prophets, apostles, preachers, and the Spirit-empowered ecclesial community.

108. Yolanda Correa, interviewed and translated by Yolanda Santiago-Correa, April 2018. Used with permission.

Mary's Pregnancy and the Spirit's Unsettling of Communal Role

In her description of Mary in Luke and Acts, Gaventa makes a point of emphasizing the multiplicity of roles that Mary plays in the text. In speaking of roles, rather than symbols or types, Gaventa grounds her description of Mary in Luke's attention to her actions, her relationships with other characters, and the way that Mary functions in the larger scope of the narrative.[109] In other words, she pays attention to the way that Mary *performs* in Luke's text—who she is and what she does in light of her relation to the characters and communal/textual expectations around her. Gaventa names three ways that she sees Mary performing in the narrative: as *disciple*, as *prophet*, and *mother*.[110] Her distinguishing of Mary's multiple roles in Luke raises a challenge for Protestant and Roman Catholic approaches to Mary that would conflate these roles by emphasizing one at the expense of others. Lois Malcolm describes how a Protestant focus on God's initiative and a Catholic focus on Mary's physical body have muted the narrative's description.[111]

But the relationships between Mary's different roles—the way, for example, that Christian discipleship informs Mary's motherhood or vice versa—is brought into focus by the Holy Spirit. The Holy Spirit is not only an agent of commissioning and power in Luke's text. As I've described, the Spirit's action creates a living dependence between one's *identity* and *agency* and the person of Christ. In so doing, the Spirit's work complicates a believer's *communal role*. In Acts 10, Peter's dynamic relation to communal norms is the result of his embodied, Spirit-empowered dependence on Christ as "Lord of all" (Acts 10:36). Similarly, Mary's embodied relation to Christ's body, made possible by the Spirit, illumines the significance of Mary's roles even as it destabilizes them. In Mary's Magnificat, her roles of *mother*, *disciple*, and *prophet* are all on display, informing each other in ways that disrupt communal expectations.[112]

---

109. Gaventa, *Mary*, 72–73.

110. Gaventa, *Mary*, 72–73.

111. Lois Malcolm, "What Mary Has to Say about God's Bare Goodness," in *Blessed One: Protestant Perspectives on Mary*, ed. Beverly Gaventa and Cynthia Rigby (Louisville: Westminster John Knox, 2002), 139–41, uses Martin Luther's "Commentary on the Magnificat," in *Luther's Works* 21 (St. Louis: Concordia, 1956); and Hans Urs von Balthasar's *The Glory of the Lord: A Theological Aesthetics*, vol. 1, trans. Erasmo Leiva-Merikakis (San Francisco: Ignatius Press, 1982), to illustrate her point.

112. I should clarify, here, that Mary's prophetic role has been embraced by Prot-

While Luke does not explicitly describe Mary's Magnificat as the speech of a prophet, many interpreters have pointed out its prophetic character.[113] Malcolm describes Mary's assertion as performing an "epistemological shift" in which she declares "a true perception of events in light of God's future transformation of them."[114] Indeed, this outpouring of prophetic speech was preceded by a Spirit-inspired affirmation of Mary's motherhood. Elizabeth's loud cry that Mary is "mother of my Lord" and "blessed among women" (1:43, 42), despite Mary's situation as an engaged, pregnant young person, instigates Mary's words. This connection between motherhood and prophesy is both familiar and foreign to Mary's tradition. On the one hand, Mary stands in the tradition of Hannah, another mother who sang a song of praise to God (1 Sam. 2:1–10).[115] Mary's motherhood, however, is not the same as Hannah's. While Hannah's pregnancy is a visible mark of God's blessing, Mary's pregnancy is invisible as "blessing," except by the Spirit's power. In significant ways, Mary does not fit the mold of Hannah or the other "barren" women who give birth in Jewish tradition.[116] And yet her affirmation of God's faithfulness "from generation to generation" (Luke 1:50) places her experience in conversation with theirs. In fact, Mary's wonder at God's favor flows from the fact that she does not fit the mold. God has, in Mary's words, "lifted up the lowly" (v. 52) in selecting her to be the mother of the Messiah.

For many interpreters, Mary's "lowliness" is a description of both

---

estants and Catholics alike who have experienced oppression, poverty, or ecclesial exclusion from the pulpit. Mary's prophetic role, for example, is repeatedly emphasized by women who have had the call to preach denied them. See Johnson, *Truly Our Sister*, 266–76; Sarah Cooke, *Handmaiden of the Lord*; and Jarena Lee, *The Life and Religious Experience of Jarena Lee, a Coloured Lady, Giving an Account of Her Call to Preach the Gospel* in *Sisters of the Spirit: Three Women's Autobiographies of the Nineteenth Century*, ed. W. Andrews (Bloomington: Indiana University Press, 1986), 36.

113. Gaventa, *Mary*, 58; and Brown, *Birth of the Messiah*, 362–63. See also Clayton Croy and Alice Conner, "Mantic Mary? The Virgin Mother as Prophet in Luke 1:26–56 and the Early Church," *Journal for the Study of the New Testament* 34, no. 3 (2011): 254–76.

114. Malcolm, *Blessed One*, 135. Malcolm borrows this language from J. Louis Martyn's discussion of the "epistemology of apocalyptic discourse." See J. Louis Martyn, "Apocalyptic Antinomies in Paul's Letter to the Galatians," in *Theological Issues in the Letters of Paul* (Nashville: Abingdon Press, 1997).

115. Johnson, *Truly Our Sister*, 264; and Brown, *Birth of the Messiah*, 258–59.

116. As Gaventa points out, for example, Mary "makes no request of God for the gift of a child." See Gaventa, *Mary*, 52.

her vulnerable sociological and sexual status.[117] She does not come from a place of privilege. For Gaventa, the term is also linked with Mary's new identity of *doulē* (v. 48). The *doulē* of the Magnificat, however, is not passive and silent. She is bold in her praise and in her proclamation of God's power and goodness. Furthermore, in embracing her role as "slave of God," Mary refuses to act as the slave to any human being.[118] Her song has a "revolutionary" ring, rejoicing in the scattering of the proud and the removal of the powerful from their thrones (vv. 51–52).[119] Johnson begins her discussion of the Magnificat by noting that it is "the longest passage put on the lips of any female speaker in the New Testament."[120] As such, the Magnificat serves as a critique of any "scripture silencing the lowly." It is, in Johnson's words, a particular "protest against the suppression of women's voices and a spark for their prophetic speech."[121]

I note here that in the space of several verses and in a single setting (Luke 1:41–55), Luke highlights all three of Mary's textual roles: Mary's role as God's handmaid and *disciple*, her vulnerable role as Jesus's *mother*, and her active role as *prophet*. Each, however, is destabilized by an "epistemic shift" brought about by the Spirit. It is the lowly *doulē* who speaks with prophetic power (see Acts 2:18); it is the powerful *prophet* whose speech flows from a Spirit-filled affirmation of her motherhood; it is the *mother* who is blessed, not because of the "fruit of her womb" but because she is God's *doulē*—because she believed "what was spoken to her by the Lord" (Luke 1:45).

This scene between Elizabeth and Mary has resonated with natural mothers as an example of the "craving" that pregnant woman have for "contact with . . . other pregnant women" to help them negotiate the com-

---

117. Foskett, *Virgin Conceived*, 127; and Johnson, *Truly Our Sister*, 265.

118. Gaventa, *Mary*, 54. See also Joel Green's discussion of how Mary's self-designation reverses social norms in "The Social Status of Mary in Luke 1,5–2,52: A Plea for Methodological Integration," *Biblica* 73, no. 4 (1992): 457–72.

119. Johnson, *Truly Our Sister*, 269.

120. Johnson, *Truly Our Sister*, 263.

121. Johnson, *Truly Our Sister*, 263. Feminist scholars describe an "implicit or structural" silencing of women in Luke's narrative. See Wilson's short summary in *Unmanly Men*, 79–80. Elisabeth Schüssler Fiorenza, for example, coins the term "Lukan silence" in *In Memory of Her: A Feminist Theological Reconstruction of Christian Origins* (New York: Crossroad, 1983). In this light, Mary's Magnificat becomes particularly significant. Her spoken response to Spirit-filled Elizabeth can be seen as cutting against the grain.

plicated new role they are embracing.[122] Johnson stresses the value of these female relationships as places to "share fears, find courage, express hopes and learn practical wisdom."[123] It is also a story that communicates the potency of female cooperation rather than competition.[124] It makes a great deal of natural sense that Mary would experience a sense of validation and integration in the presence of another pregnant woman. But finally, it is not Elizabeth's natural pregnancy that gives her insight into Mary's situation and calls forth Mary's praise. It is Elizabeth's unnatural encounter with the Holy Spirit. At the root of Mary's shifting communal roles is Elizabeth's own Spirit-empowered witness that the unwed mother before her is the mother of the Lord (Luke 1:42-45).

The Spirit's unsettling of these communal roles brings about *participation* and *differentiation* between Mary and her tradition. Many have emphasized her identification with God's "servant" Israel and her affirmation of God's remembrance of the promise God made to "our ancestors, to Abraham and to his descendants forever" (Luke 1:54-55).[125] When Mary's words are recited in present-day liturgies, they invite contemporary believers to claim a common history and a common ancestor as "ours" (v. 55). And yet her song stands as a critique of any codification of tradition that would set up the powerful on thrones or silence the lowly as suspect. It critiques any attempt to interpret God's salvation history as independent of God's saving action. As C. M. Tuckett describes in his article "The Christology of Luke-Acts," Jesus's identity in Luke-Acts fulfills God's promises to God's people, but it also involves a "redefinition of almost every aspect of those promises."[126] Christ is not codified in a textual tradition but is discerned and embraced in that tradition through the power of God. Christ's discernment requires a Spirit-empowered shift that "will not appeal to those who are satisfied with the way things are."[127] Dealing specifically with issues of gender inequality in the Cath-

122. See, for example, Renita Weems, *Just a Sister Away: A Womanist Vision of Women's Relationships in the Bible* (San Diego: Lura Media, 1988), 119. Sometimes, Weems suggests, this desire is simply a desire to feel "normal."

123. Johnson, *Truly Our Sister*, 260.

124. See Barbara Reid's discussion in *Choosing the Better Part? Women in the Gospel of Luke* (Collegeville, MN: Liturgical Press, 1996), 73-74.

125. Luke Timothy Johnson speaks of a "personification" of Israel in *The Gospel of Luke*, Sacra Pagina (Collegeville, MN: Liturgical Press, 1991), 43.

126. Tuckett, "Christology of Luke-Acts," 162.

127. Johnson, *Truly Our Sister*, 269.

olic Church, Johnson reflects on what it means to "pray Mary's song each night at Vespers" in a community where women still occupy a "subordinate position in current church structures." She states, "If [Mary's song] is applied to women's struggle for full participation in governance and ministry in the church, the reversals of the Magnificat become rife with significance for ecclesial life."[128]

In Acts 10, the Spirit's power brings Peter to a new recognition of Christ's lordship over all and a new understanding of his role in relation to gentile believers. In Mary's Magnificat, the Spirit's power, which instigates Elizabeth's blessing, allows Mary to *prophetically* claim her roles of *doulē* and *mother* as simultaneous signs of God's faithfulness. The Spirit's unsettling of communal expectations makes space for new understanding—then and now. Susana Cokanauto is an ordained Fijian Methodist pastor, a rarity for women in this South Pacific nation. She considers herself a feminist deeply committed to the preservation of indigenous culture. These intersecting roles play out in her choice of clothing on her wedding day. When she walks down the aisle, she does not only wear a woman's traditional South Pacific wedding attire, she wears her white, preaching coat. She tells me later the significance of her choice. "In becoming a wife," she says, "I am still a preacher. I wanted everyone to know that I am not giving up one for the other. I am both."[129] Susana's body witnesses to the Spirit's unsettling call, stretching the expectations of her community. Her dress testifies to a God who calls preachers to be wives and wives to be preachers, redefining the definitions of both.

The Womb and the Cross

We've gotten so focused on redeeming souls that we've forgotten that Jesus came to redeem bodies.[130]

Mary's pregnancy matters in Luke as something more than a model or symbol. It is a site of Christ's embodied relation, and as such it bears the marks of that relation. It shows us something about Jesus. In contrast

---

128. Johnson, *Truly Our Sister*, 272. Johnson's point is, of course, relevant for any number of Protestant communions as well.

129. Susana Cokanauto, personal conversation, Suva, Fiji, May 2015.

130. Interview with a pastor on the joys and challenges of preaching, August 14, 2013.

to idealizations of pregnancy that see it solely as a site of "wholeness," "union," and "life," Luke's description of Mary's pregnancy suggests that Christ's cross and Mary's labor are more connected than one would think. Certainly, Mary's womb is the site of Christ's kenotic sacrifice. Certainly, birth requires sacrifice and an ability to endure pain and danger for the sake of another. A deeper connection, however, is beautifully illustrated in Luke 14:27, where Luke's use of the Greek *bastazō* (i.e., "to carry" the cross) is language that also connotes the carrying of a child.[131] This is the same verb the angel Gabriel uses to describe Mary's bearing work (Luke 1:31) and the work of wombs more generally (Luke 11:27). Mary's experience in this case echoes the experiences of Acts's preachers. When the Spirit overshadows these followers of Christ, they carry a cross—or perhaps more accurately, they carry the Crucified One within them. When they bear him to the world, they bear his likeness, for they too are being born again. Finally, to draw on the language of Paul in Galatians, when they carry the cross of Christ, as with the work of bearing a child, they "carry [*bastazō*] the marks" (Gal. 6:17) of that work in their bodies. Through the Spirit's destabilization of *identity, agency, and communal role*, easy securities and idolatries are challenged. God's people lay aside worldly understandings of autonomy, power, and authority, and in so doing the person of the Crucified One comes into view. This body is not only a past object for imitation. By the power of the Spirit, Christ actively participates in the bodily performances of his followers. And in so doing, their faithful performances testify to that present-tense, physical relation. They testify to Christ's *absence* and *presence* in the world, relational dependence between *who one is* and *what one does* in response to Christ's call, and *participation in* and *differentiation from* their communal traditions as a sign of Christ's lordship. Each of these marks of the Spirit can be seen in Luke's description of Mary's pregnancy and his accounts of Acts's preachers. But Mary's pregnancy does more than mirror the marks of the Spirit in Acts. It focuses our attention on the labor of embodied

---

131. For this insight, I am indebted to Anna Gillette and her unpublished paper on the subject. Luke Timothy Johnson underscores the distinctiveness of Luke's language in contrast to Mark and Matthew's "taking up" the cross and "accepting" the cross, respectively. See Luke Timothy Johnson, *The Gospel of Luke*, Sacra Pagina (Collegeville, MN: Liturgical Press, 1991), 229–33; and "βαστάζω," *Greek-English Lexicon of the New Testament*, 137. In contrast to "taking up," "bearing" suggests carrying an object through time, be it a burden (Gal. 6:2), a coffin (Luke 7:14), or Christ's name (Acts 9:15)—something that bearing a child brings into focus.

relation itself. There is no script for us to follow. We cannot *be* who Mary *is*. And yet as a metaphor contextually discerned, Mary suggests a way to describe embodied relation with Christ's body—a relation that is both Spirit-inspired and fully human.

Over the centuries, women have drawn on Mary's birth of Christ to justify their call to preach. Jarena Lee is an example. When explaining her call to a skeptical nineteenth-century church, Lee drew on the Annunciation promise: "Nothing is impossible with God."[132] Pay attention to Lee's wisdom here. She does not waste time describing an essential similarity she shares with Mary, either as potent symbol or ideal woman. Lee starts with a promise about God. As J. Kameron Carter notes, Lee's understanding of her call starts with Christ, visible through his active, impossible participation in Mary's body. Through the Spirit's power, "Mary's body articulates Jesus's body at the same time that Jesus's body, abiding in her, articulates Mary's."[133] Because of this, Lee is able, through that same Spirit, to "receive herself anew from Christ" and understand her own body as "proclamation." Her "despised dark (female) flesh" becomes an articulation of Jesus "and his body hers."[134] She is neither dissolved nor dismissed. She does not loom larger than life, but she also refuses to fade away. In fact, for Lee, the act of preaching is a Spirit-empowered encounter with Christ in which one *does not* fade away.

We have seen that "starting with the body of Christ" is a theologically appropriate starting place for describing the relation between the Spirit and the preacher's performance in the pulpit. But it is important to reiterate where this insight leads. In Luke, starting with the body of Christ allows Mary, as human woman, to appear in all her particularity. To start with Christ's body in a theology of sermon performance allows human preachers to do the same. It does not suggest the unimportance of the preacher's body. It asserts the preacher's sacramental significance. Carter's "double-directional" reading of Lee's relation to Christ's body, a relation following the logic of Mary's pregnancy, is not so different from Calvin's understanding of the "mystical union" between believer and Christ in the Eucharist.[135] In Calvin's words, "Christ is not outside us, but

132. Lee, *Life and Religious Experience*, 36.

133. J. Kameron Carter, *Race: A Theological Account* (Oxford: Oxford University Press, 2008), 342.

134. Carter, *Race*, 342.

135. This understanding of Calvin's "union" as a performed, Spirit-empowered relation in time is most clearly delineated in his debate with Osiander, discussed in

dwells within us."[136] We, in turn, "do not contemplate him outside ourselves from afar ... but are engrafted into his body ... because he deigns to make us one with him."[137] For Lee and Calvin—as with Luke—God's salvation has everything to do with fully human bodies, not as essences but in their performed relation to Jesus: "a Savior who is the Messiah, the Lord" (Luke 2:11).

John Calvin, *Institutes of the Christian Religion*, Library of Christian Classics (Philadelphia: Westminster, 1960), 1:729-43.

136. Calvin, *Institutes*, 1:570.
137. Calvin, *Institutes*, 1:737.

CHAPTER 5

Fully Human Preaching

I am 5 foot 4 inches of strength, ability and power
But most of it is hidden by a wooden pulpit
Built on years of male supremacy
Reminding me, I'm only visiting.
I am 5 foot 4 inches of poise, wisdom and education
But you can't hear it because the microphone isn't pointed
     at my mouth
Don't worry, I'll move it down
It'll remind me I'm only visiting

Taylor Pryde Barefoot, unpublished poem

Katherine stands stiff in the pulpit. Her voice trembles. She doesn't like the story she is about to tell. It is the true story of a friend who died crossing the border. She is preaching about wilderness, and she wants us to know that she is not idealizing or spiritualizing her subject matter. She knows the border is both ugly and real. After telling her friend's story, she tells her own. Katherine's moonlit border crossing happened when she was a child, holding tight to the hand of her mother. Despite her fear, she tells us of the God she discovered in the dark, the God who traveled with her. It is the same God, she says, who traveled with her friend and mourned her friend's death. The congregation sits very still. Katherine does not tell us to go to the wilderness. She does not romanticize the journey or the supposed American dream. She is not asking to be imitated. She is not even asking to be believed. She tells what she has lived. She appears out of the shadows, and through her particular undocumented journey and the biblical exile of God's people, the journeys of others find voice. Finally, a different undocumented crossing comes into view: the crossing of God from heaven to earth, born in moonlight, searching for a mother's hand.[1]

How does a body matter? And how does it not? What is at stake in this academic conversation about rhetoric and revelation, Spirit and flesh? It is more than doctrinal purity. The affirmation of Christ's resurrected body, present by the Spirit in moments of Christian proclamation, is what makes fully human preaching possible and revelatory. It is what marks preachers' bodies as embodied signs of God's salvation. It's what makes preaching matter.

But the implications of this biblically grounded promise stretch beyond the personal. This assertion of a preacher's bodily value calls for the dismantling of sermon performance criteria grounded in bodies of knowledge, bodies of cultural capital, or human bodies that substitute for the body of Christ. There is the dispersing of transcendent norms and transparent shadows so that fully human preachers, in all of their diversity, can appear. There is a dismantling of a pulpit "built only for some."[2] The narratives of Luke and Acts point Christian pulpit practice away from worldly assumptions of autonomy, power, and authorization. They describe human preachers (and mothers) who exist in embodied relation to Jesus by the Spirit's power, human persons who stand in borderlands of vulnerable engagement with Christ and community. I am convinced the living relation they describe is possible today. Martin Luther said it like this: "For this preaching means, 'Fear not for unto you is born this day the Savior, which is Christ the Lord.'"[3] And Luther is not alone. A former classmate affirms the same angelic promise when our preaching professor asks what makes it possible for a preacher to be surprised, at sermon's end, by the very words she has proclaimed. "*Jesus is in the house,*" she whispers.[4]

---

1. Katherine Guerrero (sermon, Homegrown North Carolina Women's Preaching Festival, Trinity Presbyterian Church, Durham, NC, October 26, 2018).

2. To paraphrase Ahmed's description of the feminist task. See Sarah Ahmed, *Living a Feminist Life* (Durham, NC: Duke University Press, 2017),14.

3. Martin Luther, *Predigt von der Engle Lobgesang*, 1544, quoted in Karl Barth, *Church Dogmatics*, I/1, ed. Geoffrey W. Bromiley and T. F. Torrance, trans. Geoffrey W. Bromiley (Edinburgh: T&T Clark, 1975), 113.

4. Jerusha Neal, journal entry, September 9, 2013.

"Theology needs a performative lens," Kay tells us. In the last two chapters, Luke and Acts have been that lens—our spectacles of narrated human action bringing the compass needle of theology into view. Before moving forward, it is worth summarizing what we have seen. In all of this unsettling of identity, agency, and communal norms, what theological trajectories emerge? Luke and Acts show marks of Spirit-empowered relationality foreshadowed and echoed in different bodies, times, and spaces. But what do these marks reveal for a theology of preaching? What do Mary's pregnancy and birth of Christ reveal about the relational, proclamatory labor of Word and words? I sketch three, constructive implications.

The Word of God as a Performing, Embodied Person

To use Mary's pregnancy and birth of Jesus as a metaphor informing preaching performance reclaims the significance of the embodied, resurrected Jesus in the sermonic event. It forces preachers to start with the body of Christ in their understanding of their own performance in a way consistent with the Reformers' understanding of the sacraments. The Reformers parsed the problem differently, to be sure. Different issues were at stake for each. But Luther, Calvin, and Zwingli were united in their belief that Jesus's body could not be dissolved into institutional practice or dismissed by individual piety. It could not be taken for granted or dispersed by ecclesial guarantee. It was truly absent and truly present, which meant Christ's presence was a Spirit-empowered gift received through a believer's performed faith.[5] It was an *opus operantis* event brought about by divine "embrace."[6] Understanding the relationship between living Word and sermonic words through the metaphor of Mary's pregnancy affirms that there is a divine Agent who speaks and acts in the human performance of preaching. More than this, this Agent is mediated through the sermon.

5. John Calvin, *Institutes of the Christian Religion*, Library of Christian Classics (Philadelphia: Westminster, 1960), 2:1394. Calvin uses the term *gross mixture* or substitution to critique Osiander's understanding of Christ's righteousness (2:736–38).

6. Calvin uses the term *embrace* with regard to "the meaning that the Spirit of God offers" in biblical interpretation and with regard to the sacrament. See Calvin, *Institutes*, 2:1392. The term suggests his performative understanding of the "passively active" nature of human, sacramental action (2:1303, 1366).

And yet. The Otherness of this Agent from the preacher's performing body is honored, not just because of his transcendence but because of his resurrected body and bone. The *is* in Bullinger's famous definition of preaching (i.e., "The preaching of the Word of God is the Word of God")[7] is a tricky thing, in a similar way to the *is* of the Words of Institution. Calvin has an extended discussion of that eucharistic *is*.[8] He never backs off his belief that the words "This *is* my body" (Matt. 26:26) mean what they say. But because Jesus has a *particular, permeable, provisional* body, they mean what they say through the Spirit's active bridging of earth and heaven. They mean what they say in a way that never substitutes Christ's body with another. To use Mary's pregnancy as a metaphor for preaching illumines and complicates Bullinger's *is* in similar fashion. It affirms the Confession's stress on Jesus's presence. But it also affirms Jesus's absence by insisting that he has a body too. We cannot be who *he* is.

It took me a while to notice the pregnant imagery that runs all through Calvin's descriptions of sacramental participation. One sees what one expects to see. But it's there. Calvin supplements his descriptions of the sacrament as "food" for faith (i.e., something that we ingest regularly to give us strength) with images of the believer being taken up into Christ's body, through the Spirit, and feeding on him internally.[9] The image is implicitly placental. The believer feeds on Christ's body and blood while internal to Christ's person. Such an image is not a decorative gloss; it is theologically significant for Calvin. It counters the theological position that Christ loses his bodily integrity in the sacrament. Calvin is intent to avoid this point of view. By pairing the image of eating external food with an image of internally feeding on Christ's body, made possible by the Spirit, Calvin insists on both real participation and real differentiation between the believer and Christ—a "mystical union" performed in time.[10]

---

7. Heinrich Bullinger, Second Helvetic Confession, 5.004.

8. Calvin, *Institutes*, 2:1387–92.

9. See Calvin, *Institutes*, 2:1362, for his description of the sacrament as a witness "of our growth into one body with Christ" and his stress on the believer's Spirit-empowered ascent in the Eucharist. Calvin's language suggests a kind of "feeding" in which the bodily integrity of both parties is maintained: "I reject their teaching of the mixture, or transfusion of Christ's flesh with our soul. . . . From the substance of his flesh, Christ . . . pours forth his very life into us—even though Christ's flesh itself does not enter into us." See Calvin, *Institutes*, 2:1404.

10. Calvin, *Institutes*, 2:1361.

Calvin was a man of his historical moment, and he never explicitly uses the metaphor of a pregnant woman to articulate Christ's body.[11] His assumptions around the gendered particularity of Christ's humanity keep him from speculation on this front. (The Scripture, it should be noted, does not rule out intersex possibilities.)[12] But this Reformed theologian, swimming in patriarchal streams, stretching for language to describe the theological mystery of Christ's risen presence with God's people, repeatedly returns to images that evoke a mother and her unborn child. Perhaps it comes from reading Paul, who uses prepositions like *in* and *through* to describe the participation between Christ and believer.[13] Or reading Peter (1 Pet. 1:3), James (James 1:18), and John (John 3:3). We don't know. But the bodily logic of Spirit-empowered pregnancy runs through Calvin's thought, whether Christ is described as internally present in us, or we are described as internally hidden in him. Christ "refreshes" us as food,[14] even while he "abides in our flesh"[15] and "engraft[s us] into his body."[16] The homiletic question, of course, is how such images of bodily participation impact a theology of public proclamation, and finally, the act of preaching itself. Eating and digesting, even when through placental connection, do not evoke the externalized effort involved in preaching a sermon. *How is it, then, that the Word that is Christ relates to the preacher's performed words?*

11. As do, for example, various medieval mystics. See Paul Rorem, "Lover and Mother: Medieval Language for God and the Soul," in *Women, Gender, and Christian Community*, ed. James Kay and Jane Dempsey Douglass (Louisville: Westminster John Knox, 1997). Note, however, Jane Dempsey Douglass's article on Calvin's openness to using mother imagery to describe God—particularly in his appropriation of biblical imagery. See Jane Dempsey Douglass, "Calvin's Use of Metaphorical Language for God: God as Enemy and God as Mother," in *Articles on Calvin and Calvinism*, ed. Richard Gamble (New York: Garland Press, 1992), 6:91-92.

12. I would simply note, here, that the maleness of Jesus's internal organs is an assumption on Calvin's part. The biblical witness is silent on the subject. In current medical literature, persons born with intersex characteristics are not understood, by natural means, to be able to conceive or carry a child, but then, Calvin's "mystical union"—similar to the Luke's account of Mary's pregnancy—assumes an unnatural, pneumatological intervention.

13. Dorothy Martyn describes these "double-directional" descriptions as "pregnant prepositions." See Dorothy Martyn, "A Child and Adam: A Parable of the Two Ages," in *Apocalyptic and the New Testament: Essays in Honor of J. Louis Martyn*, ed. Joel Marcus and Marion Soards (Sheffield: JSOT Press, 1989), 325.

14. Calvin, *Institutes*, 2:1370.

15. Calvin, *Institutes*, 2:1368.

16. Calvin, *Institutes* 1:737.

Scholars make a distinction between the work of the Spirit in Mary's pregnancy and the Spirit's mediation of Christ in and through the words of Acts's preachers for a very good reason.[17] They fear that the divine Word of God and the human words of the preacher will be collapsed in such a comparison. They do not want the words of the preacher to be equated with the embodied revelation: Jesus of Nazareth. *But such a conflation is the antithesis of my argument.* To understand Mary's pregnancy as a metaphor for sermonic action is to see both pregnancy and sermon as entirely human, Spirit-empowered performances of relationship. The sermon is not essentialized or abstracted out of time. It is not divine content that takes on human embodiment. It is not a manuscript that requires "mixing" with rhetorical delivery. It is, most certainly, not *the baby*. From idea to page to body, the sermon is a human performance analogous to the pregnant labor of Mary, labor made possible by the Spirit that bears Christ to the world. The embodied person of Jesus, God's revelation of Godself, is made present in and through this performance.

As in Luke and Acts, however, this revealed Word is elusive. It is a sign that requires spiritual discernment. In the sermonic event, Jesus is "in the house" with salvific power, but the *doulē*'s voice and the voice of the Savior are not one and the same. Mary's pregnancy as a metaphor for preaching suggests, in this sense, a rephrasing of Bullinger's assertion, even as it affirms its core: "Through the Spirit, the preaching of the Word of God *bears* the Word of God." And, I would add, the Word of God bears human preacher and congregation.[18]

The Sermon as a Perversely Eschatological Act of the Spirit

To speak of "bearing" the embodied Christ in such a way is to speak of an entirely unnatural state of affairs, particularly because of a body's natural borders.[19] Such a bearing might be easier to explain if Christ were

17. Roger Stronstad makes this distinction in *The Charismatic Theology of St. Luke* (Peabody, MA: Hendrickson, 1988), 37.

18. Calvin describes the believing congregation as having been "begotten by the Word." See Calvin, *Institutes*, 2:1360.

19. Paul Minear describes the world of Luke's Nativity as "perversely eschatological" in his "Luke's Use of the Birth Stories," in *Studies in Luke-Acts*, ed. Leander Keck and Louis Martyn (Nashville: Abingdon Press, 1966), 125.

understood as a force or idea rather than a material reality.[20] But to argue that the living Christ performs in the act of preaching is to speak of the impossible. It is to speak of an embodied relationship with an absent Person. It is to maintain the importance of human preachers who struggle on the shifting borders of performed speech while insisting that this struggle is no substitute for the active interruption of the Spirit of God.

I was not raised in the Calvinist tradition. But one of the things I like about Calvin's sacramental thought when applied to preaching is his insistence that there is no easy fusion of material realities. Calvin takes difference and contextual particularity seriously, whether he is speaking of bodies on earth or the ascended body of Jesus. This kind of located particularity is a basic characteristic of embodiment.[21] It is a lesson that homiletics needs, especially in a season of globalization and multimedia Christian empires. The particularity of Christian communities on the ground is significant to both rhetorical practices and God's revealed Word.

But Calvin is no pessimist. He thinks bodies can experience real participation, both in human communities and in sacramental encounters, through the Spirit's work. For Calvin, robust pneumatology accounts for the uneasy participation of Christ's body with the world. The Spirit bridges the impossible divides of location and space. Luke shares this emphasis. For both, taking the physical body of Christ seriously means taking the work of the Spirit seriously, and to ignore the one is to seriously marginalize the importance of the other.

Words are wonderful creations. Rhetoric and poetry have a natural, earthly power that one might describe as analogous to the natural power of the maternal bond or to the mysterious creative capacity of the human womb. It is tempting to locate the power of preaching in this natural, linguistic capacity. It could then be scientifically studied, sociologically harnessed, and aesthetically evaluated. But to use Mary's pregnancy as a

20. This sort of Neoplatonism can be found in process-oriented homiletic projects, such as Marjorie Suchocki's *The Whispered Word* (St. Louis: Chalice Press, 1999). For Suchocki, Christ is pure, "whispered" *logos* in need of human flesh to be "incarnated again" (16–19). It can also be found in propositionally oriented homiletics, where the Word of God is understood to be "external, propositional and *sui generis*" in nature, discernable through approved methods of biblical exegesis. See Charles Fuller, *The Trouble with "Truth through Personality"* (Eugene, OR: Wipf & Stock, 2010), 127.

21. See Calvin on this point in *Institutes*, 2:1396.

metaphor for preaching is to stress that no natural power—no rhetorical, exegetical, or poetic device—can effect the embodied relation between Christ's body and the preacher's own. It turns our eyes to the necessary role of the Holy Spirit in bringing about this participation, making the presence of Christ in the sermon a gracious, present-tense gift of God. In short, a theology of sermon performance informed by Mary's pregnancy honors the "impossible" nature (Luke 1:37) of pulpit speech. Christian preaching does not simply testify to the world in linguistically natural ways. It bears a body that it has no business bearing by a power greater than its own. Given this unnatural state of affairs, a theology of pulpit performance that starts with the body of the Word should have a world-interrupting quality about it. Such a quality is, in fact, central to Luke's eschatological descriptions of the Spirit.

When Peter describes the event of Pentecost as occurring in the "last days" (Acts 2:17), he asserts the eschatological significance of the Spirit's outpouring. To be clear, this is no realized eschatology. Acts's narrative is fueled by the hope of Christ's decisive, future return.[22] But all the same, the Spirit makes this living Christ present—even in his absence—suggesting a Spirit-instigated unease between the borders of the present and future. It is an unease also seen in the similarities between the "last days" of Acts 2 and the events surrounding the birth of Jesus in Luke's Nativity.

From Luke's beginning, "young men," even babies within their mother's wombs, have been filled with the Spirit (1:15). "Old men" have seen angels in the temple and had prophetic visions of God's salvation (1:11; 2:29-32), and a *doulē* has prophesied, through the Spirit's power. Such connections suggest that Paul Minear's characterization of Luke's Nativity as "perversely eschatological" is no hyperbole. There is something apocalyptic about the Spirit's presence in these early chapters. To draw on the language of Peter's sermon, there is something of the "last days." For Luke, there is something apocalyptic about the incarnation itself—and to take seriously the incarnated God in the work of preaching means applying a similar apocalyptic understanding to God's action in the sermon.

In his article "In Support of a Reformed View of Ascension and Eucharist," Douglas Farrow suggests that Calvin does not go far enough in his thinking about the "eschatological" interruption of the Spirit in the celebration of the Eucharist. Farrow observes that Calvin's spatial orien-

22. Beverly Gaventa, "The Eschatology of Luke-Acts Revisited," *Encounter* 43 (1982): 27-42.

tation, an orientation that shaped the Reformation debate around the significance of Christ's ascension, made it difficult "for Calvin to factor *time* into his Eucharistic equation."[23] While Calvin conceived of the Spirit's ability to bend space so that a believer might ascend to Christ in heaven, he never considered a similar Spirit-empowered bending of present into future. Such a "bending," in Farrow's view, provides a sacramental "sign" of the *parousia* to come.[24]

Perhaps one way to understand the work of the Spirit in the performing bodies of Mary, the apostles, and the contemporary preacher who stands to bear witness to the Word is through this temporal lens. Farrow suggests that in faith-filled, sacramental performances, the Spirit not only brings Christ physically near in space, the Spirit brings Christ near in time. The preacher, through the Spirit's power, stands in a future hope: the time of Christ's descent to us. It is not fully realized, of course. But it is mediated, witnessed, and reflected in ordinary acts of faith, covered in the Spirit's shadow. "Were you there," the African American spiritual asks, "when they crucified my Lord?"[25] And we respond with trembling, as the Spirit folds together present and past. The witness of Luke and Acts presses the question further, finding the future under the Spirit's wing. *Were you there when Christ's Advent changed the world?*

To argue that Mary's bearing body is a metaphor for the performance of Acts's preachers—and indeed, today's preachers—is to answer yes to that question. Keeping the apocalyptic horizon of Luke and Acts in view means that the similarities between Mary and preachers come from more than imitation of tradition alone. Faithful, Spirit-empowered human performance is not the result of shared essences or a set of rehearsed competencies. Instead, their similarities reflect a common, external denominator: the advent of the embodied Jesus. Their similarities flow from an

23. Douglas Farrow, "In Support of a Reformed View of Ascension and Eucharist," in *Reformed Theology: Identity and Ecumenicity*, ed. Wallace M. Alston Jr. and Michael Welker (Grand Rapids: Eerdmans, 2003). Farrow argues that "Calvin handled the dialectic of presence and absence almost exclusively in spatial terms, and to that extent in a *non*-eschatological fashion," 366.

24. Farrow, "In Support of a Reformed View," 367-68. Again, in Calvin's "instrumental" use of the term. Farrow argues that such a Spirit-empowered "sign" of Christ's future return to earth still leaves God's gracious act in the sacrament and the provisionality of our faithful performances intact in a way that avoids Calvin's fear of "tearing Christ down from heaven" by human design or locating Christ's body directly in the world.

25. "Were You There (When They Crucified My Lord)?" first printed in 1899.

eschatological future, serving as Spirit-empowered witnesses of God's deep desire for the world. They provide a taste of our future hope: living participation in Jesus's transforming person. They provide a glimpse of a world made new.

The Preacher's Labor as Fully Human, Sacramental Sign

One might wonder where the "fully human" preacher has gone. Word of God as resurrected Jesus. Spirit-instigated shifts in time. What is "fully human" about any of this? With such grand, theological underpinnings and world-interrupting agendas, what is a work-a-day pastor to do? Have the utterly ordinary labors of preacherly study, wordcraft, and delivery disappeared?

But in Luke's Nativity texts, the body of Jesus and the Spirit's interruption are precisely what allow Mary to be herself. Because of Christ's performing body, Mary is freed from having to stand in for an other. She is freed from being defined by projected needs or patriarchal agendas. She does not need to be a universal norm or disembodied symbol. She is freed to live out the particular gift of her vocation through Spirit-empowered, embodied relation. The ordinary labor of her life becomes a witness to the greater work of God. This transformed and transforming freedom is what I believe God desires for working preachers. When Christ participates in the preacher's weekly labors through the power of the Spirit, the faithful and flawed body of the preacher comes into view. More than this, it gains sacramental significance.

Postmodernity has provided any number of philosophical reasons why the performing body matters. It has schooled us in the limits of our finite perspectives and the connections between knowledge's function and content. Feminism has further emphasized, sometimes through its failings, the significance of the performing body in recognizing and relinquishing the "master's tools."[26] Luke's account of Mary's pregnancy and the Reformers' sacramental understanding of preaching give us one reason more. The preacher's body matters because the Word's body mat-

26. Audre Lorde, "The Master's Tools Will Never Dismantle the Master's House," in *Sister Outsider* (Berkeley, CA: Crossing Press, 1984), is an oft-quoted indictment of "second-wave" feminism's complicity in ignoring the concrete, embodied experiences of lesbians and women of color.

ters, and, finally, that body is a performing body. It lives to transform the world and the preacher. To ignore Mary's performed particularity is to miss God's active presence in her life and in her context. It misses the salvation of God working through an embodied Savior—a Savior who is both "with [us]" and "Lord" (Luke 1:28) by the Spirit's power. Her body matters, in other words, because it is an eschatological site of the *Word's performance* in the world.

In my conversations with preachers, there is a recurring fear that preaching God's Word will expose them as a fraud or erase them as human. In their words, there is the fear of "shame" on Monday morning or a feeling of "inadequacy" in speaking for the divine. There is the fear of being a "charlatan" or an "impersonator."[27] There is the experience of loss when one stops experiencing hope because one "feels responsible" to make that hope a living reality for others. Whether one is trying to stand in the shoes of one's congregation or to meet those congregational needs by standing in the shoes of Christ, there is a sense that preaching requires a kind of pretense—a kind of "standing in" for a body other than one's own. For some, there is the fear that they will fail in the attempt. As one preacher describes it, "The right preaching of the Word of God is the Word of God. The hard part is figuring out 'right preaching!'" For others, the fear is that one will lose herself or her voice in a tangle of communal expectations and rhetorical traditions. Some are afraid that being a preacher finally necessitates a "concealing" of oneself or a denial of one's physical limits.[28] Behind it all is the fear that, at the end of the day, the power of God's Word in the sermon is an empty promise for all but those endowed with natural charisma and persuasive savvy, or perhaps for those pure few who have mastered the art of *fading away*. "Is the Word of God in the sermon?" a preacher says to me. "I don't know. I've heard a lot of bad preaching."

The uneasy borders between text, event, community, and performer have only heightened these tensions. It is no longer assumed that content and delivery can be crisply delineated or that the border between truth and application is impermeable. Old hierarchies between philosophy and rhetoric have broken down, and with them the belief that the ser-

---

27. All quotes taken from conversations with Baptist, Pentecostal, and Presbyterian preachers on the joys and challenges of preaching, September 11, 2013, July 23, 2013, April 23, 2012, January 14, 2013, September 12, 2012, May 6, 2012, and January 29, 2013.

28. One preacher tells the story of fainting in the pulpit because she attempted to preach through exhaustion and illness.

monic Word can be extracted and comprehended independent of rhetorical event. Bodily performance and its theological implications are not declining in significance. If anything, theology's attention to communal practices is growing.[29] And so the particularities of the Christian preacher, her doubts, fears, hopes, and humanity, are increasingly significant homiletic concerns. In a postmodern world, it becomes noticeably harder for the Christian preacher and what she "really does" in the sermon to disappear. It is even harder to imagine that whatever she does can substitute for the living presence of a living Lord.

And if the Reformers and Luke are correct, this is a gift.

To understand sermonic labor as a sacramental sign is to claim that the disappearance of the preacher is not simply unnecessary but is theologically and ethically dangerous. Such substitution collapses the uneasy border of earth and heaven. It translates the gracious interruption of God into the natural outworking of human history. And in so doing, it replaces faith in the One "hoped for" (Heb. 12:1-2) with institutions and communal practices that can be seen, controlled, and maintained. When a human body, whether Mary's body or the body of the preacher, is understood to be unnaturally transparent in the Word's mediation, a particular, practicing body becomes a norm for human performance. This body is not always the body of a pulpit prince. It may be the body of ecclesial tradition or a certain body of knowledge. But it is, finally, not the Word's body. And if mistaken for such, these bodies become dangerous in their normativity. They cut away voices of skepticism and difference. They silence questions. Furthermore, the human handmaid and her performance become, in a way very much at odds with the biblical narrative, *the point*.

And this is, finally, what is at stake. When the preacher disappears, the uneasy borders of Christ's presence and absence collapse. Christ becomes so fully present in the body of the preacher that any conception of Christ as absent Other is unnecessary. There is no need for him in his resurrected, embodied form, only his example, his teaching, his idea, and his memory. His person is expendable.

After all, the preacher is filling his shoes.

29. There is lively discussion surrounding the role and epistemological value of "practice" in contemporary practical theological discourse—from diverse theological perspectives. For a helpful introduction, see Ted Smith, "Theories of Practice," in *The Wiley Blackwell Companion Guide to Practical Theology*, ed. Bonnie Miller-McLemore (Oxford: Blackwell, 2012), 244-54.

In homiletic circles, it has become common to turn to the language of "embodiment" to describe the preacher's task. The preacher is called to "embody the Word" in the sermon.[30] But such language is relationally inadequate. Mary does not embody Jesus—just as the sacramental bread does not embody Christ. This is not Mary's call. Jesus, to put it bluntly, has a body all his own. Mary is called to be an embodied sign that lives in vulnerable relation to an embodied Savior. Furthermore, she is called to bear witness to that transformative relation in physical ways. She is called to embody the transformation that occurs in *her* when she assents to a living relation with Christ through the Spirit. The great promise of Mary's pregnancy is that this physical testimony does more than witness. Through the Spirit's shadow, it mediates the reality to which it points. Mary's Spirit-empowered, embodied performance bears Christ to the world—and if the sermon is a sacramental act, the preacher's performance does the same.

There are costs to such performances. But the cost is not being exposed as a fraud or being erased as a human. *The cost is being exposed as human.* Drawing on the work of Mikhail Bakhtin, Charles Campbell describes such exposure as the laying aside a "classical body . . . entirely finished with clear and sharp boundaries . . . hard and sculpted, taut and celebrated"—a body that is more marble than flesh. It means embracing, instead, a body "in the act of becoming," a body "never finished, never completed, . . . continually growing and created . . . [as it] also grows and creates other bodies."[31] Bakhtin describes it as a grotesque body.[32] I call it a fully human body—or perhaps, a *body performing.* When such a body is brought into vulnerable relation with the body of Christ by the power of the Spirit, it is changed. It bears the marks of an Other because God uses it to bear that Other.

On the weekend that my daughter was to be baptized, my mother

---

30. For example, see Charles Rice, *The Embodied Word: Preaching as Art and Liturgy* (Minneapolis: Augsburg Fortress, 2010). See also Ruth Pidwell, "The Word Made Flesh: Gender and Embodiment in Contemporary Preaching," *Social Semiotics* 2, no. 2 (2001): 177–92.

31. Charles Campbell, "Incarnate Word: Preaching and the Carnivalesque Grotesque" (lecture, Lyman Beecher Lecture Series, Yale Divinity School, October 19, 2018).

32. See Mikhail Bakhtin's extended description of the grotesque body in *Rabelais and His World*, trans. Helene Iswolsky (Bloomington: Indiana University Press, 1984), 18–19.

had a debilitating stroke. It was serious enough that she had to relearn to walk and talk and swallow. It left her right hand twisted for the rest of her life. It took her years to stitch together the difficulty of that experience with her lifelong trust in God. But Jesus's passion built her a bridge back to faith. His cry of abandonment on the cross gave her deep conviction that she was not alone. Jesus knew what this felt like. Through the grammar and gift of grace, my mother began to claim that God was "at her right hand" (Ps. 16:8). She never thought that God's shadow had caused her stroke. But in her questions, doubts, and inabilities, she experienced the presence of Christ. He found her hand in the dark. She was marked by his questions and by his trust. God was in her human experience of frailty. God was discovered not in the strength of her left hand but in her imperfect right. "God is at my *right* hand," she would say, her stiff fist raised like testimony.

Tragedy is no prerequisite for proclamation. But proclamation does require the exposure of being *seen*. It requires the opposite of fading away, the opposite of pretending, the opposite of embodying someone else's ideal or expectation. It requires, instead, the foolish revealing of one's imperfect, ordinary flesh as the decidedly inconclusive evidence of a loving God. *God is here—even here. Especially here.* The evidence differs from body to body. The evidence may be a limp—or the leap of a child in a womb. The evidence will be uncertain and Spirit-discerned, just like it was for Mary. But the flesh's weakness is its strength. In its particular, permeable, provisional history, there is a meeting place for earth and heaven.

Fully human preaching embraces the vulnerability and ambiguity of human life, its shifting borders and its need. It owns the particularity of its witness, its lack of transformative power, and the limits of its autonomy. And then, it names a living Savior. Such testimony requires a preacher leave behind the long shadows cast by powerful pulpit "princes" and perfect, passive "queens." It lays aside false substitutes for grace. But, if Peter's Pentecost witness is true, the promise of the Annunciation is a promise given to all God's *douloi* and *doulai*. And through the ordinary mess and witness of a preacher's life, standing beneath a different Shadow, she bears the Word to the world.

And What about That World Built Only for Some?

> What the Spirit . . . enables us to do is to be ourselves, . . . to testify
> to the Lord who bears marks and who calls us who bear marks to
> tell his story.[33]

These theological trajectories, discerned through the lens of Scripture, form an argument tied together like an Alexander Calder mobile. Pull one string and all the other pieces move. Ignore the *particular*, *permeable*, *provisional* character of Christ's body, and human preachers get ignored. Ignore Christ's body, and the Spirit gets ignored. Pay attention to the Spirit, and Christ's body will come into focus. Pay attention to Christ's body, and human bodies claim their fully human, Spirit-empowered vocations, bearing Christ to the world even as they are born again.

And now, I tug a final thread—the thread that connects this theological argument to a world of podcasts and poverty, power brokers and pawns, citizens and strangers. A world built only for some. It is not just that if Christ's body is marginalized, human bodies are marginalized, or that if Christ's body is honored, human bodies gain theological significance.

If human bodies marginalize other bodies, they marginalize Christ. When human preachers idealize or norm their performances, when their performances stiffen into static, communally accepted forms, when they fade or float, disconnected from the responsibilities of communal life, they cannot witness to a world *becoming*. Their bodies are treated like statues or smoke, neither of which can bear the marks of Christ. If it is the *particularity*, *permeability*, and *provisionality* of human bodies that allow them to testify to Christ's performance in the world, hegemonic norms in homiletics (and practical theology generally) carry a very high price. In their denial of the diversity, contextual particularity, and vulnerability of creation, they lose their fully human character. They lose their ability to witness to and be changed by an Other. They lose their sacramental function.

Herein lies the homiletician's particular labor: describing the shape and sound of an alternate way. Our theological compass has directed us to a very practical question. Are there rhetorical, hermeneutical, perfor-

33. Yolanda Santiago-Correa, unpublished reflection on the role of the Holy Spirit in preaching. Used by permission, April 2018.

mative practices that honor the *particularlity*, *permeability*, and *provisionality* of the world? What practices honor the limits of context and the vulnerability of relationship? What practices grow connection between texts and communities even as they make space for difference? What practices invite the preacher to trade false autonomy, power, and authorization for exposure of their full humanity? I don't speak here of confessional tell-alls in the pulpit or rhetorical forms grounded in a cultural fascination with individual self-expression. I don't speak of the abnegation of self or tradition through an infinite adaptation to context. Neither of these extremes describes the kind of embodied relation seen in the labor of Mary—or in the sermons of Acts's preachers. Neither describes the kind of unsettled identity, agency, and communal role that bears witness to Christ's body. These approaches simply replace one form for another. They fall short of the dependent humility necessary for rhetoric rooted in the ground of vulnerable, lived encounter. Methods of sermon performance are not static consumables. They cannot be placed in one's back pocket and carried from context to context like a sacramental guarantee. And yet, if they cannot be described at all, one surrenders the particular character of Christian speech to the rhetorical whims of the age. To leave such practices undescribed is simply another way of saying that they do not matter at all.

And here is where I find the metaphor of Mary's pregnancy particularly helpful.

Mary's pregnancy—as metaphor—allows practical theology to give descriptive contour to the human labors of rhetoric formed by embodied relation with Christ while maintaining the primacy of the relation itself.[34] In the pages that follow, Mary's human actions in pregnancy will suggest rhetorical postures, values, and tensions consistent with fully human, sacramental speech. I have already described how Mary's pregnancy witnesses to the nature of her relationship with Christ. We have seen how she is marked by that relation in ways similar to the preachers of Acts. We turn our attention now to her fully human labor in that relation.

34. It is tempting to construct descriptions of Spirit-empowered preaching that make lived dependence on Christ expendable. To draw on Mary's pregnant action as a metaphor for sermonic practice counteracts this tendency in two ways. First, it is a metaphor that does not read directly onto lived practice. It requires Spirit-inspired discernment in concrete application. Second, embodied relation is integral to the metaphor.

What does her pregnant action reveal about what is required of ordinary
Word-bearers in the grace-filled work of a sermon?

To speak about Mary's "pregnant action" at all is, of course, tricky
business. There is a sparseness to Luke's description of Mary's pregnancy
that makes any account of her experience speculative. Luke hides much
of Mary's pregnancy from our eyes. Are there swollen feet and nauseous
mornings? We don't know; Mary's body is not the Gospel's focus. But
Luke does not conceal all. His understated description, in and of itself,
suggests a pregnancy that is natural enough to provide no physical evidence of extraordinary origin, inviting a cautious engagement between
Mary's experience and others who have given birth.

Pregnancy is an experience of embodied relation lived out in time. It
spans the border of ontology and performance. Being pregnant, as I have
said, is something one *is*, as well as something one *does*. It is a liminal experience. Women who become pregnant describe uneasy, participatory
relationships between self and other, agency and passivity, and alterity
and community. In this way, pregnancies are useful descriptors of the
shifting borders of rhetorical performance. A number of feminist scholars have used pregnancy to describe the relationality of the performing
self.[35] To use pregnancy as a metaphor for preaching, however, requires
a significant disclaimer. Preaching is not only a natural, rhetorical act. It
is a natural, rhetorical act that has been unnaturally interrupted by the
Spirit, bringing about a particular relation to a particular Person: Jesus
Christ. Because of this particularity, Luke's account of Mary's pregnancy
is significant. Mary's pregnancy shares the natural relationality of other
pregnancies, but it also describes human labor that flows from and testifies to a Spirit-empowered relation to a living Savior.

In certain ways, Luke is very specific. When the angel Gabriel tells

35. Allison Weir, *Sacrificial Logics: Feminist Theory and the Critique of Identity*
(London: Routledge, 1996), 145, references Julia Kristeva's work on the material experience of pregnancy as providing a helpful "theory of identity as something that
can include difference, heterogeneity, and openness to change." For Helen Buss,
"Antigone, Psyche, and the Ethics of Female Selfhood," in *Paul Ricoeur and Contemporary Moral Thought*, ed. John Wall, William Schweiker, and W. David Hall (New
York: Routledge, 2002), 73, attending to the bodily "ambivalences" of pregnancy is
an essential component of a "philosophy of the self in connection to others." See
also Julia Kristeva's discussion of Marian veneration in relation to psychoanalytic
and linguistic theories of the self in her "Stabat Mother," in *Tales of Love*, trans. Leon
Roudiez (New York: Columbia University Press, 1987).

Mary that the Spirit will "overshadow" her, he uses three specific verbs to describe Mary's embodied response to the Spirit's power. Gabriel tells Mary that she will "conceive" in her womb, "bear" a son, and "name" him Jesus (Luke 1:31). Each of these is an active verb, with Mary the explicit subject of each. But each is also an uneasy, relational verb, complicating simple dichotomies. They describe the apparently natural actions of a human person who finds her *identity*, *agency*, and *communal role* unsettled by embodied relation to Christ.

How might these verbs inform the relational work of sermon performance? In the chapters that follow, we will look at Mary's *conceiving*, *bearing*, and *naming* of Christ as orientations toward the verbal relationality of preaching. Each calls the preacher into fully human engagement with text, community, and Christ. And we will see the distinct ways these verbs are embodied in particular contexts. They do not map onto contextually transcendent practices. Instead, similar to the unique experiences of pregnant women, they describe embodied relationships that are distinct. Christ may be the same "yesterday today and forever" (Heb. 13:8), but his mercies are "new every morning" (Lam. 3:23). And as such, the practices described are provisional. There is no one-size-fits-all solution to the puzzle of Spirit-inspired speech. And yet the specifics of Mary's experience are not random. Christ's relationship with each person and community may have a unique, present-tense quality, but these relationships are not infinitely variable. The verbs that describe Mary's action describe the action of a woman who bears Christ to the world by the Spirit's power. And as such, there is reflexivity in these verbs that foreshadows Christ's cruciform calling and reflects his character. Mary's bearing body has a particularity that matters.

When Welsh Pentecostal Ian Macpherson describes the preacher as "Mary of old" in his 1955 lectures on preaching, he makes much the same theological point that I made at the start of this chapter: "Preaching is . . . the conveyance *of* a Person *through* a person *to* a company of persons."[36] He argues, more concretely, that if a preacher's character "be such that he is not fitted to discharge homiletically the function fulfilled physically by Mary long ago, he [*sic*] can never be a true preacher."[37] Macpherson, however, like so many others who have used Mary as a symbol or a norm, never attends to the specifics of this metaphor. He

36. Ian Macpherson, *The Burden of the Lord* (London: Epworth Press, 1955), 8.
37. Macpherson, *Burden of the Lord*, 39.

never attends to the "function fulfilled physically" by Mary, and, therefore, his description of the preacher is strangely disconnected from his
theological grounding. Macpherson focuses on the preacher's essential
characteristics, the preacher's "natural attributes" and "spiritual prereq-
uisites." He describes, in other words, "what sort of man [*sic*]" a preacher
must be, down to his physical stature and good vocal chords,[38] but he
never takes seriously the messy, relational labor of Mary's pregnancy as a
sign through which Christ is mediated. The particularity of her maternal
body actively bearing and bearing witness to Jesus is never pondered.
Nowhere in Macpherson's lectures does one get the impression that he
spoke to women about what was involved in "fulfilling physically" the
acts of conceiving, bearing, and naming a child. For all of Macpherson's
talk of Mary, the preacher carries the "burden of Christ" on his "back,"
rather than in his belly.[39]

If a theology of performance starts with the body of the Word, however, the material particularity of Mary's action must be taken seriously,
not just the formal acknowledgment of her relation to Christ. Both in
its material similarity to Christ's action and in its difference, Mary's action witnesses to Christ's work in the world. And if Mary's body matters
as a site of embodied transformation, the plurivocal bodies of Mary's
interpreters matter as well. Mary's pregnant action invites the engagement of women who have conceived or borne or named children. Likewise, her unnatural, embodied relation to Jesus, made possible by the
Spirit, invites the engagement of preachers of all kinds who have been
marked by a Spirit-empowered relation to Jesus's person: women and
men, gay and straight, documented and undocumented, citizen and refugee. Spirit-shadowed preachers who allow their bodies to sacramentally
bear Christ's scandalous flesh through the mundane labors of rhetorical
speech know something crucial about Mary's call.

Acknowledging the theological import of this engagement between
Mary's account and contemporary voices implies one thing more: the
performative labor necessary to interpret biblical texts in a world where
the body of Christ intersects the bodies of his followers. Such performative labor is familiar to the preacher. It is labor that knows its limita-

38. Macpherson, *Burden of the Lord*, 37-72. Ironically, given Macpherson's focus
on Mary, the manhood of the preacher is a recurring theme. While left undefined, the
category clearly indicates more than the preacher's humanity.

39. Macpherson, *Burden of the Lord*, 4.

tions even as it knows its import. It offers no proofs and "writes with an eraser." But, when shadowed by the Spirit, this uneasy, interpretive labor bears witness to the Crucified One; indeed, it bears him to the world. This is no small thing. In fact, such labor affirms the far horizon of another birth, when a world in which certain voices count—and others do not—is made new.

....

CHAPTER 6

Conceiving

The Labor of Hospitality

> Not so much a thought as a pinpoint on the horizon of thought;
> not so much appearing, as the world slowly rolling to reveal it;
> not so much the world, but a breath of eternity, releasing this in-
> finitesimal "Yes."
>
> Debra Rienstra, Great with Child

It is the second week of my second term teaching preaching at Davui-levu Theological College, and I am carrying a Fijian mat down a puddle-filled road. The mat, woven from pandanus leaves, was given to me by Akanisi Tarabe, a ground-breaking Fijian sociologist who happens to be my next-door neighbor. Akanisi has written her master's thesis on women's funeral rituals in her beloved Cu'u, and she has a great deal to say about mats.[1] I have sat on her mats. I have eaten dinner on her mats. We have prayed together on her mats. But it wasn't until I read her book that I realized how much I had yet to learn about a mat's meaning—how much I had yet to learn about this *ibe* that I carried.

I roll out the mat on my classroom floor. My students are bemused. *Vulagi*, or outsiders like myself, usually prefer chairs.

"What is the *meaning* of this mat?" I ask.

Weaving a mat is women's work, but my students—most of whom are

---

1. Akanisi Sobusobu Tarabe, "Re-Assessing Gender Roles: A Study of Indigenous Fijian Women's Role in Funerals" (master's thesis, School of Social Science, University of the South Pacific, September 2015). In addition to her constructive description of Cu'u funeral practices, Tarabe's work offers a unique critique of the androcentrism in Asesela Ravuvu's seminal, *The Fijian Way of Life* (Suva, Fiji: University of the South Pacific Press, 1983).

men—respond quickly. Mats are significant objects in Fiji, and there is much to say. "A mat means that you are welcome," one of them tells me. "A mat is what they gave to chiefs years ago who crossed oceans to reach new lands. Mats were provided so they could sit on the shore and dry themselves." Mats are still given to honored guests in formal ceremonies of welcome. But welcome ceremonies are not the only times when mats are given. My students' answers fly around the room. "You are wrapped in them at your wedding." "You're buried in them." "Mats are given at baptisms." Any ritual of commitment or faith. Any moment that marks life or death. "They keep our *vanua* connections strong."[2]

The stories affirm Tarabe's argument that mats are more than material, temporal objects. The hospitality they facilitate when functioning as a table, bed, or gift of honor mediates the spiritual labor of communal connection. They regenerate spiritual relationships between kinship groups and create new connections when these relations are disrupted by death, birth, marriage, or stranger.[3] They serve the life-giving function of creating family ties, and then they stretch and strengthen those responsibilities beyond the duties of blood, time, or proximity alone.[4] It is no wonder, then, that Tarabe highlights the ways in which mats carry women's "substance." The front side of a mat is called its "belly." This belly is respectfully folded so that it is not exposed when being carried outdoors. The work of this belly is intimate work—intimate labor. It creates spiritual family, and in so doing, it shapes identity.[5] It may seem strange to speak of a mat as an active, animate object. But in its giving and its acceptance, in its gracious holding of the community in times of change—in its *performance*—a mat's substance testifies to, maintains, and even transforms social relationships. It does more than remind one who one is. It changes who one is.

At the end of chapter five, I suggested that the three verbs given to Mary by the angel to describe her vocational labor are significant as metaphors for the actively passive labor of the preacher. "You will conceive . . .

2. *Vanua*, most simply, is the land and all the land sustains, including human communities and cultures. See I. S. Tuwere, *Vanua: Towards a Fijian Theology of Place* (Suva, Fiji: University of the South Pacific Press, 2002).

3. In "Re-Assessing Gender Roles," Tarabe states, "The mat equals women's substance, which is the basis for kinship relations," . . . the exchange of mats "keeps the doorway of kinship relations open," 82–83.

4. Tarabe, "Re-Assessing Gender Roles," 82–83.

5. Tarabe, "Re-Assessing Gender Roles," 82–83.

bear . . . and name," the angel tells Mary (Luke 1:31). How might these actions inform the fully human, sacramental labor of sermonic speech?

The first verb, *conceive*, complicates this effort from the start. *Conception* doesn't seem to be an active verb. It is not something one does but something that happens to someone—a strange place to begin a conversation about the human labor of the preacher. In a memoir describing her experience of waiting to conceive, Debra Rienstra recounts her feelings of surrender to a process outside of her control, even in a world of increasing medical intervention. Conceiving, as is clear to those who have had their expectations altered by infertility, miscarriage, or pregnancy itself, is quite different from the act of intercourse. In the natural course of things, sexual relations may lead to conception or it may not. Conceiving is not something that a woman can make happen by her will, or, for that matter, always prevent.[6] When Serene Jones discusses the significance of "reproductive loss" for the 35 percent of women of child-bearing age who experience infertility or miscarriage, she emphasizes the feeling of powerlessness than can surround the issue of conception.[7]

But even when a hoped-for pregnancy comes to fruition, conceiving confronts the illusion that one's future is one's own to construct. For Rienstra, who describes both miscarriage and live birth in her account, the lack of control one feels in waiting to conceive foreshadows the experience of parenthood generally. In conceiving, there is an embodied relation formed with a stranger other than oneself, and one's future becomes marked by that other. "Children will defy the places, plans and schemes we make for them in our lives," she states. And this is at odds with the fact that "at bottom, I have quite a particular idea of what I want . . . and am not truly open to whatever comes."[8] There is,

6. Even the various reproductive technologies that have increased a woman's agency in this process offer few fail-safe guarantees.

7. Serene Jones, "Hope Deferred: Theological Reflections on Reproductive Loss," in *Trauma and Grace: Theology in a Ruptured World* (Louisville: Westminster John Knox, 2009), 130, carefully defines the term as "the experience of women who desire to have biological children, who are biologically unable to do so and who experience this bodily inability as a failure, a desire thwarted, a loss of a potential child that they hoped for and expected." Her statistics, which do not include abortions, come from the American Society for Reproductive Medicine (128).

8. Debra Rienstra, *Great with Child: Reflections on Faith, Fullness, and Becoming a Mother* (New York: Penguin Putnam, 2002), 26–27.

for Rienstra, a kind of "recklessness" in being open to such an unknown trajectory, a recklessness that makes sense for her only in light of her Christian faith and the "trust I have in the sense of this universe and in the compassion and power of the Creator."[9] Such openness is not causally linked to conception, of course, but it is descriptive of conception's attempt and conception's vulnerability. In the context of an action that is not brought about by an act of will, a woman's willingness to conceive represents an openness to the wonder and wounding of an unknown future. It represents a willingness to live in embodied relation to someone else.

One way that Luke's description of Mary's Spirit-empowered conception is different from natural pregnancy is Mary's *inactivity*—most notably, her sexual inactivity. Mary's virginity can increase the sense that her conception is an act of passive submission, an experience of being acted upon rather than an act in its own right. This sense is amplified by Protestant interpretations of Mary's submission as flowing from God's gracious initiative, a view my reading of Luke supports. It is the promise of God (Luke 1:35, 37) that enables Mary to respond with faith (v. 38), opening up space for her to conceive a new reality through the Spirit's power.

But Luke makes a point of acknowledging Mary's willing response. "Let it be with me according to your word," Mary says (v. 38), a spoken assent that is unique in Scripture's description of supernatural birth narratives. Her assent does not bring about creation, but similar to Rienstra's description, it is an act of openness and engagement. Mary agrees to embrace and be changed by the spoken promises and overshadowing presence of God. She agrees to allow her body to participate in and be transformed by the body of the Messiah. For Rienstra and Mary, to conceive is to embrace and be changed by an other. And Luke makes sure that we understand that, for Mary, it is an *active* embrace. In its most basic sense, *it is an act of hospitality*.

Hospitality has a domesticated connotation in many United States church circles. It is the work of potluck coordinators, parking-lot attendants, and front-door greeters. Its value is touted, but its telos is blurred by flurries of volunteer sign ups and church kitchen policies. The risks involved in creating liminal spaces of vulnerability are papered over with

9. Rienstra, *Great with Child*, 10.

politeness. It is a far cry from Tarabe's assertion of the spiritually regenerative significance of spreading a mat[10] or the resonances she describes
between Fijian practices of hospitality, new life, and death.[11] Her appreciation for the active sacrifices of those who do the work is undeveloped
in white, Western spaces.[12] But Fijian protocols of how to sit, speak, and
move on a mat express an often forgotten truth. Genuine hospitality is
serious business. It is tender, trying, even dangerous work, and something is risked for guest and host alike.

Mary's pregnancy gives imagery for this. To understand hospitality
through the lens of conception and pregnancy is to describe hospitable
action as having a participatory, transformative border. This is hospitality with a "belly." It is a picture of hospitable relationship that unsettles
the identities of both guest and host. Jacques Derrida argues that when a
guest is truly welcomed without conditions, there is a fluidity that emerges
in the encounter. There are changes in power and control as well as self-
knowledge. In a genuine hospitable encounter, the guest becomes "the
one who invites the one who invites, . . . liberating the power of his host
. . . host[ing] the host."[13] It is just such a "fluidity" that Amos Yong sees
in Mary's pregnancy, flowing from the hospitality of God. In Luke, Yong
explains, "Those who welcome Jesus" become, in turn, "guests" of God's
redemptive work.[14] In short, Mary's conception changes who she is.

And yet *who she is* is not lost. The metaphor of pregnancy resists ide-

10. Tarabe, "Re-Assessing Gender Roles," 143.

11. Tarabe, "Re-Assessing Gender Roles," 14. Tarabe notes the connections between birth, death, and the ritual work of women—including the spreading of mats.
In Fiji, "women's bodies are tropes for periods of transition: from conception to birth,
from the period between death and the afterlife" (82).

12. Tarabe, "Re-Assessing Gender Roles," 80, 92. Tarabe speaks about the risk of
"pollution" in hospitality rituals surrounding the liminal spaces of death and mourning, underscoring the vulnerability required to keep the doorway of kinship relations
open (110).

13. Jacques Derrida, *Of Hospitality* (Stanford, CA: Stanford University Press,
2000), 123. Derrida's words ring with theological overtones, and so it is no surprise
when he supports his ideas with biblical narratives and stories like "The Legend of St.
Julian Hospitaller," who welcomes a leper Christ into his home, providing food, drink,
and a shared, warm bed. See Jacques Derrida, *Acts of Religion* (New York: Routledge,
2002), 363-64.

14. Amos Yong, *Hospitality and the Other: Pentecost, Christian Practices and the
Neighbor* (Maryknoll, NY: Orbis, 2008), 102.

alizations of hospitality that "deconstruct" the self[15] or collapse the self into the other "to the point of substitution."[16] Contrary to romantic idealizations of pregnancy as a "transcorporeal, transpositional" identity, feminist scholars have stressed the relationality of the pregnant body, a body marked by particularity, as well as participation and vulnerability.[17] When Graham Ward describes the church as being enfolded within the body of Christ, an argument that draws on the same pregnant imagery as my own, he ends up concluding that "to understand the body of Jesus, we can only examine what the Church is,"[18] exchanging pregnancy's uneasy, relational borders for a more totalizing description.[19] There is a collapsing of the two—a collapse that flows from his imagery into his theology. Feminist thinkers, however, describe pregnancy's "separation,"[20] the "continuous . . . division of the very flesh,"[21] and the significance of touching and being touched by an other in the body's interior.[22] They stress, in other words, pregnancy's capacity to image a theory of identity where the self is, in Paul Ricoeur's language, "enjoined."[23]

15. Derrida, *Acts of Religion*, 364.

16. Emmanuel Lévinas, *Totality and Infinity* (Dordrecht: Kluwer Academic, 1992), 113. Derrida expresses his skepticism that such substitution is possible without the deconstruction of the concept of hospitality itself. See Derrida, *Acts of Religion*, 9.

17. Graham Ward, *Radical Orthodoxy: A New Theology*, ed. John Milbank, Catherine Pickstock, and Graham Ward (London: Routledge, 1999), 176.

18. Ward, *Radical Orthodoxy*, 177.

19. Douglas Farrow, "In Support of a Reformed View of Ascension and Eucharist," in *Reformed Theology: Identity and Ecumenicity*, ed. Wallace M. Alston Jr. and Michael Welker (Grand Rapids: Eerdmans, 2003), 360, notes that Ward is trying to avoid totalizing narratives in favor of a more "aporetic" description of grace, but he finally critiques Ward's metaphor of the pregnant Christ as being unable to explain "how or in what way the savior can be distinguished from the church." I suggest that this lack of clarity in Ward's ecclesiology flows, in part, from inadequate reflection on pregnancy's lived experience—an experience that includes differentiation and otherness.

20. Allison Weir, *Sacrificial Logics: Feminist Theory and the Critique of Identity* (New York: Routledge, 1996), 190.

21. Julia Kristeva, "Stabat Mater," *Tales of Love*, trans. Leon Roudiez (New York: Columbia University Press, 1987), 166.

22. Iris Marion Young, "Pregnant Embodiment: Subjectivity and Alienation," in *On Female Body Experience: "Throwing Like a Girl" and Other Essays* (Oxford: Oxford University Press, 2005), 50, describes the significance of the "movement of a body inside me."

23. Paul Ricoeur, *Oneself as Another*, trans. Kathleen Blamey (Chicago: University of Chicago Press, 2002), 354. Ricoeur's attempt to describe the "enjoined" self

When Mary says yes to the work of the Spirit, she agrees to live in this uneasy place: welcoming Christ's body, feeding and nurturing Christ's body, magnifying and living in relation to Christ's body. All of which assume her differentiation from that body. In conceiving, she refuses to fade away, and yet she agrees to be changed. She agrees to carry the marks of an other.

How might Mary's act of conception serve as a metaphor for the rhetorical labor surrounding biblical exegesis and sermon delivery? The following descriptions are suggestive answers to this question. They are not comprehensive. The specifics of hospitality differ depending on the persons involved. But each suggests ways that the fluid borders of hospitable practice are discerned in distinct settings, unsettling the borders of the church, the text, and the preacher's own identity. Each suggests how practices of fully human relationship open preachers to a different Guest and Host, through the work of the Spirit. A contemporary preacher describes it this way: "I feel like, in preaching, Christ is dwelling in me. Christ is not me, but comes in from the outside."[24] How might this mystery be witnessed in the pulpit?

Testimony: Hospitable Labor and the Biblical Text

I brought the mat to my Davuilevu preaching class for a reason. We were discussing Anna Carter Florence's article "Put Away Your Sword! Taking Torture Out of the Sermon," and there was one particular line that was hard to translate. "Don't tell us what the text means!" she says, "Tell us what it says to you!"[25] It's a tricky enough sentence for students who share Florence's mother tongue. But it's a critical idea, whatever a preacher's language. What is *meaning* after all? And what does that meaning have to do with the function, character, and revelatory power of the scriptural witness so central to preaching?

I ask students to imagine themselves as employees at the Fiji Museum in the nation's capital. "Pretend this mat is going to be hung in a

---

resonates with Weir's feminist attempt to affirm a self-identity that does not repress "difference" or "connectedness to others." See Allison Weir, *Sacrificial Logics*, 1.

24. Conversation on the joys and challenges of preaching, January 29, 2013.

25. Anna Carter Florence, "Put Away Your Sword! Taking Torture Out of the Sermon," in *What Is the Matter with Preaching Today?*, ed. Michael Graves (Louisville: Westminster John Knox, 2004), 101.

display, and you have to describe the mat's meaning on one of those little 5" by 7" plastic rectangles bolted to the wall. What would you say about the meaning of this mat?"

They tell me that the mat's meaning is related to the woman who made it, when she made it, and where she made it. Fijian folklore and flora would have influenced the materials and patterns she used. The mat's function is revealed in its size and edging. Its meaning is influenced by the rituals in which it had been used and the occasion on which it was given and received. A mat given at a baptism has a different meaning than a mat given at a funeral. It's a lot to describe. "How would one fit all of that meaning onto that small plastic rectangle?" I ask. "How would you decide what was most important to say?" Silence descends. They are starting to figure out what this exercise has to do with preaching.

"Let's say you were able to do it," I say. "Let's say you were able to fit all of that information into very small writing and put it on that placard, and let's say I had the time and sharp eyesight to read it all. After reading your description of this mat's meaning, would I know the meaning of this mat?" And from the back of the room, a tentative answer comes. "No. You wouldn't know. Because a mat isn't supposed to hang in a museum. You learn about a mat by sitting on it." Another student adds, "You learn about a mat by sitting on it *together*."

It's this *togetherness* that I think is finally at stake in Protestant theologies of the Word: a moving beyond objectified meaning and an opening of oneself to living, vulnerable encounter. The most significant, of course, is the encounter with Christ himself. Until we spread Scripture like a mat on the ground of a particular community and invite Christ to sit with us—until Christ speaks from that particular textual location—we do not know the Scripture's meaning for preaching. We do not know what it says to us, or more accurately, what Christ says to us through it. The belly of the text creates space for us to hear the voice of an Other who changes who we are. But we must be open to being changed.

In her book *Preaching as Testimony*, Florence stakes her claim that "everything for me begins and ends" with "sola scriptura."[26] It is a strange place for Florence to begin a homiletic theology grounded in "testimony," a category that has become synonymous with "sharing

---

26. Anna Carter Florence, *Preaching as Testimony* (Louisville: Westminster John Knox, 2007), 61.

my story."[27] But Florence argues for a sermonic definition of *testimony* that does not simply describe experience generally. Her definition describes an "encounter with God" when living in and interpreting a biblical text.[28] She draws deeply on the language of hospitality: "We read the biblical text in order to *hear* it, in the fullest sense of the word, and then to *welcome* it and *host* it in our lives and in our bodies."[29] But she clarifies that she is not talking about the domesticated hospitality of a dinner party. She describes a hospitality akin to Tarabe's description of the spiritually regenerative "belly" of the Fijian *ibe*—or, perhaps, more akin to pregnancy and conception itself. Hospitality with the biblical text, for Florence, requires a bodily engagement that "alters our routines like a new baby."[30] It conceives a new identity. Note that neither image (i.e., mat or mother) collapses guest and host into the same entity, recreating text, stranger, or family members into one's own likeness. The point is to live in relationship with the other and describe what one has seen in that relation. More than this, the goal is to be "affected, even changed by what we see."[31]

What does that bodily engagement look like? It includes Florence's creative practices of "attending" to the text, practices like physically "blocking" the text, "pushing" the text through dialogue with others, drawing the text, and describing the text through poetry and song.[32] Sally A. Brown and Luke A. Powery add prayer and spiritual practices like *lectio divina* to the list.[33] But whatever the practice, the preacher does not stay on the sidelines. Florence insists the vulnerable, messy engagement of embodied participation is not optional; it is part of what it means to take the text, in its particularity, seriously. True hospitality, like the act of conception itself, requires self and other to exist in an unsettlingly vulnerable relation.[34] When this happens, it is not only the preacher who

27. Florence, *Preaching as Testimony*, 60.

28. Florence, *Preaching as Testimony*, 68. See Paul Ricoeur, "The Hermeneutics of Testimony," in *Essays on Biblical Interpretation*, ed. Lewis Mudge (Philadelphia: Fortress Press, 1980).

29. Florence, *Preaching as Testimony*, 76.

30. Florence, *Preaching as Testimony*, 77.

31. Florence, *Preaching as Testimony*, 144.

32. Florence, *Preaching as Testimony*, 144. See Florence's full list on pages 139–50.

33. Sally A. Brown and Luke A. Powery, *Ways of the Word: Learning to Preach for Your Time and Place* (Minneapolis: Fortress Press, 2016), include prayerful practices of spiritual engagement at the start of their description of homiletic exegesis, 130–33.

34. Some have described Florence's homiletic through the lens of Lévinasian

is changed. Because the preacher is connected to a human community, the dynamism of her identity will impact the identities of her listeners.

A preacher begins her sermon on Jeremiah 29 by describing her mother's immigration to the United States, comparing that experience to Israel's exile in Babylon.[35] She is already unsettling a particular geographic narrative in her sermon: the identity of the United States as promised land. For her white congregants, the promise of the United States is a familiar trope, and her sermon places them on startlingly different ground. As she continues, however, her sermon confronts a deeper conviction in the psyches of her listeners. Speaking primarily to those raised in their country of origin, the preacher insists that the scriptural promise of this passage is not a promise for those in the security of their homeland. It is a promise given to the alien. "I know the plans I have for you," God says to Israel in Jeremiah 29:11, an assurance of hope that has been embossed on any number of eBay trinkets. It is a "life verse" that the congregation would appropriate for itself. But the preacher is clear: "This text is not about us." It is a text written to dislocated people far from home.

Notice how she carefully negotiates self and other in her interpretation. She does not lay claim to this verse, and in fact, she pushes back against a conflation of context that does not honor the text's particularity. This is a verse written to people who are mourning the loss of a homeland, the loss of blood relations, familiar constellations, and the smells of a particular soil. But her appreciation of this particularity depends on what she has learned at her mother's knee. She would not know the particularity of this text without the story of her life and the story of her mother. There is an uneasy border between text and experience, and she refuses to give either the upper hand.

"substitution." See John McClure, *Otherwise Preaching: A Postmodern Ethic for Homiletics* (St. Louis: Chalice Press, 2001), 120–23. Florence herself draws on Rebecca Chopp's language of the Word as "perfectly open sign" as the theological grounding of her project. See Rebecca Chopp, *The Power to Speak: Feminism, Language, God* (Eugene, OR: Wipf & Stock, 1991), 31. Both of these descriptions, however, seem inadequate descriptions of Florence's method. Florence's hermeneutic practices and her description of the tensive, tactile character of testimony suggest a border between self and other that is considerably more uneasy than either of these philosophical approximations.

35. Kelsey Faul (sermon, Princeton Theological Seminary, Princeton, NJ, November 5, 2013).

And into this tension between text and life, there is a promise that does speak into a contemporary room filled with comfortably settled citizens. The text does more than "mean"; it speaks—and the preacher testifies to what she hears. She does not hold the text at arm's length. She pulls the text, in its particularity, into the present and presses it back into our empty hands. It *is*, in fact, a text about us. We are just not playing the part in the narrative we expected to play. We are, in fact, Babylonians. Our identities have shifted. There is a biblical promise in this text, but not the promise we expected. The promise is found in a God who desires "welfare" (*shalom* [Jer. 29:7]) for all, including the people of Babylon. This welfare, however, flows from the prayers and well-being of the aliens who struggle to make a new life in a new land. The promise is a gift of grace flowing through their lives, worship, and witness. *Is it a gift we are ready to receive?*

Similar to the lived performances of Acts's preachers and Mary herself, an *unsettling of identity* fills the room. The preacher could have said, "This text is not about *you*," instead of "not about *us*." But she has done deep work of her own, differentiating her second-generation immigrant experience from her mother's first-generation story. Her life has been shaped by immigration, but she acknowledges the blind spots she shares with her listeners. She stands with us in our ignorance and privilege, a Babylonian as well. She has grown up in this country too. "There are things about my mother's experience," she says, "that I will never know." Her vulnerability humbles us. It bears the marks not only of a particular text and a particular mother but a particular Savior who knows something about life in a "far country."[36] She has welcomed the Word into her life through a spiritual conception that has made her identity dependent on God's grace and the grace of the outsider. She has even gone so far as to throw her lot in with *us*. Her willingness to stand by our sides and allow her heart to be pierced by a similar sword resembles Christ's own vulnerable witness.[37] Through the Spirit, her words mediate the relational identity they describe. As she allows herself to be unsettled by this Spirit-empowered dependence, we find a similar unsettling in ourselves. Her labor blesses and breaks the words of Scripture in a fresh, sacramental

36. Karl Barth, *Church Dogmatics*, IV/1, ed. Geoffrey W. Bromiley and T. F. Torrance, trans. Geoffrey W. Bromiley (London: T&T Clark, 1956), 192.

37. Christ becomes vulnerable in entering the world as a baby, but also by allowing the ambiguity and scandal of the cross to define him. He does not justify himself.

encounter, and we receive the Word with hearts stripped of entitlement and chastened by gratitude.

Florence underscores that such radical, hospitable testimony leaves preachers with conviction, but no interpretative proof. Mary's openness to the Spirit's work marks her with the scandalous opacity of God's "sign" (Luke 2:34–35), and preachers who live in embodied relation to Christ through Spirit-led engagement with Scripture experience a similar vulnerability. The congregation may suspect that the preacher has sat on the mat of Scripture with Jesus. But we have no guarantee, and neither does she. That is what it means to follow One who leads by faith and not by sight. There is an unsettledness to the entire enterprise. Finally, we have a preacher's testimony of what she has heard Jesus say, we have her embodied witness of how she was changed, and we have the witness of the Spirit burning in our hearts.

There is more to be said in the chapters that follow about what it means to spread the mat of Scripture wide in the work of biblical exegesis for preaching. The preacher's encounter with Jesus is not the only relational encounter on that mat. Preaching is about more than earnestness and risk. But none of those other relations and methodologies matter if risk never enters the equation. None of them matter if a preacher's desire for authoritative proof keeps her from welcoming a living God into her embodied performance of scriptural exegesis. None of them matter if the preacher is too afraid to speak what she hears. It is no easy thing to relinquish authoritative proof and substitute "meaning" with encounter. But that is finally what the labor of hospitality in the work of biblical interpretation requires. It requires, first and foremost, a willingness to lay aside epistemological seals of approval, respectability, and control for the sake of a Spirit-empowered conception that witnesses to Christ's cruciform call.

Dialogical Delivery: Hospitable Labor and the Sermon Event

The fluid hospitality between the self of the preacher and the Other of Christ in the conception of preaching does not only play out on the mat of Scripture. It plays out in the sermon event itself. The Other of Christ meets the preacher in the biblical text. But by the power of the Spirit, Christ also meets the preacher in and through the gathered community. To say yes to the labor of conceiving Christ is to say yes to the labor of congregational dialogue. As Christ speaks to the congregation through the preacher, Christ speaks to the preacher through the congregation, unsettling fixed categories of guest and host and creating robust, dynamic relationships among God's people. To be open to this voice of Christ, then, the preacher must be open to the voices of the faithful, exchanging the false security of autonomy for a permeable, present-tense relationship.

Different homiletic traditions live into this dialogical labor in distinct ways. Evans Crawford's classic description of the African American church's call-and-response tradition describes the congregation's active participation as a means of grace. The "responsive chord" of the congregation is more than a theological signifier of the priesthood of all believers—though it is that.[38] "The particularity of the hum thought that moves between preacher and congregation as they affirm and celebrate the gospel together" is a medium of truth.[39] It is a sacramental relationality, facilitated by the Spirit, that allows for fully human encounter with Jesus. The laity "reminds preachers that they are not gods, but persons who themselves need to be spoken to as hearers."[40] The congregation's participation witnesses to a risen God on the loose.

The silence of many white congregations during the sermon can suggest a lack of appreciation for this sort of dialogical participation. But congregations shape sermon content through various means. Attentiveness to nonverbal cues, the use of inductive sermon forms, and participatory liturgies have all been used to embody a hospitable embrace of the congregation's presence and role in constructing sermonic content.[41] Sermon preparation groups or sermon feedback circles provide additional opportunities for dialogue.[42] Bakhtin argues that all communication is dialogical in the sense that "addressees explicitly or implicitly play an

38. Evans Crawford, *The Hum: Call and Response in African American Preaching* (Nashville: Abingdon Press, 1995), 55–56.

39. Crawford, *Hum*, 60.

40. Crawford, *Hum*, 60.

41. Fred Craddock, *As One without Authority* (St. Louis: Chalice Press, 1981), 52–53, for example, insists that inductive preaching is grounded in an understanding of the hearer as more than a "destination" and the "handing over a conclusion."

42. Leo Hartshorn, "Evaluating Preaching as a Communal and Dialogical Practice," *Homiletic* 35, no 2 (2010). Lucy Rose draws on Rebecca Chopp's hermeneutic of "mutual interpretation" between text, faith, and community in *Sharing the Word: Preaching in the Roundtable Church* (Louisville: Westminster John Knox, 1997), 131.

active part as co-authors."[43] A preacher's sermon preparation does not take place in a vacuum. The "already-said" and the "not-yet-said" of the congregation influence a preacher's preparation even if they appear silent in the worship space. Indeed, the congregation's witness is critical for the preacher's voice to emerge.[44]

Many years ago, when I was teaching young seminarians how to read Scripture in the pulpit, a young woman came to me who was supposed to read Romans 8:9–17 in class. She had practiced. She had studied the meaning. She had marked up the text—and she could not say the words. They stuck in her throat. She didn't know how to say "Abba Father." She didn't know how to say any of it. One pays attention when a person says something like that. It usually means that God is very near.

We talked about the logistics of the passage. We talked about different ways to say the text comfortably. But when she stood at the front of the room, she read the passage in a monotone voice that was not her normal demeanor. "I know I should feel something," she said. "But I don't. They are just . . . words."

I put an empty chair in front of the lectern, and I asked her to read the passage again, but this time, imagine a person sitting in the chair. "Let's call her a woman," I said. "She's been through struggle. She's suffered. I don't know what she's been through—but you do. You can imagine. She doesn't quite believe that God is for her—that she is really God's child. She's been crying to God, and she's heard nothing. She's close to giving up on the whole business. Tell her about Romans 8. Tell her that even her crying out is proof that God's Spirit hasn't given up on her. She needs to hear it, and she's tired."

The student started again, looking out at the empty chair in front of her. When she got to the words, "It is that very Spirit bearing witness with our spirit that . . ." her voice broke and a physical change came over her body. Her eyes got teary; her face flushed. She paused and continued, "we are children of God." And then she laughed and cried at the same time.

I will never know who that student imagined to be sitting in that empty chair. Perhaps it was herself, "seeing herself seeing," in the words of Augusto Boal.[45] But this simple exercise of connecting the words of

43. Marlene Ringgaard Lorensen, *Dialogical Preaching: Bakhtin, Otherness and Homiletics* (Bristol, CT: Vandenhoeck & Ruprecht, 2014), 15.

44. Lorensen, *Dialogical Preaching*, 15.

45. Augusto Boal, *The Rainbow of Desire: The Boal Method of Theatre and Therapy* (New York: Routledge, 2003), 13.

Scripture to the needs of a listener opened her up to the promise of the text, and it released her voice. She discovered the promise of God for herself when she turned her eyes on the need of another.

The trouble, of course, is that it is possible to deny this dialogical reality its power. It's possible to use the words and input of a congregation "as scaffolding" rather than allowing it to deeply shape one's own sense of call and the "architectural whole" of the sermon.[46] It is possible to simply imagine the needs of one's people rather than hear them in their particularity. It is possible to collapse the other into the preacher's own self, creating pews full of convenient figments of one's own pastoral imagination. The temptation is great. Allowing actual congregational voices to disrupt and redirect the preacher's words requires an entirely new level of vulnerable hospitality, especially in the sermonic event.

Church planters like Megan Pardue and Molly Brummett Wudel have been experimenting with just such a risky, dialogical sermon form. Pardue and Brummett Wudel preach in different churches with different ecclesial visions, but they share something in common. Each allows her voice to be decentered in the sermon event to invite the congregation into the labor of meaning-making. When Pardue and Brummett Wudel speak to my introductory preaching classes about their methods and exegetical processes, it is clear that they have thought long and hard about how text and community intersect. They craft questions that open up different entry points for various members, and they think through how the sermon will land and connect other portions of worship—like the eucharistic table. They have done their homework, as any good host would. But when they preach, they ask the congregation to join them in verbal reflection in ways unusual in many worship spaces.

In a sermon at Emmaus Way Church, Brummett Wudel asks her congregation what it would mean to "bear witness and reclaim kinship" by engaging the text of Luke 7:36–50.[47] This story of the woman who kisses Jesus's feet and washes them with her tears at a dinner party of men brings up the ambiguous imagery of the table in the church's community and worship. "What does the word 'table' call up for you?" Brummett Wudel asks. The stories that follow are ambivalent and jarring. Tables are not always

46. Lorenson, *Dialogical Preaching*, 15.

47. Molly Brummett Wudel, "Bearing Witness at Table: Not What We Expect, Luke 7:36–50" (sermon dialogue, Emmaus Way Church, Durham, NC, September 2, 2018).

places of welcome. The congregation describes "tables of power" that exclude and tables of painful conflict. The most positive image comes from a congregation member describing a card table where her family played games in the evening. Brummett Wudel's ultimate goal in the sermon is to encourage her congregation to break bread together outside of worship, and to a certain extent these unsettled images disrupt that end. But rather than simplify the images, she weaves them into the table described in the text, which is also an ambivalent, exclusionary space. Her congregation's voices resist idealizations of this table and idealizations that would make table fellowship in and of itself a panacea for a broken world.

Brummett Wudel negotiates her voice and the voices of her congregation, allowing space for both. She has come prepared with her own image of a table, the true story of a meal shared across the US-Mexico border. "What might a table that imagines life without a wall look like in this place?" she asks. The congregation enters into a time of shared discernment, giving their own testimonies of what radical hospitality might look like in their North Carolina community. But then, a member turns the conversation on its head. Rather than imagine the many ways the community might serve as hosts to broader swaths of their neighbors, he gives an account of being received as a guest when he was an outsider. Given the tenor of the prior conversation, the story is remarkable. It recognizes a fluidity between guest and host that lays aside entitlement and control—a fluidity that makes hospitality generative. The point is not only to host others but to embrace the vulnerability of living as a guest. The point is not only to welcome the outsider. The point is to receive grace as an outsider oneself.

Brummett Wudel never makes this point directly, but she doesn't have to. She has been modeling this fluidity from the beginning of her sermon. She has been modeling a hospitable inversion between guest and host, preacher and congregant, speaker and listener through her performance. At the close of her sermon, she shifts her attention not to the table but to Jesus himself. She acknowledges the risk of the space where the congregation finds itself, now in the shoes of the woman who weeps at Jesus's feet. "Breathe," she says. "This is what it is supposed to be about . . . showing up . . . fully yourself. A woman with an alabaster jar being fully welcomed and loved by the One with whom she has an encounter." Her dialogical approach has been about more than modeling hospitable table fellowship. It has been about preparing her congregation to be welcomed by the One waiting for them at the table.

Dialogical preaching, as Pardue and Brummett Wudel describe it, is not for every setting. Relinquishment of autonomy in the sermon event looks different in different locations. But however it looks, such relinquishment is part of what conceiving by the Spirit implies. To be open to the Otherness of Christ is to be open to the surprise of Christ's presence among God's people and particularly open to the disruptive ways Christ's body works through those bodies. When a preacher comes with that openness, Pardue explains, "it doesn't matter if you have a manuscript. You will have to improvise."[48]

Vulnerability: Hospitality and the Stranger

To *conceive* the Word in the performance of preaching is to open oneself to an encounter with Christ through the scriptural text and gathered congregation. But no chapter on preaching's hospitable labor would be complete without reflecting on the Other of Christ in the stranger. To allow Christ to mark one's embodied witness in the pulpit is to live in embodied practices of relationship with those outside the congregation as well. Hospitality is not simply a discursive act. It requires actual relationships with those who are different than oneself, and no metaphor should skirt the point. It is not only words, spoken and read, that shape sermons. It is shared meals, interreligious conversation, protests, and prayer vigils. All of these are part of the sermon *performance*—what Alma Tinoco Ruiz calls "la vida del sermón"—the life of the sermon.[49] It is welcoming into sanctuary the immigrant about to be deported. It is gulping hot AA coffee in the church basement and remembering a transgender youth's requested pronouns. It is initiating the conversation about race with a white neighbor after another shooting of an unarmed black boy. It is breaking bread with the clergyperson with whom one deeply disagrees. As Amos Yong states, "The orthodoxy of Christian proclamation" is connected to "the orthopraxis through which the Spirit of God accomplishes the eschatological transformation of the world."[50] If Christ disrupts the

48. Megan Pardue, "Dialogic Preaching" (lecture, Duke Divinity School, Durham, NC, November 6, 2018).

49. Alma Tinoco Ruiz, "La Entrega o Presentación del Sermón," in a Spanish language preaching manual commissioned by Asbury Theological Seminary, forthcoming.

50. Yong, *Hospitality and the Other*, 140.

borders of the church even as he touches down within them, a preacher who agrees to conceive God's Word must be open to embracing God outside of the borders of the gathered congregation's expectations and comfort, even when that embrace is costly. Such conceptions bear testimony to an embodied God. The Easter angel's declaration "He is not here" (Matt. 28:6) throws down the gauntlet for any church that would treat God's temple as a tomb where Christ's body is sealed and secure. The Easter proclamation asks believers to see Christ, through the power of the Spirit, alive and active outside the church walls on street corners and park benches. "Christ is elsewhere," the angel tells us, and he cannot be boxed in or managed—not if he is truly alive.

The church my husband pastored in New Jersey had shrunk to fifteen worshipers when he arrived. They were all faithful, committed followers of Christ, but the church had forgotten what it meant to live in hospitable engagement with its neighbors. The front doors of the church were locked because "everyone" knew to use the back door, or so my husband was told. An act of hospitality began the church's revitalization: an ordinary soup supper for the many persons on the street struggling with opioid addiction. Wednesday night supper expanded to Sunday lunch, and then the church began to experience growing pains. These persons in recovery had begun attending worship, and they did not know the congregation's rules, stories, or faith. They interrupted the sermon. They disrupted the family feel of the fellowship hour. They did not belong. The conflict surrounding this labor of conceiving was real. But as Amos Yong describes, this conflict ultimately led to a "deepening of the home tradition brought about by the gifts of others."[51] Three years into my husband's tenure, the church crafted a new mission statement, painted on a banner by a recovering addict and hung in the sanctuary: "A place of healing and new beginnings." The church had been disrupted by others outside their walls, and in the disruption, they had met Jesus.

In the process, my husband's preaching—his performative style, his content, his use of Scripture—had also been disrupted. He left the pulpit. He learned to go off script. He started preaching in points because they were easier for second-language speakers to follow. Most of all, he opened his heart to relationships that left him changed. Opioid addiction is serious business, and I watched his preaching grow increasingly urgent, committed, and connected. None of it was easy. But these others

51. Yong, *Hospitality and the Other*, 133.

reminded the church of who it was called to be, and they reminded my husband who he was called to be. Just as Mary claimed her identity as "*doulē* of the Lord" in her willingness to conceive, that little congregation claimed its identity as God's servant in its embrace of others—and in its willingness to be embraced.[52]

I don't romanticize the process. Disruption can quickly become deconstruction and dissolution. There were times when the identity of that little church was hanging by a thread, overwhelmed by needs outside its walls. For all its talk of "Self" and "Other," postmodern philosophy has struggled to describe a relational vulnerability that makes space for genuine, transformative encounters that do not collapse the difference of each.[53] And yet there is something about lived practices of negotiation, solidarity, and risk that press communities beyond these polarities. And, of course, there is a living God who responds when a community decides, "Let it be with me according to your Word."

Annunciations stretch beyond the personal. They have a political edge. The active embrace of conception disrupts the powers that be. In her analysis of Luke's first chapter, Brigitte Kahl describes how the conceptions of Elizabeth and Mary disrupt the imperial narrative of time. Luke's references to political-historical time, religious-cultic time, and even the promised messianic time are bracketed out of the Annunciation. "In the sixth month," the angel appeared to Mary (Luke 1:26), referencing the sixth month of Elizabeth's pregnancy. This "gynocentric" view of time shifts the reader's vision away from narratives of power and authority and toward the work and witness of mothers and children.[54] There is privileging of a new age. It is no wonder that the angel tells Mary, "Do not be afraid" (Luke 1:30). The labor of hospitality decenters the foundations and timetables of the imperial world.

52. My thanks to Wesley Neal for letting me share his story.

53. Both postfoundationalist and antifoundationalist responses to postmodern epistemology have fallen into polarities that undermine the transformative capacity of participatory relationships. For one description of what is at stake in the impasse, see Weir's discussion of feminist identity models in *Sacrificial Logics*. Weir suggests that the central question of feminist philosophy is this: "Is it possible to affirm some sort of self-identity which does not repress the differences within the self, or the connectedness of the self to others and to do so without making false claims to authority and authorship?" See Weir, *Sacrificial Logics*, 1.

54. Brigitte Kahl, "Reading Luke against Luke: Non-Uniformity of Text, Hermeneutics of Conspiracy and the 'Scriptural Principle' in Luke 1," in *A Feminist Companion to Luke*, ed. Amy-Jill Levine (London: Sheffield Press, 2002), 76–77.

This chapter began by discussing Fijian mats and the Fijian commitment to relational hospitality. For this island nation, finding a way to welcome the other without fading away is no philosophical exercise. Welcome, too, has a political edge. For years, the British colonial government in Fiji worked to keep Indian Fijians and indigenous *iTaukei* Fijians separate and distrustful of each other. It was illegal for Indo-Fijians, whom British colonists brought to the country as indentured laborers, to visit an *iTaukei* village.[55] Ethnic conflict has marked the relationship between the Indo-Fijian and indigenous communities since Fijian independence, fueling a series of military coups.

On July 9, 2016, using proper indigenous protocol, the chief of Rewa officially welcomed the Indo-Fijian community into her tribal confederacy.[56] It was a radical conception challenging a century of distrust. Into a fraught conversation about lineage, land, religion, and culture, the mat of hospitality was formally spread in hopes that a new relational identity might be conceived. The broader consequences of that hospitable act for Fiji's common life are still being negotiated.

Several months after the ceremony, in a sermon preached in an *iTaukei* village, Reverend James Bhagwan, an Indo-Fijian pastor, interpreted the chief's extension of tribal identity through a theological lens.[57] Bhagwan drew on two texts involving Samaritans (Luke 10:25–37; 17:11–19), noting how the Samaritan community was ethnically and religiously cut off from the Israelites but bound to them by land and history. What is striking in Bhagwan's sermon is the way he resists mapping the identities of the Samaritans and Israelites onto the current Fijian context. The parts his listeners play in the story keep changing. They are fluid. In the first text, the Good Samaritan describes the indigenous community. In the second, the Samaritan praised by Jesus describes an Indo-Fijian.[58] The play of biblical metaphors mirrors the shifting borders of identity in the room. The sanctuary is filled with saris and *sulu jabas*.[59] I*Taukei* Christians play Indian instruments and Indo-Fijian Christians sing indigenous

55. Sashi Kiran, "For Peace Which Is True," *Fiji Times*, September 29, 2016, https://www.fijitimes.com/for-peace-which-is-true.

56. Maika Bolatiki, "Girmitiyas Accepted as Rewans," *Fiji Sun*, July 10, 2016, http://fijisun.com.fj/2016/07/10/girmitiyas-accepted-as-rewans.

57. James Bhagwan, "Gratitude" (sermon, Girmitiya Welcome Service, Nabudrau Village, Rewa, October 9, 2016).

58. Bhagwan, "Gratitude."

59. The *sulu jaba* is the traditional dress worn by *iTaukei* women.

hymns. Difference is visible and intermingled, and yet the congregation worships together, many seated on *iTaukei* mats.

For Bhagwan, a theologian who draws on postcolonial resources, this disruption of identity binaries cuts at the heart of the Western imperial project, a project that has invested much in maintaining and regulating the category of the other. His goal is not a "naïve syncretism" or the dissolution of cultural particularity.[60] His goal is honoring the relationality (*veiwakani*) at the heart of *iTaukei* self-understanding and the relationality in his own understanding of Christian faith. To deny Christ in the other is to deny oneself. It submits to false definitions of embodied life that serve the manipulations of the powerful. In the humble, Spirit-shadowed labor of hospitality, those manipulations are muted. An "infinitesimal 'yes' can be heard" and a fragile creation conceived.[61]

60. Yong, *Hospitality and the Other*, 159.
61. Rienstra, *Great with Child*, 1.

....

CHAPTER 7

Bearing

The Labor of Dependency

The words "she gave birth" evoke . . . women's pain and strength involved in laboring, sweating, counting, contractions, breathing deeply, crying out, dilating, pushing hard while riven to the very center of one's being with bursts of unimaginable pain, until slowly, slowly, the baby's head finally appears.

Elizabeth Johnson, *Truly Our Sister*

I guess when God is ready to birth something in you, nothing can stop it.

A preacher reflecting on her labor pains

This chapter is going to be messy. *Bearing* is a sprawling verb that spans nine months and connotes all manner of content. It is not a single thing. It is the waiting, carrying, and nourishing that allows a child to grow. It is the willingness to allow one's embodied relationship with that child to become visible to the world. It is not a momentary decision but something done over time. And yet, in English, *bearing* also connotes the fierce struggle of childbirth itself. It is both the patient work of carrying another body in one's own and the interruption of that work with the determined, difficult press of release. Part of this chapter's messiness comes from the broadness of the metaphor's meaning.

A different kind of messiness comes from the ways this verb intersects and overlaps with the labor of hospitality described in chapter six. Conceiving and bearing are braided together: a willingness to do one indicates a willingness to do the other. There are themes and practices that will circle back between this chapter and the last. Fully human preaching that is marked by Christ requires vulnerable, embodied relationships to material others—the biblical text, the gathered community, and the stranger. Conceiving and bearing share this common relational telos. But as descriptive lenses, they bring different aspects of the work into focus. I have used the labor of conceiving to describe practices of hospitality that unsettle the borders of a preacher's *identity* in fully human ways. In this chapter, we will examine the labor of bearing to describe practices of dependence that create a similar unsettling of a preacher's *agency* and power. Dependence is, of course, inseparable from true hospitable practice, but it is regularly absent from what passes as hospitality in the church. One can imagine oneself as the perfect sermonic hostess, expertly shifting identities in the preaching moment through adept performances of cultural competency. And yet one might never release control. One might never experience the weakness and joy of labor that exchanges autonomous power for power of a different sort.[1] As such, the labor of dependency helps to identify when real hospitality is occurring. Hospitality is not only about spreading a mat and welcoming outsiders but being silent long enough to hear those outsiders speak and lead. It is about relinquishing one's agenda and risking dependence in the performance of the sermon.

Perhaps the messiest part of this chapter is that it acknowledges the painful cost of proclaiming life. The goal is not to lionize that cost for its own sake but to underscore the fact that bearing a Word is no easy labor. There are all sorts of mundane practices that are part of bearing a sermon, just as there are mundane practices that are part of bearing a child. But there are also practices that require courage and a deep dependence on God. They unsettle our agency in ways that mark us with Christ's passion. This passivity—this willingness to be acted upon—is not apathetic or disconnected. It is "a kind of passivity that is responsive, responsible, response-able."[2] It unsettles us in ways that require committed cleaving and active embrace. The practices described are not comprehensive or

1. Curtiss DeYoung, Michael Emerson, George Yancey, and Karen Chai Kim, *United by Faith: The Multiracial Congregation as an Answer to the Problem of Race* (Oxford: Oxford University Press, 2004), discuss the difference between "power sharing" and "power releasing" in multiracial congregations—and how the former often describes a naive hospitality that masks assumptions of privilege and ownership.
2. Marcia Mount Shoop, *Let the Bones Dance: Embodiment and the Body of Christ* (Louisville: Westminster John Knox, 2010), 84.

applicable in every circumstance. And of course, none of these practices replace the unsettling work of the Spirit. But to the extent that they resist false grounds of autonomy, power, and authority, they keep our performances fully human. And in so doing, they keep us dependent on that deeper hope.

In her article "Mary and the Artistry of God," Cynthia Rigby describes an artist's "extrinsic energy" to create as something that cannot be "managed, [or] achieved." Instead, Rigby emphasizes the connection between what artists *do* and who they *are*. She argues that, for the Christian artist, the "particular concrete actions . . . [through which] finite creatures realize their participation with God" are not autonomously chosen. Instead, they allow one to "exist in consistency with [one's] essence" through the living out of a call.[3] The artist may birth a creative work. But that creative work, if it carries the marks of the Spirit, also bears the artist into a God-given, vocational identity. *It is a* doing *that both affects and is affected by a new, relational way of* being.

One of the great challenges in the homiletic classroom is how to teach rhetorical practices fueled by this relational dependence. What are the things that pastors *do* that press them further into embodied relation with Christ—the source of their true identity? Likewise, what impact does *who they are*, called and claimed as preachers, have on their actions? Does this lived dependence on Christ affect their lived dependence on others? Bearing a child is an active process, but there is much about the experience that cannot be managed or controlled. One is acted upon, even as one engages in the work. There are experiences of responsibility and agency alongside experiences of surrender and transformation. What might such dependent labor look like in the pulpit?

Waiting: The Labor of Patient Dependence

Sermons do not live on the page. They live in time. They are material, embodied events that unfold, moment by moment. They are streams of experience that are always new. One never steps into the same water, even if one has returned to the same riverbank. This stress on a sermon's lived performance has been a core conviction of this book. But often

3. Cynthia Rigby, "Mary and the Artistry of God" in *Blessed One: Protestant Perspectives on Mary*, ed. Beverly Gaventa and Cynthia Rigby (Louisville: Westminster John Knox, 2002), 154.

when preachers think of the *time* in which the sermon lives, they think of the twenty minutes in which the preacher stands in the pulpit. The *performance* of the sermon is limited to the moments in which the sanctuary fills with the sound of the preacher's voice, and the performance finishes when the preacher takes her seat. Performance, in this view, is an act of agency, power, and speech.

But the metaphor of bearing a child complicates the borders of this sermonic labor. Bearing a child certainly does include the day of birth itself and the moment of delivery. But it also describes a longer process. One does not bear in a moment. One bears a child over months—and that *waiting* is part of the labor too. As with so many other aspects of Mary's pregnancy, this ordinary aspect of maternal experience—the bearing of a child in time—is part of her witness. One imagines that a God responsible for a miraculous birth could have sped the process along, but Luke says nothing to make us think this is so. In fact, when "the time came for her to deliver her child" (Luke 2:6), Mary and Joseph were in decidedly inconvenient circumstances. The lack of control that Mary has in this process is striking; she does not determine the time. The time *comes*. And Mary—who has been waiting and growing and traveling and pondering for months—bears her son.

This lack of control that preachers have over the timing of sermonic insight can be maddening. Sermons don't come on cue. They cannot be forced to fit a schedule. One cannot snap one's fingers and evoke God's punctiliar in-breaking. Because Christ is born in time, bearing witness is a time-bound practice. It involves preparation, space, and expectancy. It involves Advent waiting, no matter the ecclesial season. For certain traditions, the liturgical calendar makes sermonic waiting a communal experience. One waits to hear the lilting familiarity of Luke 2 read in worship. One waits to hear the "Early in the morning" promise of John 20. And in the waiting, one prepares—which is the strange part about waiting. Relinquishing one's agency over how and when the process of sermon creation unfolds does not mean relinquishing one's responsibility. For mothers, preachers, and congregations, waiting is often an actively attentive time.

The work of waiting is especially apparent in Pentecostal traditions that emphasize the importance of "waiting on God" in the act of sermon preparation and worship. Describing the Pentecostal experience of "tarrying," Marva Williams describes a communal practice of intense prayer and expectation at the altar, sometimes lasting for hours. Williams makes clear that this waiting is not about forcing God's hand. "The understanding is that God is sovereign and the waiting is with expectation . . . to learn discipline and patience in one's prayer life."[4] Ironically, Williams defines this discipline as the ability to release control over a situation, learning to "surrender the will of self."[5] But this surrender does not take place in a vacuum. Keri Day emphasizes the "sociality" of this dependence. Tracing the grammatical links between the tarrying at the Azusa Street Revival and the "prays" houses of slave religion, Day describes how this dependence on God radically reorients the "pneumatological imagination of white Christianity," particularly in how it centers the wisdom and leadership of African American women.[6] Day argues that the reason Azusa Street was so scandalous for many white Christians was that this dependent waiting on God required a dependence on the anointed facilitation of black female bodies.[7] Waiting, in this case, not only destabilized individual power, but it also created human dependence in community, disrupting spiritual practices grounded in autonomy, control, and hierarchy. It was a dependence that disrupted the assumptions of white supremacy.

Day's point extends the significance of waiting practices in the church beyond the pietistic. Communal acts of dependence have political and social consequence. For Mary, the process of waiting allowed time to visit her cousin Elizabeth and receive Elizabeth's blessing. The Magnificat's fiery witness to a world turned upside down flows from Elizabeth's anointed proclamation. Practices that develop a preacher's ability to "wait on God" allow for those who are outside the ecclesial power structure—whether unordained or unembraced—to bring their spiritual gifts to bear in the sermonic work, making visible the Word's communal gift. Indeed, when preachers do not have ready answers, they find themselves in the shoes of Elizabeth herself, calling forth the gifts of other Marys in the community. Pastors who lean into their own need discover their need for those around them—including persons deemed transgressive or scandalous by the powers that be.

---

4. Marva Williams, "Tarry Service—Is It Still Needed?," *Pentecostal Family*, March 16, 2017, https://www.thepentecostalfamily.org/blog/tarry-service-is-it-still-needed.

5. Williams, "Tarry Service?"

6. Keri Day, Pauli Murray/Nannie Hellen Burroughs Lecture on Women and Religion, Duke Divinity School, Durham, NC, March 5, 2018. The Azusa Street Revival, stretching from 1906 to 1915, is widely understood to be the catalyst for the contemporary Pentecostal movement.

7. Day, Pauli Murray/Nannie Hellen Burroughs Lecture.

An empty chair sits in the sanctuary of CityWell Church in Durham, NC. It is reserved for Samuel Oliver-Bruno, a pastor in training, faithful husband, and father deported to Mexico on November 29, 2018.[8] Nearly a year prior, Samuel made the difficult decision to enter sanctuary at CityWell. His wife suffered from a chronic illness, and he had a teenage son. "I am here in sanctuary because I want to fight for my family," Oliver-Bruno had said.[9] A year later, under false pretenses, government officials convinced Samuel to leave sanctuary in order to officially appeal his deportation order. He was arrested by undercover ICE agents along with twenty-seven church members and supporters who nonviolently resisted his arrest.[10] When CityWell members talk about Samuel, they describe how their community changed because of the year he lived within the congregation's walls. In the words of Reverend Cleve May, Samuel "formed us in powerful ways. . . . He brought his gifts to bear in ways that literally mark our communal life."[11] The empty chair is a reminder of his loss and a silent prayer for his return.

Several months have passed, and it is the first Sunday of Lent. The Reverend Crystal Des Vignes is preaching.[12] As she reflects on that empty chair, she notes that waiting is something the CityWell congregation knows a bit about.[13] She is preaching about Jesus's temptation in the wilderness (Luke 4:1–13), but given her congregation's present wilderness season, she finds that she cannot move quickly past the first verse. She takes her time describing the setting. "Jesus," she reads, stopping to reflect on the meaning of Jesus's name. "Full of the Holy Spirit," she

---

8. For a description of Oliver-Bruno's participation in Duke Divinity School's Hispanic Latino/a Preaching Initiative during his season in sanctuary, see Alma Tinoco Ruiz and Tito Madrazo, "Preaching from Sanctuary" (paper, *Societas Homiletica*, Durham, NC, August 5, 2019).

9. Samuel Oliver-Bruno, quoted in Pilar Timpane, "After Samuel Oliver-Bruno's Deportation, a Sanctuary Community Suffers Together," *Sojourners*, December 3, 2018, https://sojo.net/articles/after-samuel-oliver-brunos-deportation-sanctuary-community-suffers-together.

10. Meagan Flynn, "Feds Deport Undocumented Immigrant Whose Church Supporters Went to Jail to Protect Him," *Washington Post*, November 30, 2018, https://www.washingtonpost.com/nation/2018/11/30/feds-deport-undocumented-immigrant-whose-church-supporters-went-jail-protect-him/?utm_term=.17cd539f9e1d.

11. Timpane, "After Samuel Oliver-Bruno's Deportation."

12. Crystal Des Vignes, "Luke 4:1–13," March 10, 2019, https://citywell.org/audio-items/3-10-19-crystal-desvignes.

13. Crystal Des Vignes, interview, April 8, 2019.

stops again, noting the Spirit's presence in this unexpected place. "Returned from the Jordan," she says. And again she stops, this time noting the significance of that watery border. "And was led by the Spirit *into the wilderness*." She has reached the heart of her message. "This is a sermon that has been in process for five years," she tells her church. She speaks of her own transitions and wildernesses—the KKK threats that her East Carolina congregation received when it was discovered that she, an African American woman, would be pastoring in that community. And she speaks of her new congregation's wilderness, drawing on womanist Delores Williams's description of Hagar's exile to claim that God is present in and through this dry, waiting season.[14] "God is not only a liberator," Des Vignes states. "God is a sustainer," who offers more than "popcorn theology." Never doubt the Spirit's work, she preaches. "God will never leave you, and you will come out [of the wilderness] with power." For Des Vignes, this power allows churches like CityWell to "speak a word in due time . . . to speak to your government and tell them that this church of a living God will be a sanctuary. We shall be a safe haven for all of God's people." Des Vignes's words testify to the experience of a black woman pastoring in predominately white, Southern, denominational conference, as well as a community grieving the deportation of a faith-filled friend. Her testimony to her congregation, many of whom come from places of privilege, is to not be afraid of the wait. "Springs of living water will come up," even in the wilderness, she tells them. And at the end of the day, God has given them each other. Unlike Jesus in the wilderness, there is a communal "holding each other" that will bear them through this season.

Finally, practices of waiting do more than develop discipline in prayer. They grow the humility, conviction, and communal networks necessary to sustain witness to justice over the long haul. When the church stands against entrenched structures of injustice and violence, a discipline of putting in time is required. Change can happen quickly, of course, but social transformation rarely comes by reacting to a moment. Secular movements like Black Lives Matter can be a model to the church in this regard. When the protests of Ferguson finished, the work of Black Lives Matter was just getting started. "People were hungry to galvanize their communities to end state-sanctioned violence against Black people," which required the infrastructure behind the Black Lives Matter

14. Delores Williams, *Sisters in the Wilderness: The Challenge of Womanist God-Talk* (Maryknoll, NY: Orbis, 1993).

Global Network.[15] In the words of cofounder Alicia Garza,[16] this work of "building bridges" requires a surrender to a larger commitment and calling.[17] It requires a patience that roots such work in hope.

From this intersection of surrender and commitment, I speak to young preachers who ask me whether preparation time is necessary for *overshadowed* sermons. Indeed, some students wonder whether preparation time impedes the Spirit's work! Mary's experience makes clear that Spirit miracle and preparation time work together. God can give a sermon to a preacher on a Saturday night—thank goodness. But if a preacher is called to witness to the bodily engagement of Christ in the church and in the world, she will put in hours, often without seeing immediate fruit. She will put in prayer, relationship, and commitment to God's larger work in the community. She will "tarry in Jerusalem" (Luke 24:49), at ICE protests, and at prayer vigils with brothers and sisters in wait for the Spirit. She will attend to wordcraft and biblical study with the expectant grit of Jacob, who said to God's angel, "I will not let you go, unless you bless me" (Gen. 32:25). She will wait, committed and connected, knowing she is dependent on God's response.

Carrying: The Labor of Differentiated Dependence

What if bodies refused to be invisible?[18]

Changes appear in the waiting—changes that can be seen. To bear a child is to carry the weight of another person and become visible in that carrying. Carrying a child allows one's pregnancy to come into view. The work of carrying affects one's energy and one's relationships. It affects one's sleep and appetite. Everyday tasks require more effort, and everyday interactions more forbearance. Pregnant women speak of their bellies being touched by strangers and having the fears and joys of others projected onto their experiences. They can receive unsolicited advice based on

15. "Herstory," *Black Lives Matter*, accessed April 5, 2019, https://blacklivesmatter.com/about/herstory.

16. Alicia Garza is a cofounder along with Patrice Khan-Cullors and Opal Tometi.

17. Janell Ross and Wesley Lowery, "Black Lives Matter Shifts from Protests to Policy," *Chicago Tribune*, May 4, 2017, https://www.chicagotribune.com/nation-world/ct-black-lives-matter-trump-20170504-story.html.

18. Shoop, *Let the Bones Dance*, 66.

"how [they] are carrying" as they become increasingly vulnerable to the world's gaze. But it is not only the pregnant woman's body that becomes visible. Her child's physical presence takes on increasing particularity. This child has its own flesh—its own body. A small foot presses into the mother's rib cage. A kick wakes her up in the middle of the night. To carry a child is to remember this child's difference—to feel that difference in one's body and make space for it. Carrying a child is an act that makes one vulnerable to being acted upon.

For preachers, carrying the Word invites a similar bearing of weight. It may mean carrying the congregation in intercessory prayer. Sleep and appetite can be affected. A preacher may find herself waking in the middle of the night and stumbling for a pen in the dark. She might crave quiet or a particular piece of music. The borders between her heart and the world may seem increasingly permeable—tears and delight more accessible. Preachers who carry a Word can glow, or on difficult weeks look green around the gills. Carrying God's Word makes a preacher vulnerable. It risks visibility in the public sphere. Ask any woman nervous about wearing a clerical collar.[19] Invisibility has its comforts.

But finally, as with pregnancy, carrying the Word is not only about the visibility of a preacher's body. It is also about offering embodied testimony to the particularity of the One being born. The Word is also coming into view, and the Word's body is distinct from the preacher's own. As the work of carrying the Word continues, this differentiation can become uncomfortable, requiring changes in the preacher's daily rhythms and theological contours. To carry the Word is to commit to living as an embodied witness to this difference.

One concrete way that preachers demonstrate this commitment to difference is by attending to the particularity of the biblical text. The careful study of a text, its context, its history, and its difficult edges has ethical implications for the performance of preaching. It reminds the preacher that, finally, the Word a preacher bears is Other. Embodied relation with the Word does not remake the Word in one's own image, even when Word and preacher bear a family resemblance. It means allowing for a differentiation that can challenge and change the preacher. Ellen Davis describes "holy preaching" as preaching that is "oriented toward the biblical text and characterized by a willingness to acquire new habits

19. Barbara Brown Taylor talks about her challenges with clerical collars in *Leaving Church: A Memoir of Faith* (San Francisco: HarperSanFrancisco, 2006), 21.

and categories of thought."[20] It is preaching that allows the text to change a preacher from the inside out. Similar to carrying a child, carrying the Word means acting in ways that make a preacher vulnerable to being acted upon.

The labor of *conceiving* described in chapter six emphasized a welcoming of the biblical material into one's lived experience and community. It invited the biblical text near. Practices of imagination, prayer, and connection were emphasized. *Bearing* the Word stresses a complementary, costly commitment to differentiation. It includes the time-consuming, world-altering work of carrying a text—not to own it or hide it but to make space for it to be seen. Alexander Deeg notes an "astonishing...homiletic loss of the text" in much Protestant preaching, where the "biblical text increasingly disappears" after the reading of the biblical passage for the day.[21] Drawing on Hebrew rabbinic tradition, Deeg argues that imaginative preaching is fueled by a "meticulousness" that attends to a text's concrete details.[22] When I ask my Fijian students to describe a mat's meaning, they may emphasize a mat's shifting eventfulness, but they also note the mat's size and edging. They note the quality of the work and what the pattern indicates about the woman who wove it. They note the materials used—whether store-bought or naturally available. They pay attention to details and specifics, letting those details shape their reading.

When it comes to the labor of biblical interpretation, some of that detail work can take place at a desk. Careful study pays attention to nuances in translation and echoes of recurring themes and metaphors. It asks what is at stake for the text's original community, and to the extent one can ascertain, the stakes for the original author. But as Fernando Segovia has effectively argued, careful study of a biblical text also pays attention to other biblical interpreters—particularly those from different social locations. Segovia chronicles the ways that the historical-critical method has draped itself in a "guise of neutrality and impartiality" rather than acknowledge its own cultural particulars.[23] Historical research is itself an interpretive performance influenced by one's class, conventions,

20. Ellen Davis, *Preaching the Luminous Word: Biblical Sermons and Homiletical Essays* (Grand Rapids: Eerdmans, 2016), 90.
21. Alexander Deeg, "Imagination and Meticulousness," *Homiletic* 34, no. 1 (2009): 146.
22. Deeg, "Imagination and Meticulousness," 146.
23. Fernando F. Segovia, "The Text as Other: Towards a Hispanic American Her-

and ideological stance. Given this, embracing the otherness of the text requires an embrace of "other readers of the text," intentionally privileging the voices of those who can subject "our respective view of one another and the world to critical exposure and analysis."[24] Segovia describes a hermeneutic of "otherness and engagement," where our understanding of the Bible depends on the perspectives of those unlike ourselves.[25] A preacher doesn't know what she doesn't know—and neither does a religious community, which is why inviting a familiar community into conversation about a text is not enough. To carry the Word is to let the mystery of dislocation confront us in ways that invite our silence and change.

A South Pacific student reminds me that the critical exposure Segovia describes might be more necessary for a Western white woman than himself. His whole education has required him to listen to voices outside his community. He doesn't particularly feel the need to engage those voices further, and I see his point. But what of South Pacific biblical scholars? I wonder with him. And what about the voices in his community that are different in other ways? What about his wife's understanding of the text? Or his lay Bible study group? What about an ostracized youth or a homebound elder? Communities are not monolithic. They have multiple social locations. "Whom will you invite to sit on your mat?" I ask. Christ is there, sitting on the mat of Scripture by his faithful promise and the Spirit's power. He is ready to speak. "Whom will you invite into conversation with him?"

The indigenous Fijian word for discernment through conversation is *talanoa*. The *talanoa* of scriptural interpretation includes the voices of the original community and communities of the faithful over time. These are part of Scripture's weave and texture. A preacher gives these voices space to speak and lets them mark her testimony. A preacher may note the conversation between the call stories of Isaiah 6 and Luke 5—between Isaiah's "unclean lips" and Peter's "I am a sinful man!"[26] She may notice how James and John answer Jesus's question "What would you have me do for you?" differently than Bartimaeus does just verses later (Mark

---

meneutic," in *Text and Experience: Towards a Cultural Exegesis of the Bible*, ed. Daniel Smith-Christopher (Sheffield: Sheffield Academic), 285.

24. Segovia, "The Text as Other," 293, 297.

25. Segovia, "The Text as Other," 297.

26. Sarah Seibert, (sermon, Goodson Chapel, Durham, NC, February 7, 2019), for example, intersplices these Scriptures in her performance to amplify the resonance.

10:36, 51).[27] She might wonder whether there are similarities between those talkative Corinthian women and the brave Hebrew midwives. She could invite them all to the mat and have a fantastic, intertextual conversation. She could even add her favorite theologian to the mix.

But a robust *talanoa* of biblical interpretation does more than listen to voices familiar to text and tradition. It also includes voices overlooked or actively silenced. It is one thing for theologians and biblical scholars to grapple with David's rape of Bathsheba. It is quite a different thing when a young woman sits on a pastor's couch and admits she is pregnant by a man who is not her husband—and that the father is a powerful church elder. It is different when she tells the preacher how hard it is to say no to the Davids lionized by her community. In the face of such honesty, the other voices on the preacher's interpretative mat grow still and the preacher's eyes turn to Jesus. Does he have anything to say about this difficult scrap of text, sitting with this hurting woman on this particularly painful piece of earth?

Honoring the otherness of the text means honoring others. It means carrying the mat of Scripture to unusual places and spreading it wide enough to include conversations with unexpected people. Such carrying of difference makes a preacher dependent on persons she does not know to shape her biblical interpretation, which is risky business. But she is not alone. Jesus is on the mat, too, and he will have his say. The point is not to showcase a sufficiently diverse group of interlocutors. Mats are finite, and voices will always be excluded. The point is to risk a scriptural *talanoa* particular enough to change us, challenge us, and mark us with gospel. Sometimes, an unexpected conversation partner is precisely what brings the particularity of the biblical text into view.

"I have called you by name, you are mine" (Isa. 43:1), a preacher proclaims. It's a favorite, familiar passage. But I'd never heard the text in conversation with the experience the preacher describes: the experience of a transgender woman who realizes that her name is Joanna—rather than John.[28] Speaking God's promise to Joanna, the preacher tells us, "I will call you by your true name. I will speak the name you really are." You do not belong to those who told you to hide, she continues. "You belong to

27. Leigh Curl (sermon, Goodson Chapel, Durham, NC, October 25, 2018), imagines how these status-conscious disciples might overhear Bartimaeus's response to the same question Jesus asked of them.

28. Margie Quinn (sermon, Duke Divinity School, Durham, NC, March 19, 2019). Used with permission. Joanna's name has been changed.

me." The verse, previously vague in its promise of belonging, snaps into focus. This specific promise is a protest against earthly powers that refuse to learn or use one's name. It is not just Joanna who comes into view. Isaiah's exiled people come into view, those who have been displaced and given Babylonian names (as in Dan. 1:7). One might imagine that these names do not rest easy on Israelite tongues. They are names designed to make the powerful comfortable and the particularity of God's people invisible. "I have called you by your name," says the God of living, "and I will do so again. You are not theirs. You are mine." Joanna's otherness gives us eyes to see Israel's otherness and *carry the weight* of the text's claim. Her presence is not just an affirmation of inclusive politics (though I praise God for inclusive politics). Joanna's voice, combined with the preacher's attention to detail, brings the text's context into clarity. Her presence allows the text to be seen—and by the power of the Spirit leave its mark.

That mark calls forth "repentance" and a seeing of oneself, something that is not always easy.[29] I was teaching a Bible study for Fijian pastors' wives about Dorcas, also called Tabitha (Acts 9:36-37), when the group began talking about the reasons Dorcas might have had a name in two languages. Without thinking, I asked, "Have you ever had to change your name to make someone who didn't speak your language comfortable?" The room fell quiet. I flushed, realizing these women had been using shortened forms of their Fijian names for months—for my benefit. A kindness that I *hadn't seen*. Carrying the Word commits to the work of rendering bodies visible—the body of the text and the bodies of those who hear that text differently from ourselves. It allows one's body and practice to be changed by that difference, stretching in witness to an embodied God.

Nourishing: The Labor of Communal Dependence

Strong is what we make each other.
Until we are all strong together,
a strong woman is a woman strongly afraid.[30]

29. Davis, *Preaching the Luminous Word*, 90.
30. Marge Piercy, "For Strong Women," in *The Moon Is Always Female* (New York: Knopf, 1980), 56.

If it isn't yet clear, "bearing the Word" is hard. It takes energy, patience, and courage. But for all of its cruciformity, there is a difference between bearing a cross and bearing a baby. When one bears a child, one has to nourish and care for one's body. And this is one of the most important words I give to young preachers: nourish yourself. Bearing a Word requires the preacher's sustenance because the Word's thriving depends on a preacher's own.

Mothers-to-be require sleep and food to give them strength for the work. Preachers are no different. "Are you getting enough rest?" I'll ask a struggling preacher. "Are you putting good things in your body?" It's a decent place to begin. But preachers know that sustenance and nourishment come in many forms. Nourishment comes from sabbath, a book of poetry, and loudly playing one's favorite playlist on repeat. In Fiji, nourishing the Word means fasting for the sermon. It means prayer and hymn-sings at family devotions after dinner. To bear a child means honoring one's limits and sitting down when tired. It means paying attention when something doesn't feel right. Many preachers convince themselves that bearing the Word looks more like a heroic quest than communal dependence. But sometimes the most heroic work a preacher can do is ask for what she needs. For preachers who root their worth in productivity, admitting a need for rest is a radical act of self-love. To admit that one is lonely or depressed is a courageous act of trust. It is no small thing to share one's weakness with those who may not know what to do with it.

Admitting weakness can be particularly hard for communities whose survival has depended on a performance of strength. In *Too Heavy a Yoke: Black Women and the Burden of Strength*, Chanequa Walker-Barnes describes the dangerous burden of the black Superwoman, building on the work of Michele Wallace. This Superwoman is "a woman of inordinate strength, with an ability for tolerating an unusual amount of misery and heavy, distasteful work. This woman does not have the same fears, weaknesses, and insecurities as other women, but believes herself to be ... the embodiment of Mother Earth, the quintessential mother with infinite sexual, life-giving, and nurturing reserves."[31] For Walker-Barnes, the archetype is a racialized variation of "the cult of true womanhood—a

---

31. Chanequa Walker-Barnes, *Too Heavy a Yoke: Black Women and the Burden of Strength* (Eugene, OR: Wipf & Stock, 2014), 6, quoting Michele Wallace's *Black Macho and the Black Superwoman*, 107. Walker-Barnes notes that the ideal of "strength" can burden women and men of various ethnicities, but "what is unique for Black women is the degree to which these are a prescriptive function of one's fixed public identity" (8).

White, middle-class ideal characterized by piety, purity, domesticity and submissiveness."[32] In enacting the Superwoman ideal, black women become the "embodied locus of atonement for the imputed sins of the race as dictated by White racism."[33] The effects on the bodies of black women are deadly, and these effects are often ignored or romanticized. There can be dangerous silences or rationalizations of black women's suffering, particularly if they find themselves in church leadership.

Drawing on Jeremiah 17:5–7, Reverend Chalice Overy notes her suspicion that there is "something about the work [of church leadership] that causes emotional distress."[34] There is an impression that "going through the things that make us human disqualify us from the work." The result is isolation and shame. In her sermon to future clergy, Overy emphasizes the importance of "root work, . . . digging in and reaching out." Nourishment that is vital to preachers is found in those who would "want us around . . . even if we were not producing." Let your roots go deep into these resources, Overy tells those gathered. Too many preachers smile and say "I'm good" when they're not.

For all of her unsettled vulnerability, Mary has faithful companions in Luke's Gospel. She does not get to Bethlehem alone. Joseph finds space for Mary to deliver. Elizabeth affirms Mary's vocation even before Mary finds the words to name it. A preacher's Joseph and Elizabeth take many forms. They are not always relatives or spouses. But these protectors and prophets are necessary for a preacher's bearing work. They nourish a preacher's call. When I speak to a group of women beginning their calls to ministry, I know that some in the room have support. They come from denominations that have ordained women for decades and have mentors cheering in the wings. But I also know this call will separate some from those they love. Their family does not understand. Their faith community is embarrassed. There might be celebrations for others, but there are no neighbors and relatives to rejoice with them (Luke 1:58). I tell them to "find your Elizabeth." It may not be whom you expect or whom you would have chosen. You may have to travel to find her. But God doesn't give a call without providing a witness. God knows you need nourishment. God knows you need support. Find those who will love you for

32. Walker-Barnes, *Too Heavy a Yoke*, 11.

33. Walker-Barnes, *Too Heavy a Yoke*, 11.

34. Chalice Overy, "Planted (Jeremiah 17:5–7)" (sermon, Goodson Chapel, Durham, NC, February, 12, 2019).

who you are in your particularity. You don't need a crowd. You need one or two who can be counted on. Find your Elizabeth. Find the person who tells you that something leaps inside her when she sees the Word shining in your eyes. And when she prophesies blessing over you in the Spirit's power, receive it.

Finally, Reverend Overy tells her listeners, the roots that connect us to others reveal a deeper connection—a deeper dependence. We realize that we have not come this far because of "how tight we have held on to God." We have come this far because God has been "holding tight to us." And this God desires our nourishment, body and soul.

Giving Birth: The Labor of Costly Dependence

Birth is the poetic embodiment of self-assertion and surrender. It is the dance of power and passivity.[35]

There is no getting around it. Giving birth is risky. It is painful—even with the assistance of modern medicine. And Mary didn't have modern medicine or give birth with proper help in a proper place. There are certain ecclesial traditions that claim Mary did not feel pain during her labor, but the simplicity of Luke's words (i.e., "she gave birth" [Luke 2:7]) suggests otherwise. Luke doesn't give us proof of the Annunciation's miraculous claim in the extraordinary painless labor of Mary. It is located in the child himself, interpreted through the inspiration of the Spirit (Luke 2:25–35) and the witness of the angelic host (vv. 11–12). Luke's very reticence concerning Mary's labor suggests that Elizabeth Johnson's description of being "riven to the very center of one's being" is more consistent with Luke's meaning.[36] There is much we don't know about Mary's labor, but if it is ordinary enough to be described in a single verse, it was a struggle.

Ricoeur has noted that living one's life in embodied relation to others brings suffering—a difficult word to swallow. To live in enjoined relation is to live as both agent and "patient," and such "intimate passivity" has

35. Shoop, *Let the Bones Dance*, 84.
36. Johnson's description can be found in this chapter's epigraph. See Elizabeth Johnson, *Truly Our Sister: A Theology of Mary in the Communion of Saints* (New York: Continuum, 2003), 277.

a cost.[37] Physical dependence creates a vulnerability to the other, an *unsettling of agency*. It opens oneself up to the hurt of the world. The "power and passivity" of a laboring woman provides a potent visualization of Ricoeur's claim.[38] It also reframes and focuses his point. One bears the cost of embodied relation *for the purposes of life*. Joy can be found in the struggle. But one should not minimize the cost of this "self-assertion and surrender."[39]

It is similar to the cost of bearing the Word. If a preacher has been joined by the Spirit in embodied relation to Christ and world, she finds her body marked by those relations. Her body witnesses to a God who bears suffering for the sake of life, which is no easy dependence. The metaphor has a significant biblical pedigree. Paul's description of his "travail" for the sake of the gospel suggests the costly press and pressure of proclamation (Gal. 4:19).[40] And yet there has been resistance to such visceral images in the teaching of homiletics. Similar to traditions surrounding Mary's pain-free labor, there can be a denial of tears in the preaching of gospel hope. But an unwillingness to acknowledge the pain of life can lead to sermons that are less than fully human. Such denials can lead to an inability to enter into the pain of the congregation and world—or even the aching heart of God.

Luke Powery begins his book *Spirit Speech: Lament and Celebration in Preaching* with a description of a funeral that took place for his ten-year-old niece during Advent 2005. He notes that "there were those, even ordained ministers and preachers of the gospel, who appeared afraid to lament . . . evidenced by their overemphasis on celebrating the fact that my niece was now in glory."[41] The inadequacy of this response would shape the trajectory of Powery's ministry and witness. For Pow-

37. To be patient means being passive or being acted on. See Paul Ricoeur, *Oneself as Another*, trans. Kathleen Blamey (Chicago: University of Chicago Press, 1992), 320. While Christ's passion is not Ricoeur's subject matter, his reference to this passivity in terms of "passions" (i.e., experiences of otherness and suffering that accompany enjoined relation) is evocative for a Christian reader.

38. Shoop, *Let the Bones Dance*, 84.

39. Shoop, *Let the Bones Dance*, 84.

40. Beverly Gaventa discusses Paul's maternal imagery in *Our Mother, St. Paul* (Louisville: Westminster John Knox, 2007), 29-40. See also Susan Eastman's discussion of Paul's "labor pains" in *Recovering Paul's Mother Tongue: Language and Theology in Galatians* (Grand Rapids: Eerdmans, 2007), 89-126.

41. Luke A. Powery, *Spirit Speech: Lament and Celebration in Preaching* (Nashville: Abingdon Press, 2009), xiii.

ery, the lament of preaching is a necessary part of its ability to speak a word of hope. A willingness to touch pain is connected to one's ability to speak promise. Developing this idea further in *Dem Dry Bones: Preaching, Death, and Hope*, Powery argues that the tension between death and hope is at the heart of the gospel. In proclamation, "present death is proclaimed boldly and the future of God is declared courageously because at their intersection, in this liminal space, hope lives."[42] For Powery, such a tension between pain and hope is a mark of the Spirit's work. It is "the Spirit's song."[43] Significantly, it is a tension that is not simply preached *about* but that a preacher preaches *within*. Drawing on the lived experience of African American spirituals, Powery argues that spiritual preaching existentially engages the pain of the world and the promise of God's future. It places the preacher on a "homiletical tightrope."[44] More importantly, it requires the intervention of a "present God" who encounters those in the pews. The preacher's balancing act is not hope's source—God is.[45]

A seasoned preacher tells me about her preparation process. "There are times when I read the Word and sob. I feel the pain of the people before I preach it. . . . I experience the people's anguish first."[46] From this preacher's perspective, such an engagement with human suffering is "a vulnerable place. It is not the place where everything seems good and holy." It is active engagement with the wounds in her community and simultaneously a moment of surrender. She explains, "God uses a broken vessel . . . and so I say 'God, I trust you' . . . even if I don't know if I have anything to give. Those are usually the times God uses me the most." This preacher takes an unmistakable joy in her work. Even as she speaks of pain, she acknowledges her "amazement that God chooses me to proclaim such a wonderful, powerful Word." In describing the tension between joy and pain in her preaching, she draws on her experience of bearing children. She takes a breath and beams, "The joy surpassed the pain." She stretches to describe the paradox theologically, settling on a

---

42. Luke A. Powery, *Dem Dry Bones: Preaching, Death, and Hope* (Fortress Press: Minneapolis, 2012), 93.

43. Powery, *Spirit Speech*, xiii.

44. Powery borrows this image from Cornell West's *Hope on a Tightrope: Words and Wisdom* (Carlsbad, CA: Smiley, 2008).

45. Powery, *Dem Dry Bones*, 100.

46. Conversation with a preacher on the joys and challenges of preaching, January 7, 2013.

christological analogy. "I took the pain for them," she says, emphasizing the love that lay beneath the labor.

She is not the first to make the connection. In her book *Cross Talk: Preaching Redemption Here and Now*, Sally A. Brown draws on this intersection of pain and generative hope in pregnancy to reframe the sacrifice of Christ on the cross. Drawing on the work of Mary J. Streufert, Brown suggests, "The sacrifices involved in pregnancy and motherhood are generative sacrifices: they are life poured out to another to generate life."[47] Through this lens mothers like Debra Rienstra interpret Mary's pain in labor as "a kind of foretaste, of Jesus' later suffering." For Rienstra, the image is reflexive: "Good Friday was, in a sense, the concentrated labor of God, the transition to the New Creation."[48]

There is danger in such language. The cross can be used to romanticize oppressive pain or justify the status quo with indefinite calls to resilience. These abuses twist the metaphor and mock God's liberating love. Pain, in and of itself, is not redemptive. Neither does a preacher's willingness to experience the pain of her community make her a substitute for Christ. Jesus's sacrifice on the cross is salvific, and the sacrifice of Mary in bearing Jesus is not. All the same, Mary's sacrifice does bear a Savior. Furthermore, similar to how a sacramental sign resembles the reality it mediates, Mary's sacrifice bears a resemblance to her Savior's own. She bears in her body the marks of the One she carries. Her body, her commitment, and her love matter.

When I speak to young preachers, I often draw on Mary McClintock Fulkerson's description of a wound as the redemptive space where theological insight occurs.[49] Rather than thinking of the function of the sermon, our attention will be drawn to the particular wound that the sermon addresses and how the sermon might speak hope to that wound.[50] Such wounds may be emotional, physical, or epistemological in nature. They may exhibit themselves inside the congregation or outside its walls. They

47. Sally A. Brown, *Cross Talk: Preaching Redemption Here and Now* (Louisville: Westminster John Knox, 2008), 116.

48. Debra Rienstra, *Great with Child: Reflections on Faith, Fullness, and Becoming a Mother* (New York: Penguin Putnam, 2002), 157–58.

49. Mary McClintock Fulkerson, *Places of Redemption* (Oxford: Oxford University Press, 2009), 13.

50. *Function*, as developed by Thomas G. Long, *The Witness of Preaching* (Louisville: Westminster John Knox, 1990), 78–91, is a helpful category that allows preachers to articulate a sermon's purpose in a given context.

often have a public and private face. Such reflection can move preachers toward greater vulnerability and specificity in exegeting their context, inviting greater empathy. In so doing, many preachers acknowledge their own lack of answers and their inability to heal. As they engage deeply with the wounds of the world, they find themselves on the tensive border of their own agency and passivity, dependent on a Spirit-born Word from God. Such engagement leads to a greater dependence on a Savior, which is, finally, where hope resides.

The Tuesday after Samuel Oliver-Bruno was deported, a student who knew him well stood to preach in a Divinity School classroom. Because Samuel was part of the seminary community, many in the room were still in states of shock and grief. The preacher looked particularly exhausted. Even in the best of circumstances, this class had not been easy for him. English was not his first language, so preaching to his English-speaking classmates meant a whole different level of "unsettled agency." He could not always find words to say what he needed to say. But there are days when words are not the best descriptor of wounds. And on those days, mother-tongue facility can get in the way.

About five minutes into the sermon, the preacher takes a pair of handcuffs from his pocket.[51] His text is John 18:28–40, Pilate's inquisition of Jesus, and he wants us to imagine the Good Friday scene. He wants us to imagine that Roman courtroom and shift uncomfortably in our seats in the position of Pilate. He wants us to see Jesus's apparent helplessness in that place of power. Since the preacher is unable to handcuff his own hands behind his body, he asks for help from one of the listeners in the room, underscoring the "intimate passivity" of the act. The room grows very still because the preacher is doing more than setting the stage. He is touching a wound. We are not only remembering Good Friday. We are remembering the Friday prior—the Friday after Thanksgiving when Samuel had been handcuffed and taken into custody. In US parlance, the day of Samuel's arrest is called "Black Friday," and the preacher does not overlook the irony. Black Friday and Good Friday bleed together.

We see Jesus and Samuel standing bound before us, imaged through the preacher's body. But the preacher doesn't objectify them. He doesn't let us stabilize the categories of powerful and powerless. This is John's Gospel, after all, and the preacher is going after a deeper wound. Finally,

---

51. Saul Gastelum Flores (sermon, Duke Divinity School, Durham, NC, November 27, 2018). Used with permission.

the handcuffs are not meant to describe the pain of Samuel or the passion of Christ. They are meant to describe *us*. Just as John describes Pilate as bound by his fear and political machinations, we are bound. We have been shackled by economic privilege and a fear of dependence—by *idolatry* and *nationalism*. "We are handcuffed," the preacher tells us, "when we oppress minorities." And what is worse, "We are comfortable being handcuffed."

The preacher does not stand in the position of Jesus; he acknowledges the handcuffs of his own privilege. Neither does he sensationalize redemptive suffering. Instead, he bears witness to a question he cannot answer: "What would it mean to depend on each other again? Documented and undocumented alike?" "There are times over these past days when I have felt like there was no hope," he tells us. "I have thought, *we are screwed*." But then the preacher describes the tears of a fellow congregation member—a male, white US citizen—who wept with him over the weekend. "Perhaps there is hope when our brothers and sisters help us," the preacher says.

Throughout the sermon the preacher has needed the help of his listeners to turn the pages of his manuscript, and now he needs their help again. He looks at his peers and asks a listener to unlock his handcuffs. There is nervousness in the room as the preacher twists his body so that the key can fit into the mechanism. His dependence makes us feel our own. We feel the discomfort of handcuffs we didn't know we were wearing.

A deep longing emerges in the preacher's final prayer. "Thank you, Jesus, for talking to us in ways that hurt sometimes," he says. There are days when "it is hard to see you are there." In response to this opacity, the preacher calls on the Spirit. "Holy Spirit, move in this place, in this Divinity School, in every church and state in this nation.... We need you here. We want to see you."

This lament-filled prayer is costly. It is intercession that embraces the pain of the community and models a dependence we cannot match. We do not know what this sermon has cost the preacher. Most in the room have never risked the weakness of preaching in a language other than our own. Most have not risked such a vulnerable embodiment of sin and suffering. But in this costly labor, the bodies of our Christian brothers and sisters come into view. And by the Spirit's power, the wound in the room finds voice. We not only feel Samuel's absence; we feel Jesus's absence. It is "hard to see" that Jesus is here. As the preacher asks the Spirit for new vision, we risk hope—and pray this hope "does not disappoint" (Rom. 5:5).

To Bear and Be Born

The sermons in this chapter take fierce postures of resistance, which may seem strange given the chapter's emphasis on dependence. For all of my talk of being acted upon, these are *active* sermons. Like a laboring woman, they are sermons fighting for life. The logic of labor tells me that these two categories—power and dependence—are not mutually exclusive categories. In *Dem Dry Bones*, Powery describes the story of a woman who bears a child. In March 2000, in the midst of the horrible floods that covered Mozambique, a woman in labor climbed a tree. Many of her family had already died, and her home had been destroyed. She was in the tree for three days, and at the end of that time, she gave birth to a daughter. Powery states, "Crying could be heard from those dying in the floods, but life and hope, in the form of a newborn baby, was crying too."[52]

To bear Christ is to embrace the pain of a broken world and relinquish the illusion that one can master that pain. Such proclamation clings to a tree of life in the midst of death and listens for the cry of a coming Redeemer. But, finally, the world's hope is not constituted by the preacher's labor any more than Mozambique's hope was constituted by the labor of that bearing woman and the life of her baby. It is Christ's labor on a tree and his continuing labor at God's right hand through which the world is born into new life. As the preacher embraces this labor through the Spirit's power, God's people are born again.[53] Indeed, the preacher herself is reborn.

I started this chapter with Cythnia Rigby's description of how an artist is changed through Spirit-driven, creative work. Such work requires an *unsettling of agency* in responding to flashes of creative insight. But more significantly, such work requires an embrace of vocational identity—a living into one's created "essence."[54] In such cases, to be free is to act in

---

52. Powery, *Dem Dry Bones*, 98.

53. Powery repeated this story in a sermon on Romans 8, making explicit the labor of God amid the "groaning" of the world. See Luke A. Powery, "Groaning for Love" (sermon, Miller Chapel, Princeton Theological Seminary, May 2, 2012).

54. Cynthia Rigby, "Mary and the Artistry of God," in *Blessed One: Protestant*

concert with the person one was made to be. Such resonance between identity and action is precious. It is the holy labor of life.

A woman sits in my office and tells me that she has been running from a call to preach for ten years. She knows that the faith community that formed her will reject her if she claims this call. I've seen her preach. I've seen her face light up with delight when she breaks open the rock of Scripture and shows us the honey inside. I've seen her eyes come alive when she tells a room about Jesus. But bearing the Word is not easy, and I don't want her to think there is only one way forward. "Perhaps you can teach," I say. "Perhaps you can write. Are you sure that preaching is your call?" She looks at me with quiet simplicity and says, "It is what I was born to do."[55]

Is this "self-assertion" or "surrender"?[56]

Or is it the power of a daughter of God, born in the crook of Christ's tree and held in the cradle of Christ's arm, crying a full-throated cry—fighting for all she's worth to greet the sun?

Perspectives on Mary, ed. Beverly Gaventa and Cynthia Rigby (Louisville: Westminster John Knox, 2002), 154.

55. Conversation with a seminary student, March 28, 2019. Used with permission.
56. Shoop, *Let the Bones Dance*, 84.

CHAPTER 8

Naming

The Labor of Discernment

> I distanced from religious language last year, not because I didn't believe, but because I've seen an awful misuse of religious terminology. . . . I needed a healing of these words so I could use them again. . . . [My sermon] was very much me. There was very little religious talk.
>
> Seminary student conversation, May 15, 2012

> The sermon emerges from the language of the believing community.
>
> Richard Lischer, *The End of Words*

To speak of Mary's naming of Jesus is to focus on the social embodiment of that relation. It is to move from conversations about bearing to conversations about mothering. It is to interact with rituals embedded in particular traditions and perform one's calling "in full view"[1] of one's community. It means dealing with something thicker and thornier than *identity* and *agency* alone. It means dealing with family—and one's *role* in that family.

Metaphors have limits, and Mary's pregnancy may seem ill-equipped to describe the particularity of a preacher's role or the ecclesial function of a sermon. The metaphor is most obviously an interior picture of the relationship between preacher and Word and less explicitly about a preach-

---

1. Anna Carter Florence, *Preaching as Testimony* (Louisville: Westminster John Knox, 2007), xviii.

er's relation to tradition and congregation.[2] It says more about the body of the Word than the slippery specifics of speech. Is there anything in Luke's description of Mary's labor to help preachers discern the distinctive content of the words they say and the communal role they play?

Luke's text—and particularly Mary's naming of Christ—provides a place to start. When the angel Gabriel describes Mary's pregnant action, *naming* is part of the labor to which she is called. Naming the Word in a particular community is descriptive of preaching's goal when it flows from a Spirit-empowered relation with Christ. Mary's naming of Jesus is a linguistic act that claims God's salvation is near. As such, it holds the uniqueness of her experience in unsettled relation to her community's narratives and norms. Mary's naming of Jesus uses language in ways that participate in her tradition, as well as differentiate from that tradition. A preacher's *naming* of Jesus requires a similar commitment and risk.

What's in a Name?

Mary's naming of Christ can seem almost perfunctory in the biblical account. Luke tells us that eight days after his birth, Jesus was circumcised and "called Jesus, the name given by the angel before he was conceived" (Luke 2:21). In Elizabeth Johnson's view, the verse stresses the importance of religious tradition in Luke's account and his depiction of Mary and Joseph as "active parents committed to the heritage of their ancestors."[3] This verse connects Jesus to the covenant of Abraham, making clear his Jewish specificity. Jesus is a participant in his communal tradition.

Jesus's naming and circumcision, however, also points to a disruption

---

2. In contrast, see Mary Catherine Hilkert, *Naming Grace: Preaching and the Sacramental Imagination* (New York: Continuum, 1997), 183, for the image of the preacher as midwife. Hilkert addresses the role of the community more directly, locating the birth of the Word in the congregation. Hilkert's image, of course, does not speak to the Spirit-empowered birth happening in the preacher. The congregation can act as midwife, as well.

3. Elizabeth A. Johnson, *Truly Our Sister: A Theology of Mary in the Communion of Saints* (New York: Continuum, 2003), 279. In Fred Craddock's words, "Jesus' parents represent the best of Jewish piety and obedience to the law of Moses." See Fred Craddock, *Luke* (Louisville: John Knox, 1990), 37. The timetable for a child's circumcision is provided in Lev. 12:1-4.

of expectation. First of all, Jesus's mother, rather than his adopted father, provides his name.[4] Also, similar to Luke's account of Zechariah's naming of John (Luke 1:59-63), the name of Jesus does not have an apparent corollary in Mary and Joseph's family. It is the name given to Mary by the angel (Luke 1:31). Her naming of Jesus is an act of obedience that fulfills the angelic promise of the Annunciation. In this terse description of Jesus's naming and circumcision, then, there is an attention to communal religious practice, as well as particular alterations to that practice in light of God's action and call.[5]

In a sense, the naming of any child carries with it this fulfillment and disruption of expectation. Naming a child is a "performative utterance" that converses with communal traditions, even as it disrupts and transforms those traditions.[6] Naming is a practice impacted by social narratives and familial norms. But it is also a practice that allows parents to assert their child's particularity. Sometimes, this is through the choice of an unusual name. But even when a child's name is a common namesake, family tradition is disrupted. When parents match a name to a child, they are not only allowing that name to shape the child's identity but are allowing the child's particular identity to shape the meaning of the name. More than this, the name influences, and is influenced by, the identities of the parents themselves. There is much at stake. One mother describes the "naming summits" that took place between herself and her husband in order to arrive at a name on which they could both agree.[7] Naming a child foregrounds the complex social context in which pregnancy occurs and the competing claims within the parental role. Ellen Klein worries, "I am unsettled in my new role. . . . I am in awe of the fact that within me lives a person who is the collective sum of all

4. Luke's account is different from Matthew's Gospel, in which Joseph is told to name the baby (Matt. 1:21).
5. Raymond Brown, *The Birth of the Messiah: A Commentary on the Infancy Narratives in Matthew and Luke* (Garden City, NY: Image Books, 1979), 447-50, points out several inaccuracies between Luke's account and traditional Jewish practice that Brown attributes to Luke's gentile unfamiliarity with Jewish custom. Brown's point raises the question of the purpose behind the text's emphasis on Mary and Joseph's Jewish piety, given the fact that, apparently, Luke does not follow these Levitical practices himself.
6. J. L. Austin, *How to Do Things with Words* (Cambridge: Harvard University Press, 1962), 9-11.
7. Interview with a mother on her experience of pregnancy, birth, and naming, September 19, 2012.

my ancestors."[8] Naming a child is a performative act that negotiates one's relationship to that role: *Will one parent act in a way that is expected? Will one break with tradition? What does a child's name say about oneself and one's relationship to past and present?*

Mary, of course, has no naming summits. She has an angelic birth announcement. She is called to give her child a specific name. In this way, Mary is more like a preacher than a parent. Preachers of the gospel do not come to the task of naming the Word with the same freedoms as most mothers and fathers. David Lose describes the classic Christian confession "Jesus is Lord" as foundational for the Christian preacher.[9] In David Buttrick's words, "Christian preaching tells a story and names a name."[10] If Mary's experience of naming is used to describe preacherly action, a similar specificity is required. The name of Jesus is, itself, significant.

Jesus's name is, at first glance, ordinary enough. It is the Greek form of the Hebrew word for Joshua, meaning "salvation."[11] The name was common, and unlike Matthew (1:21), Luke does not provide its etymological significance. However, Jesus's name is a clue to the overarching theme of Luke's Gospel: Jesus as Savior. By emphasizing Jesus as the embodiment of salvation in historical time, Luke holds human history together with God's sovereign "supremacy . . . over the world."[12] Thus, "salvation itself" and "not salvation-history" is Luke's focus.[13] This salvation intersects the world in the person of Jesus, and the world is transformed. There is tension here, participation in and disruption of the norms of lived human experience.

Mary's act of naming reflects this tension. When Mary gives her child the name Jesus, she faithfully participates in her tradition. At the same time, she affirms God's promise for that tradition. Jesus (i.e., God's "salvation") has come into the world, which means that human customs, traditions, and roles are subject to change. Mary's obedience in giving

8. Ellen R. Klein, "Birth of a Woman," in *The Spirit of Pregnancy*, ed. Bonni Goldberg (Chicago: Contemporary Books, 2000), 84.

9. David Lose, *Confessing Jesus Christ: Preaching in a Postmodern World* (Grand Rapids: Eerdmans, 2003), 108.

10. David Buttrick, *Homiletic: Moves and Structures* (Philadelphia: Fortress Press, 1987), 17.

11. I. Howard Marshall, *Luke: Historian and Theologian* (Exeter: Paternoster, 1970), 98.

12. Marshall, *Luke*, 104.

13. Marshall, *Luke*, 92.

Jesus his name implies that she believes the angel's words about who this child is: the "Son of the Most High" (Luke 1:32). In this light, all human traditions are provisional, even as they are a necessary part of what naming requires. Mary's action is one of piety, prophesy, and personal testimony. It claims a reality she cannot prove: God's saving presence and transformative power in the world.

I have lingered on this description of Mary's naming because it underscores the particular, performative way that I am using the word *name* in this chapter. When I describe Mary's naming as a metaphor for Christian preaching, I am not advocating the simple pronouncement of a label or linguistic formula. I am not saying that every sermon should speak the name Jesus. The sons of Sceva attempted to use that name as a guarantee of spiritual power independent of Jesus's person, and they suffered the consequences (Acts 19:11-20). Similarly, contemporary preachers can use Jesus's name as a proof of their purity and authority, or for the advancement of a cause that is antithetical to Jesus's teaching. Jesus's name can "congeal 'into traditionalism and conservatism, paving the way to a tyranny of custom.'"[14] When this happens, the name of Jesus loses its connection to the presently active Lord it represents.

When Mary names Jesus, however, her act performs something of the name's meaning, suggesting an embodied relation to the One named. Her naming is marked by the kind of *unsettling of role* and communal practice that occurs when a Savior comes into living relationship with the world.[15] For preachers who wish to draw on Mary's example, naming Jesus requires more than saying the word *Jesus* in a sermon. A preacher's sermonic performance should demonstrate what this name means in the context of a particular community's common life. In order to name Jesus, a preacher must participate in this common life and speak its language. But, if Luke is correct, she must also be prepared to disrupt and challenge communal expectations in response to God's call. It is a provisional, risky place to stand. It requires that preacher to simultaneously embrace her community and her own unique experience, not because

---

14. David J. Lose, *Confessing Jesus Christ: Preaching in a Postmodern World* (Grand Rapids: Eerdmans, 2003), 55. Lose cites the work of Calvin Schrag, *The Resources of Rationality: A Response to the Postmodern Challenge* (Bloomington: Indiana University Press, 1992), 65.

15. Similar to my discussion of Peter's sermon to Cornelius (Acts 10:34-48) and Mary's Magnificat (Luke 1:46-56).

of who she is but because of who Jesus is. It is a tension that flows from a Spirit-empowered, lived discernment of Jesus himself.

Other practical theologians have argued for the importance of a preacher's participation and differentiation within a tradition on philosophical or ethical grounds.[16] Strong arguments can be made in this regard, but they are not Luke's arguments. Rather, for Luke, Mary's naming of Jesus—and all the ways that act resonates with and disrupts her traditional role—flows from Jesus's identity and his living relationship with her. Naming Jesus, then, is an act of lived *discernment*, making sense of his relationship to the community into which he comes. How might that labor of discernment mark a sermon's performance?

Authenticity: Discerning the Call within the Role

Doing or not doing whatever some think they mean by "black preaching" or even "women's preaching" is risky business.[17]

Richard Ward describes the perennial question of new preachers as a question of authenticity: "Can I be myself as a preacher and proclaimer of the Word?"[18] It is a deep question, echoing my own questions about fully human preaching. For some preachers, the question is one of scriptural authority and what they believe about revelation. *Am I allowed to be myself given what I believe about God's Word?* For others, the question is about power and exclusion. *Is it safe for me to be myself given what I know about my congregation and what they expect from me?* And then there are those who know the question itself assumes some definitions. *What is "myself," after all?* Is the true me some isolated soul, floating free from communal obligation? Or is it the product of that obligation? Is my fully human self the effective performance of an expected, predetermined role?

In his book *The Journey and Promise of African American Preaching*, Kenyatta Gilbert stresses the significance of the particular needs and ex-

16. See, for example, Elaine Graham, *Transforming Practice: Pastoral Theology in an Age of Uncertainty* (Eugene, OR: Wipf & Stock, 2002), 142–72.

17. Lisa Thompson, *Ingenuity: Preaching as an Outsider* (Nashville: Abingdon Press, 2018), 3.

18. Richard Ward, "Finding Your Voice in Theological School," in *Preaching and Performance*, ed. Clayton Schmit and Jana Childers (Grand Rapids: Baker Academic, 2008), 140.

pectations of the church in shaping a preacher's "functional identity"—particularly in the African American church.[19] Gilbert rejects static, simplistic models of that tradition, noting responsive shifts in the history of African American preaching during periods of social change. He argues for a diversity within the tradition itself and the necessary role of discernment in negotiating the preacher's "tri-vocal" role.[20] In thinking about the challenges facing contemporary black churches, Gilbert suggests multiple "masks" that allow African American preachers to adopt the communal personas necessary to speak to these shifting concerns.[21]

When I teach Gilbert in US classrooms, his metaphor of masks can be challenging. In dominant US culture—and particularly white culture—an individual model of authenticity is near sacrosanct, and Gilbert's insistence that the preacher's identity be shaped by the needs of the community pinches those assumptions. At this point, certain preachers get cold feet. For some, speaking one's truth in the pulpit is far easier than yoking one's identity and language to a broken, imperfect community. Gilbert's suggestion that faithful preaching adopts a "persona or *prosopon*, meaning 'face' in Greek" that is intimately connected to a community's need can seem a dangerous denial of individuality.[22] But my experience teaching Gilbert in the South Pacific was decidedly different. In that context, Gilbert's insistence that true authenticity grows out of communal relationship was readily embraced. Upolu Lumā Vaai describes how the relational epistemology of the Pacific *itulagi* (worldview) prioritizes embodied knowledge, the interconnectedness of life and relationships with ordinary people.[23] To be authentic is to honor these connections. One's true self and one's communal role are not in opposition; they are related.

And yet for preachers whose bodies disrupt communal expectation, this relationship is fraught. Foregrounding the particular experiences of African American woman preachers, Lisa Thompson describes the ex-

19. Kenyatta Gilbert, *The Journey and Promise of African-American Preaching* (Minneapolis: Fortress Press, 2011), 139.

20. Gilbert lifts up the prophet, priest, and sage as three vocal registers within the preacherly role. See Gilbert, *Journey and Promise*, 57–64.

21. Gilbert, *Journey and Promise*, 131–40.

22. Gilbert, *Journey and Promise*, 132.

23. Upolu Luma Vaai, "Relational Hermeneutics: A Return to the Relationality of the Pacific Itulagi as a Lens for Understanding and Interpreting Life," in *Relational Hermeneutics: Decolonizing the Mindset and the Pacific Itulagi*, ed. Upolu Luma Vaai and Aisake Casimira (Suva, Fiji: University of the South Pacific Press, 2017), 23–24.

clusions that flourish when a tradition's expectations are collapsed into preaching's definition. "Does one preach like other bodies within the tradition?" community gatekeepers ask. "If the answer is yes," Thompson notes, "then 'that's preaching.'"[24] The bodily practices of "outsiders" do not count.[25] This limiting of diversity leads to a theological danger. When communal expectation becomes synonymous with a preacher's role, "we potentially close off . . . the possibility of sacred in-breaking through the practice of preaching itself."[26] Maintaining the stability of communal practice takes precedence over naming the disruptive solidarity of the risen Christ. This tension is precisely what makes concepts like authenticity difficult. Both a preacher's relation to and differentiation from the community matter. Thompson is no advocate of isolated individualism. She, too, wants preachers to "mine life" in ways that are true to listeners' experience.[27] Her feet are firmly planted on communal ground. "We are constantly attempting to mediate expectations and retain some form of authenticity in preaching," she notes, all "while helping listeners connect with what is said."[28] What, then, defines a preacher's authentic speech? More provocatively, who decides when the preacher has been "herself"?

For outsiders, Ward's question is not just one of permission. Such preachers wonder whether authenticity is even possible given their bodily disruption of a community's expectation. *Can* one be oneself in a situation where that self is consistently misread?[29] An African American student tells me of the catch-22 in which he finds himself when he preaches in his predominately white seminary. If he performs as if he were in a black church, he risks his listeners misinterpreting or caricaturing his tradition. If he adjusts his performance for his white audience, he fears accusations of inauthenticity—not being true to himself.[30] In

---

24. Thompson, *Ingenuity*, 25.

25. "Outsiders" is Thompson's self-description: "Our status is often that of forced outsider." See Thompson, *Ingenuity*, 4.

26. Thompson, *Ingenuity*, 4.

27. Thompson, *Ingenuity*, 37.

28. Thompson, *Ingenuity*, 6.

29. A question related to Gayatri Chakravorty Spivak's formidable inquiry, "Can the Subaltern Speak?" in *Marxism and the Interpretation of Culture*, ed. Cary Nelson (London: Macmillan, 1988), 271–317.

30. Michael Eric Dyson discusses the ways that the "hidden logics of multiculturalism . . . obfuscate the incredible heterogeneity and the raucous diversity that is contained in black identity—or any minority identity." See Sidney Dobrin, "Race and

his experience, black preachers in white spaces are "damned if they do and damned if they don't."[31] For black women, gender complicates the equation. Thompson tells of an encounter with a woman who admits to not liking women preachers. But, "I like you," the woman tells her. "You don't sound like a man, but you don't sound like a woman either." Thompson doesn't know whether to be flattered or offended.[32]

The particularity of this struggle for minoritized preachers has unique contours and implications. These are dangerous shoals for preachers excluded from safer channels of community affirmation. But to some extent, all preachers who name Christ in the sermon negotiate these waters—because naming Christ is embodied, traditioned, performative work. The problem of pulpit authenticity has a long history. Alan of Lille, a medieval homiletic theorist, describes how the performance of "holy simplicity" is crucial to a preacher's role. It is not "enough merely to *be* humble; to [be] effective, the preacher must *project* his own humility."[33] Every preacher's body, then, is "always an actor's body," performing for the community as well as the divine.[34] In such a vocation, is authenticity even possible?

When Mary is asked to name Jesus, something remarkable happens. She gives herself a name. She is God's *doulē*, a designation beyond individual preference or communal expectation. Mary's experience suggests that authenticity is not defined by whims of passion or scripted roles. *Authenticity is defined by one's call.* In naming Jesus, a preacher discerns who *she* is called to be in the shifting performative spaces that she finds herself. Any parent knows that naming a child changes oneself. One becomes "Jessica's mother" or "Micah's father." When one has an embodied relationship with Jesus, his salvation shapes the preacher's role and identity, giving it navigational trajectory and movement. Who one truly is and who a community needs most overlap in the body of a preacher who

the Public Intellectual: A Conversation with Michael Eric Dyson," in *Race, Rhetoric and the Postcolonial*, ed. Gary Olson and Lynn Worsham (Albany: State University of New York Press, 1999), 93.

31. With gratitude to Corie Wilkins for his willingness to share his experience and his words.

32. Thompson, *Ingenuity*, 3.

33. Claire Waters, *Angels and Earthly Creatures: Preaching, Performance, and Gender in the Late Middle Ages* (Philadelphia: University of Pennsylvania Press, 2008), 46. Waters specifically references Lille's discussion of *a propria persona* in his *Summa*.

34. Waters, *Angels and Earthly Creatures*, 50.

knows who she is called to be: an embodied witnesses to God's salvific mission. A preacher might affirm or disrupt an expected role in fidelity to that calling, but the calling itself doesn't change—and it is finally outside of the congregation's control. A community may shape a preacher's role, but her call is Christ's to define.

Late in his volume, Gilbert notes that, despite the significance of communal practice, it is "Jesus's vision" that finally makes the preacher's voice "authentic."[35] Faithful preaching might be intricately connected to the expectations of the community, but it is not determined by those expectations. The "*prosopon* of Christ" takes precedence.[36] Christ's face, discerned through the labor of the Spirit, helps a preacher hold her alterity and community in generative tension. After all, Christ transcends and touches down in both. "To speak about the cross truthfully and persuasively," Gilbert asserts, "is to be drawn into [Christ's] image of vulnerability and come face to face with the God undergoing death to defeat all that is dead." Such "drawing in" shapes an authenticity that is not static. It is less like an anchor that holds one still, and more like a sail that holds one on course. It is relationally discerned through a living faith—what Gilbert calls a "rigorous spirituality."[37] When a preacher witnesses to this authentic call, particularly when she has been previously silenced, there are redemptive consequences. In the words of Mary Donovan Turner, "It is a mysterious and sacramental moment."[38]

A young woman describes her Eastern European culture as a place where women "are never close to the pulpit," which makes the pulpit in which she stands a place of risk and vulnerability.[39] She has agreed to lead one of the seminary's daily chapel services, and her Advent text is Luke's account of the Annunciation. Her words are simple, her body straight. When she speaks the angel's command, "Do not be afraid," she smiles as if she knows something of the challenge and joy of these words. When she speaks the angel's announcement of God's favor, she

---

35. Gilbert, *Journey and Promise*, 133. Particularly Jesus's inaugural vision in Luke 4.

36. Gilbert, *Journey and Promise*, 133.

37. Kenyatta Gilbert, "Decolonizing the Homiletical Mind: Religious Hypocrisy and Cultural Invasion," Howard University School of Divinity, April 8, 2019. https://www.youtube.com/watch?v=vNjTmoqSMHE&feature=youtu.be

38. Mary Donovan Turner, "Reversal of Fortune," in *Performance in Preaching*, ed. Jana Childers and Clayton Schmit (Grand Rapids: Baker, 2008), 96.

39. Conversation on the joys and challenges of preaching, May 15, 2012.

comes alongside the congregation, reframing Mary's question to voice the questions of her listeners. "'How can this be,'" she asks, "when I have a complicated past—when I do not feel so good about myself today?" Then she voices her own question, "'How can this be since I am a woman and women are supposed to have babies and organize tea parties and not stand in the pulpit?" Her answer is the same as the answer of Gabriel: "Nothing is impossible with God" (Luke 1:37). "Nothing is impossible for this God who chose me," she continues, "[this God] who saved me, who gave me life—this God who is my life."[40] At no point in the preacher's sermon is the name of Jesus explicitly mentioned. And yet the person of Jesus is given descriptive content through her performance. She *shows* us who Jesus is by standing on the borders of her community's expectations and responding to a divine, interruptive call that presses beyond those boundaries. She reveals who she really is in relation to that call. In so doing, she testifies not only to God's transformative power in the world but also to a power that is transforming her.

The labor of naming requires the discernment of a new name for oneself and the adoption of authentic speech grounded in God's call. But here we have come full circle, for the community is not passive in this process. Authenticity and community *are* related. Our communities may not define our call, but they are discerning alongside us. Mary, after all, is not the only one in Luke's Gospel doing the naming. Elizabeth also names both Jesus and Mary in her Spirit-filled affirmation that Mary is the "mother of [the] Lord" (Luke 1:42-43). What follows is Mary's Magnificat: the longest string of words uttered by any woman in Luke's Gospel. Like this seminary preacher's Annunciation sermon, the Magnificat never mentions Jesus's name. But in holding together Mary's faithfulness to her tradition with a Spirit-inspired disruption of that tradition, the Magnificat explains who Jesus is and what he means for Mary's people. Mary's song gives descriptive content to salvation for the community and for Mary personally. God is not only *the* Savior in Mary's text. God is "*my*" Savior (v. 47), the One for whom "nothing will be impossible" (v. 37).[41]

40. Andreta Livena (sermon preached in Miller Chapel, Princeton Theological Seminary, December 5, 2011).

41. Note, for example, that after the opening verses (vv. 46-49), Mary's song moves away from first-person pronouns and focuses specifically on God's action in the world. When she returns to the first-person at the song's end, she uses the plural form, "our" (v. 55), connecting God's action on her behalf with God's action on behalf of her community.

Reflecting later, this preacher notes that her sermon had very little "religious talk." It was, in her words, "very much me." And yet it wouldn't have been possible without the affirmation of fellow students who encouraged her to "trust the Holy Spirit [with her] words."[42] She was not embodying a traditional role, but her sermon was rooted in communal discernment. The congregation played a vital role in naming God's call in her.[43] The point underscores, among other things, the theological significance of homiletic pedagogy. Honoring the offerings of preachers across broad intersections of the Spirit's call brings God's saving work into view. When Mary says that generations will call her blessed (Luke 1:48), this blessing is not for her alone. The great things that the "Mighty One has done" for Mary (v. 49) are a fulfillment of the "promise he made to [Mary's] ancestors" (v. 55). Mary's call depends on God's Spirit-filled work in her tradition and vice versa, a dependence that requires differentiation and commitment. But Luke tells us the Spirit makes these authentic spaces possible. It is here where "preacher, hearer and the Spirit-driven-Word dance."[44]

Metaphor: Discerning the Poetry of the "Not-Yet"

> Words strain,
> Crack and sometimes break, under the burden,
> Under the tension, slip, slide, perish,
> Decay with imprecision, will not stay in place,
> Will not stay still.[45]

The discernment required to name Jesus in a community does not only play out in a preacher's unsettled relation to her role. It also plays out in her unsettled relation to language. Language is, in certain ways, the water in which a community swims. To honor the "verbal womb" of a community is intimate, world-affirming work.[46] It brings the truth of incarnation

42. Conversation reflecting on Livena's sermon, June 3, 2012. Used with permission.

43. For example, she mentions the name of the seminary chaplain who "invited me into the story" by inviting her to preach.

44. Lose, *Confessing Jesus Christ*, 141.

45. T. S. Eliot, "Burnt Norton," *Four Quartets* (New York: Houghton Mifflin Harcourt, 1943).

46. Dyson, "Race and the Public Intellectual," 90.

close, until it is felt like breath on the skin. But it is also one of the most significant mediums through which a preacher, "tethering . . . history and the not-yet," witnesses to a transcendent God.[47] To name Jesus in the rhetorical performance of the sermon is to stretch the possibilities of that linguistic womb and offer an "alternative to the normative view of reality."[48]

Sometimes this takes place through nonlinguistic signifiers. Donyelle McCray describes preachers who break a sweat in their performance or let spittle fly from their mouths in proclamatory fervor, disrupting expectations of Western propriety.[49] They stretch the preacher's performance beyond the "mores of polite and respectable speech," refocusing the telos of the sermon on a "higher call." In these performative disruptions, McCray sees a "wild notion of holiness" emerge, testifying to an unmanageable gospel.[50] But critically, these performances of disruption honor Christian preaching's deep DNA. Through these normally impolite excretions, "listeners encounter a God made known through weak and profane human flesh. . . . [The] foolish things of the world make God known rather than human perfection."[51] There is not only disruption in these practices but also submission to a gospel tethered to Jesus—an incarnate, crucified, living Lord. The permeability of the preacher's body testifies to a Spirit-empowered permeability with this risen Body. McCray describes the preacher as becoming "lost in the Word or captivated by its transformative power."[52]

McCray's discussion turns explicitly linguistic in her discussion of cursing. She notes the ways that profane words can, in certain contexts, become the "husk of the sacred."[53] In both their ability to bring undiluted, "underground" truths into conversation with the gospel and in their ability to "crack brittle understandings of what constitutes sacred

47. Thompson, *Ingenuity*, 23.
48. Donyelle McCray, "Sweating, Spitting and Cursing: Intimations of the Sacred," *Practical Matters* 8 (April 2015): 62–72.
49. McCray's work demonstrates how the performing body adds layers of meaning to linguistic content, drawing on Judith Butler's description of the "excess" of speech. See McCray, "Sweating, Spitting and Cursing," 55. See Judith Butler, *Excitable Speech: A Politics of the Performative* (New York: Routledge, 1997), 155.
50. McCray, "Sweating, Spitting and Cursing," 55.
51. McCray, "Sweating, Spitting and Cursing," 55.
52. McCray, "Sweating, Spitting and Cursing," 54.
53. McCray, "Sweating, Spitting and Cursing," 56.

speech," curse words can glorify God.[54] When Tony Campolo tells an audience that they "don't give a shit" that thirty thousand children died of malnutrition while they were sleeping, and "you are more upset with the fact that I said 'shit' than the fact that thirty thousand kids died," he uses the "affront of the curse word to reveal an even greater outrage."[55] These words are not static in their meaning and purpose. They perform differently in different contexts. And here, McCray brings up the critical issue of discernment, comparing this decision-making process to a preacher's consideration of an illustration or metaphor. "Will the illustration (or curse word) propel the message, distract from it, or take on a life of its own?" McCray asks. Finally, the use of image or explicative is not tied to propriety or disruption for its own sake. It is tied to its usefulness as a signifier of good news, a salvation that stands in the present and cracks open God's future.[56]

McCray's work on sweat, spit, and cursing highlights metaphor's performative quality. It highlights how words like *holiness* are given specificity and breadth through unexpected material signifiers *and* congregational interpretation. There is labor involved. Congregations discern, sometimes unconsciously, the ways these signifiers draw on and disrupt their spoken language systems. If this work is absent, a metaphor simply stands in for what it signifies, and its efficacy atrophies. If Christian holiness is defined by sweat, perspiration becomes one more performative proof text, justifying certain performances and excluding others. In her description of preacher, Word, and congregation, McCray describes a more active interplay.

When preachers describe their use of metaphor in a sermon, they generally describe its function in two ways. They may describe it *apocalyptically*, honoring its ability to break open calcified linguistic forms to reveal new insight.[57] Alternately, they might stress its *incarnational* function, making abstract concepts accessible and tactile.[58] There is overlap

54. McCray, "Sweating, Spitting and Cursing," 57–58.
55. McCray, "Sweating, Spitting and Cursing," 58.
56. McCray, "Sweating, Spitting and Cursing," 59.
57. Paul Ricoeur, "Between Rhetoric and Poetics," in *Essays on Aristotle's Rhetoric*, ed. Amélie O. Rorty (Berkeley: University of California Press, 1966), 333, argues, for example, that a metaphor simultaneously "recognizes and transgresses the logical structure of language," specifying metaphor's disruptive function.
58. Janet Soskice extends and critiques Ricoeur, suggesting that metaphor can "disclose genuinely new realities" beyond itself, providing a way to gesture toward

between these seemingly divergent goals, as McCray's work shows. But what preachers often miss is that both of these functions depend on the performative discernment of the congregation. There is no power in the metaphor itself. A metaphor's power lies in its weakness. It cannot name, grasp, define, or pin down. It can only testify and unsettle, inviting a listener toward discernment of and dependence on Christ. Like Mary, it names in ways that require a Spirit-empowered relation with a Savior who is both near and new.

In her classic study *Metaphorical Theology: Models of God in Religious Language*, Sally McFague emphasizes the communal discernment process necessary for religious language to avoid the twin dangers of "idolatry and irrelevance."[59] McFague argues that naming God "can never be simply a baptizing of the tradition," nor can it be an isolated, individualistic assertion.[60] Naming God should affirm the "relational . . . interdependent, relative, situational" nature of our knowledge.[61] Finding alternative metaphors for God's disruptive, transformative presence in the world (i.e., God's salvation) allows for this dual affirmation of interdependence and difference. Again, the point is not propriety or disruption for its own sake. The point is to demonstrate the meaning of Jesus's name in the context of communal religious speech: God's salvation *in* history and *of* history.

These conversations on metaphor and the naming of Jesus are given pedagogical specificity in the conversations I have with classes on whether a preacher should refer to God as *he* in a sermon. I do not make ontological arguments in these discussions; I make theologically performative ones. I ask preachers how the pronouns they use will further or hinder their primary call: to name God's salvation in the community. How will those pronouns touch down in the linguistic systems in which their congregations operate, and how will they disrupt those systems? How will they witness to the salvation of those systems? Some preachers decide that, in their local contexts, gendered pronouns are already being

God without defining God. She is less concerned with metaphor's ability to disrupt linguistic form and more concerned with appropriate imaging of the divine. See Susan Eastman's concise summary in *Recovering Paul's Mother Tongue: Language and Theology in Galatians* (Grand Rapids: Eerdmans, 2007), 91–92.

59. Sally McFague, *Metaphorical Theology: Models of God in Religious Language* (Philadelphia: Fortress Press, 1982), 22.

60. McFague, *Metaphorical Theology*, 29.

61. McFague, *Metaphorical Theology*, 194.

read metaphorically by their congregation and, in fact, testify to God's ability to transcend *all* language. There is no pronoun big enough for the task, they reason, so one might as well use the masculine pronouns familiar to the community's text, tradition, and habit. I think this argument is valid. There are congregations who have this kind of nuance in their understanding of religious language.

I thought mine was one of them.

I was raised in an increasingly rare religious ecosystem: a progressive, evangelical home. I grew up singing praise songs based on biblical texts and excelled at memory-verse challenges. This meant that I grew up referring to God as "he." But my parents taught me early and explicitly that God was neither male nor female. God was bigger than the pronoun we used. There was an intersex fluidity to our religious language, which also grew out of scriptural immersion. God gave *his* Son so that we could be *born again* by God's Spirit (John 3:1–16). I didn't see any contradiction. I knew inclusive language mattered a great deal to my seminary peers, and in that context, I was happy to oblige. But when I began copastoring with my husband in our first congregation, I didn't give it much thought. Surely, these mainline churchgoers knew that God was not literally male. I would have bet money on it.

But then, John 3 appeared in the lectionary, and I preached what I considered to be an innocuous sermon on Jesus's use of mother imagery for God. I'm sorry to say that this was no prophetic takedown of patriarchy. The choir was singing "Sometimes I Feel like a Motherless Child," and I gave the congregation a word of pastoral encouragement: "You have a divine Mother." Jesus said so.

I have served congregations through tumultuous seasons. I have preached sermons on everything from preemptive war and immigration policy to white privilege and climate change. But in my twenty years of ministry, that sermon was the only one that provoked congregation members to go behind my back and ask my husband whether I was right. That sweet, pastoral sermon was the only time my congregation felt threatened enough to confirm that my biblical interpretation met with my husband's approval.

They *didn't* know. They didn't know that the words we were using were metaphors—which meant that for years, I hadn't been doing my job. I had not been naming Jesus with the proper specificity—as a Savior who stands within and beyond our communal language games. I had not shown them a God bigger than the pronoun.

These days, I tell preachers not to take their congregation's theology of language for granted. If a preacher is wedded to using masculine pronouns for the Godhead, she must be especially proactive (and provocative) in embracing a scriptural boldness in her disruptive imagery for the divine. *What pictures witness to the unexpected scandal of the God revealed in Jesus Christ?* Is God like a female clown,[62] or a wailing woman,[63] an emaciated man,[64] or a fat Jesus?[65] Such images confront preachers like grace—through street graffiti, hospice prayers, and kindergarten crayon. And like grace, they crack open the "prose of the probable" with the "poetry of the impossible."[66] They create spaces of resistance, reorienting a congregation to God's "upside-down" future.[67] Naming Jesus does not flatten metaphors into morals. It uses language's categories to press language's limits. It stretches words to reveal their weaknesses and strengths, and through the work of the Spirit, discerns the "uneasy vibrancy" of God's salvation.[68]

Sometimes, it feels like joy.

When I met her, Erin Kinlock was a resident of the North Carolina Correctional Institution for Women. She was part of a Duke Divinity School program in which incarcerated residents and divinity students took classes together. For the final project of this "Women Preaching" course, students were asked to present a creative expression of their preaching theology. Kinlock brings a poem. She reads the poem aloud, stringing together a series of images to describe the preaching task.

---

62. Charles Campbell and Johan Cilliers, *Preaching Fools: The Gospel as a Rhetoric of Folly* (Waco, TX: Baylor University Press, 2012), 57.

63. L. Juliana Claassens, *Mourner, Mother, Midwife: Reimagining God's Delivering Presence in the Old Testament* (Louisville: Westminster John Knox, 2012).

64. John Donne, "Death's Duel" (sermon, St. Paul's Cathedral, Whitehall, February 25, 1631). Called his "owne funeral sermon," Donne creates a conceit between the body of the dying Christ and his own wasted flesh. He would die a month later.

65. Lisa Isherwood, "The Fat Jesus: Explorations in Fleshy Christologies," *Feminist Theology* 19, no. 1 (2010): 20–35.

66. Charles Campbell, Revelation 7:9–17 (baccalaureate sermon, Duke Chapel, Duke Divinity School, May 11, 2019). Campbell quotes Stephen H. Webb, "A Hyperbolic Imagination: Theology and the Rhetoric of Excess," *Theology Today* 50 (April 1993): 56–67.

67. Campbell, Revelation 7:9–17.

68. Theodore Gill, describing Donne's dialectical view of truth and his use of conceits. See John Donne, *The Sermons of John Donne*, ed. Theodore Gill (New York: Meridian Books, 1958), 14.

Preaching is like "shucking oysters" and "drinking music." It's like "passing through color" and "taking a whale for a walk on a leash."[69] That last image leaves the room in upheavals of laughter, several of us wiping away tears. We'd never imagined such a description before, but what could describe it better? When a preacher is tethered to God's not-yet, she is pulled into all manner of depths. A serious preacher knows she better hang on for the ride.

Promise: Discerning the Particularity of Hope

Why didn't you reach out, touch us with your soft fingers, delay the sound bite, the lesson, until you knew who we were?[70]

To name Jesus "salvation" in the sermon is to relinquish the expectation that the preacher can fill his salvific role. The preacher is not the congregation's Savior. Neither can the congregation save itself. All prior talk of unsettled practices and disrupted grammars flows from these theological tributaries. To name Jesus "salvation" is to say something about God's action and character, which is a bigger promise than the promise of one's own charisma and leadership. It is grounded in sturdier stuff than congregational piety. Naming Jesus names God's salvific promise for the world—and more particularly, God's promise for a specific community listening to a specific text of Scripture in a specific place and time.

"Say something about God," Fred Craddock said.[71] It was decades ago, and he was giving a series of preaching lectures at the seminary in which I was enrolled. I still remember his reedy voice piercing the chapel's silence. There was no inductive guessing game involved. His command was short and clear, and I've carried it with me. Say something about God.

There are no hard and fast rules in preaching. Apparently, God takes pleasure in disrupting homiletic prescriptions with Spirit-filled sermons

69. Erin Kinlock, "It's Like," a poem written for Project TURN *Women Preaching* course, North Carolina Correctional Institution for Women, Raleigh, NC, April 25, 2019. Used with permission.

70. Toni Morrison, *The Nobel Lecture in Literature, 1993* (New York: Alfred Knopf Publishers, 1994), 28.

71. Fred B. Craddock, "In Service to the Gospel" (lecture, Macleod Lectures, Princeton Theological Seminary, October 16, 1996).

that break the mold. But Craddock's words are ones I repeat. They are the first thing that needs saying. To name Jesus in the sermon, a preacher speaks a promise grounded in God's work rather than our own. I'm surprised by how often preachers neglect this sermonic function. They are more comfortable assessing the faithfulness of the congregation than proclaiming the faithfulness of God. It is a reticence that can grow from a liberal ambivalence to naming the divine at all. Phil Snider describes a postmodern fear of "God-language as . . . too intertwined with superstitious beliefs" and progressive congregants who "don't do the supernatural well."[72] But it can grow as easily from holiness traditions, progressive and conservative alike, that collapse salvation into moralism. It can grow from a preacher's own performance anxiety in leading a compromised congregation. Whatever the reason, God is too rarely the subject of the sermon.

But Craddock's words only scratch the surface, for it is possible to say something *about* God and not proclaim a living promise *from* God. Even when God is the sermon's subject, that Subject is often objectified. Preachers speak *about* God's faithfulness like the topic of a well-exegeted essay, rather than saying the direct, present-tense promise at the heart of that teaching. They forget to look into their listener's faces and say, "God is faithful." Teaching about God's character is laudable and necessary. But it stops short of proclaiming God's active presence in a risk-filled world. It stops short of naming Jesus. Such naming does not just describe something. It does something. Like Mary's naming, it promises something unproved, something that takes the Spirit's foolish wisdom to discern: God's salvation is alive and loose in the world. David Schnasa Jacobsen explains that promise is not "a premise behind which something stands, . . . a reality behind the word." It is "a reality created by a word."[73] And the creator, of course, is God. The promise is not authenticated by the preacher. It is trustworthy only to the extent that God is trustworthy. But if God is truly the Savior named, then that Savior's promise changes everything—including the preacher.[74] When Mary names Jesus, she goes

---

72. Phil Snider, *Preaching after God: Derrida, Caputo and the Language of Postmodern Homiletics* (Eugene, OR: Cascade, 2012), 6.

73. David Schnasa Jacobsen, "Promise as an Event of the Gospel in Context: Toward an Unfinished Homiletical Theology of Grace and Justice," in *Toward a Homiletical Theology of Promise*, ed. David Schnasa Jacobsen (Eugene, OR: Cascade, 2018), 112.

74. See James F. Kay's discussion of promissory narration in relation to Jürgen Moltmann's theology in *Preaching and Theology* (St. Louis: Chalice Press, 2007), 121.

public with her private testimony, in ways that change how she sees her community and herself. She participates in work that God is currently doing, claiming salvation that is scandalously concrete and powerless by the world's standards. It is a promise that resembles the Savior. One might say it bears his marks.

Mary's experience underscores that preaching God's promise is not the same thing as keeping the peace. In the Magnificat, divine promise has a way of carrying good news and challenge at the same time, which can sound strikingly different in different ears. Just ask the hungry who get filled and the rich who get sent away empty (Luke 1:53). Preaching a promise like "God surprises us with grace" may provide listeners a pastoral word of acceptance. But it might also call a congregation to rethink long-held assumptions about outsiders. "God refuses to white-wash white supremacy" is a discomfiting promise for a congregation unused to owning up to their privilege—but it is good news all the same.

Neither does this sort of naming bless a congregation's passivity. Practical exhortation and Monday morning takeaways matter. There is a quotidian quality to Jesus's name that keeps preachers grounded in the efforts of common life and justice-seeking engagement with the world. Emilie Townes notes the power of "apocalyptic vision" for womanist spirituality, but never at the expense of a God "working in history and through human agency."[75] Jesus's salvation of history plays out in history's ordinary, Spirit-shadowed labors.

More provocatively, God's power is not intended to reconcile God's people to evil. One of the great critiques of preaching *promise* is that it can paper over scriptural and societal complexity with a reductive gospel. It can make bearable what should never be born. Hortense Spillers wonders whether the black church tradition in which she was raised "makes alright" the violence and violations of racism through the preacher's repeated promise of resurrection. She fears that the sermon's "rhetorical tenacity of form" creates a false resolution to a congregation's ongoing experience of terror.[76] Spillers's critique underscores the dangerous consequences of misunderstanding where the power of a promise lies. Prom-

---

Kay quotes from Jürgen Moltmann's *Theology of Hope: On the Ground and Implications of a Christian Eschatology* (New York: Harper & Row, 1965), 103-4.

75. Emilie Townes, *In a Blaze of Glory: Womanist Spirituality as Social Witness* (Nashville: Abingdon Press, 1995), 123.

76. Hortense Spillers, "Moving on Down the Line," *American Quarterly* 40, no. 1 (1988): 94-95.

ises are no stand-in for a Savior. The words and form of promise, in and of themselves, do not save. It is the *particular, permeable, provisional* Christ who makes salvation a reality—and Jesus does not paper over anything. True to his name, through the power of the Spirit, he enters his people's present need.

In my experience, this is often where a preacher's real resistance to naming God's salvation for a congregation lies. To truly name God's living promise, one has to touch the pain that needs saving. It turns out that "saying something about God" has everything to do with saying something about the specific humans to whom one speaks because God's salvation touches down in actual lives. Promises are not general. They are particular. They are events in time, with consequences for real communities. Discerning this particularity makes one vulnerable to those communities.

In her 1993 Nobel Lecture in Literature, Toni Morrison tells a folktale about a group of young people who approach a blind, wise woman. The woman is known for having answers to difficult questions, and the youth, with smirks and shuffling feet, decide to stump her. They ask her the one thing she cannot know: "This bird that we hold in our hands . . . is it alive or is it dead?" The woman pauses to consider their arrogance and disregard for life. She knows their trick. "I don't know," she replies, "but it is in your hands. It is in your hands."[77]

For Morrison, the folktale is a parable about words. She sees language, fragile and feathered, ready to have its neck snapped by an ignorant generation in order to best an opponent and prove a point. She berates a society intent on linguistic control, a society that wishes to "monumentalize," "sum up," and have the "final word," as if language could ever "'pin down' slavery, genocide, [or] war."[78] She explains the consequences of this reckless stewardship and all that is at stake. Whether the words in our hands are alive or dead, she argues, we are responsible for them. "We *do* language," she concludes, and "that may be the measure of our lives."[79]

Morrison could sit down at this point, her lecture complete. Her astute critique of the looting and weaponizing of language has issued a pointed call to responsibility. But she pauses instead. And then, she

77. Morrison, *Nobel Lecture*, 11.
78. Morrison, *Nobel Lecture*, 20–21.
79. Morrison, *Nobel Lecture*, 22.

continues in an entirely new direction. "Suppose there is nothing in their hands," she wonders. Then the old woman's "gnomic pronouncement" makes no sense. What if these young people had come, not with a trick, but in sincerity, asking the most important question they knew? "What is life? What is death? . . . Is there no speech you can give us . . . [to] break through your dossier of failures? . . . Is the nothing in our hands something that you could not bear to contemplate or even guess?"[80] Morrison skewers her own insightful prose and allows her critical sword to pierce, not the youth, but wise, blind women who keep their "good opinion of [themselves] . . . in sophisticated, privileged space."[81] The devastating question at the heart of her lecture is placed in the mouths of the young people: "Why didn't you reach out, touch us with your soft fingers, delay the sound bite, the lesson, until you knew who we were?"[82]

In chapter seven, I encouraged preachers to respond to the wounds in their congregations and not shy away from lament and grief. A preacher's willingness to engage the pain of the world is connected to her ability to name God's promise.[83] But *discerning* that wound is often a difficult task. Preachers are quick to identify any number of symptoms: sporadic giving, unhospitable treatment of guests, gossip and arguments, poor worship attendance. The list can get long, and preachers are quick to give sermonic pointers on how to fix the list. They advise congregations to be less selfish, to control their tongues, to believe more, to hope more, to love more. They tell their congregations, "The bird 'is in your hands.'" But more often than not, they say very little about God. They don't really know what to say. God's promise is unclear because they don't yet know the extent of the wound the promise is intended to heal. They haven't asked, for example, why the division and gossip exists, or why the congregation's love has grown cold. They haven't wondered why the stewardship numbers are down or why the congregation is so protective of its space. *What is the wound beneath the symptom?* To reach out and touch that emptiness is to admit one's blindness, and what is more, to know that one does not have the resources to fix the problem. Astute critique has its place, but it cannot create life. Only God can do that, and preachers don't control God. They can only testify to God's promise and let promise

80. Morrison, *Nobel Lecture*, 24–25.

81. Morrison, *Nobel Lecture*, 24.

82. Morrison, *Nobel Lecture*, 28.

83. Jacobsen explicitly connects lament and promise in "Promise as an Event of Gospel in Context," 111.

testify to a God "hidden and revealed—known yes, through crucifixion and resurrection, but still mysterious."[84]

I tell my classes that they will know they are getting close to the wound beneath the symptom when nothing but a promise from God can heal it. This is the wound one takes to the mat of Scripture. This is the wound one takes to Jesus. If a congregation doesn't know what to do, then by all means teach them. Their wound is a lack of information. But most congregations know what is required. They are simply too afraid, too proud, too bitter, or too tired to do it. They don't need information. They need salvation. They need a promise that creates a new reality.

Peace Lee is a Korean American homiletician who theologizes on the borders of language's necessity and danger. "Language . . . protects us from . . . things with no names," Morrison tells us.[85] But language also obscures and categorizes the not-named. It decides who deserves naming—and who does not. Lee stands in her divinity school's pulpit, preaching on a famously difficult biblical text: Matthew's genealogy of Jesus (Matt. 1:1–17).[86] Appropriately, the entire passage is about names. But it is also a passage about scars, status, and patriarchal power. It is a passage about who matters in the story and who gets left out. Lee has some experience with a culture that honors genealogy. She remembers being told as a child that she was a "royal Lee" with an eight-hundred-year lineage. She remembers wondering, with youthful fasciation, whether there was some ancient scroll on which her name was recorded. Lee also knows something of genealogy's dangers. It took time for her to realize that, as a woman, her name would never have been written down.

Preachers who exegete this Matthew passage can jump quickly to the unexpected countertestimony of Tamar, Rahab, Ruth, the "wife of Uriah," and Mary. These outsiders provide a "miraculous counter-song to the prevailing hymn of patriarchy." Lee honors them, as well, but not before naming the wound at the heart of the text. She does not rush past the "systematic erasure of mothers and wives." She doesn't paper over the wound.

Joseph Winters argues for language's value in "tell[ing] stories about events forgotten or never spoken," but also language's insidious ability

84. Jacobsen, "Promise as an Event of Gospel in Context," 111.

85. Morrison, *Nobel Lecture*, 28.

86. Peace Lee, Matthew 1:1–17 (sermon, Goodson Chapel, Duke Divinity School, Durham, NC, October 30, 2018).

to domesticate and sanitize those events. "We need stories," he argues, "that disconcert our trust in language . . . in the face of the unspeakable."[87] And this is Lee's difficult task. She is working to honor the women in Matthew's genealogy at the same time that she is deconstructing genealogy's premise, a premise that defines family by blood—particularly, male blood.

Lee knows what is at stake. Before she was born, she tells us, her mother made a customary visit to Lee's paternal grandfather to ask him to name the unborn child. He had a chosen a name for the baby if it was a boy, but if the child was a girl, he said, "name her whatever you want. Dog [excrement], for all I care. It doesn't matter."

Lee speaks this story with the matter-of-fact calm of a woman who has done deep spiritual work. She has chosen to name the unnamed in her family and in Matthew's Gospel. In so doing, she reaches out to her listeners, showing us the unspeakable erasure in every line of biblical text. We breathe together, disconcerted, seeing the emptiness in our hands and in our tradition. In Matthew's genealogical memory, with the exception of five miraculous outliers, the names of women do not matter.

From this empty place, Lee names God's promise. God loves the unnamed so much that "their names are inscribed in the palms of Her hands." Their names are written in the blood of a wounded Christ, who "lived and died for the purpose of claiming all persons as Christ's own." The promise claims the significance of names at the same moment that it disrupts human definitions of lineage. "God has taken it on Godself to be born among broken, messy, complicated, irregular, indecent, queer, wild outsider peoples," Lee tells us, "making them God's own family." And here, she pivots her gaze from God's action to our own—for these outsider peoples are our family as well. "We have been called from the beginning of time," she tells us, "to serve . . . those unnamed, undocumented, unbelieved and unheard."[88] In naming Jesus, she invites us to honor the names of each other.

And finally, that is the paradox of Mary's naming work. Saying something about God, whether through the Magnificat or through the very word *salvation*, means saying something about particular human lives. It means naming the exclusions and skeletons of a *world built only*

87. Joseph Winters, "The Gift, and Death, of Blackness," *Journal of Africana Religions* 6, no. 1 (2018): 22.

88. Lee, October 30, 2018.

for some—a world that needs a Savior. And it also means treasuring the names of brothers and sisters who are part of God's outsider family. Their names are not only marked by God's salvation; they mark God's body, inscribed on her palms.

At her sermon's close, Lee shows us what it might look like to honor the unnamed. She tells us the story of the woman who named her. "I think of my mother," Lee says, a woman "whose own call to preach would be thwarted by the claims of misogyny." Lee shows us a woman who received less protein than her brother at the dinner table and no financial assistance for education. She shows her working the night shift at a factory to fund her dream of being a pastor. "She will be the only person in her family to attend college," Lee tells us.[89]

"I see this twenty-six-year-old woman . . . walking home shaken from what she's been told. She strokes her belly, as large as a moon . . . whispering gentle words of assurance because she knows with a woman's instinct that she will bear a daughter." Lee's mother prays for a name that will protect her child from the "curses and death dealings of powers and principalities, a name that expresses her deepest desires, not just for the child but for the child's world. A world where no persons will be forgotten or lost or erased or unbelieved, but embraced, treasured, fiercely loved, and protected." And then, discernment comes. "She names her . . . the name of God's shalom."[90]

Mothers have been preaching for a very long time.

89. Lee, October 30, 2018.
90. Lee, October 30, 2018.

Epilogue

The Overshadowed Preacher

not fossilized, hardened, stiff, unshaken,
not contained in creeds and testimonies,
judgements and stone tablets,
but in the wound breaking open.

Christine Valters Paintner, "Please Can I Have a God"

Every attempt to define [the ascended Jesus] as something other
than a human being is really an act of violence designed to force
him to yield his meaning on our terms.

Douglass Farrow, *Ascension and Ecclesia*

This book began with a gamble. What would it mean to replace our
sanitized approximations of Jesus's risen body—whether fully present in the church's performance *or* safely removed from those uneasy
negotiations—with an actively performing Christ? In allowing for the
possibility of his absence, might we discover that he is indeed faithful?
In risking a Spirit-mediated relationship with him, might we find the uneasy borders of our bodies and communities marked with his own?

The woman who stands in the pulpit is a *radini*, a Fijian minister's
wife. As part of the tenth anniversary of the training program for pastor's
wives at Davuilevu College, the faculty has agreed to offer these women
a preaching course. Women can preach in the Fijian Methodist Church,
but it is uncommon. In our three-week seminar, women have shared their

fears of looking scandalous or foolish. Many are afraid they do not have the skill, holiness, or power to pull off the task. But when we read the story of Mary together, they silently nod. Maybe God is in the business of using "the lowly" after all. Their gambles have real-world consequence. The woman in the pulpit is betting her reputation on it.[1]

The sermonic marks described in the previous chapters are not comprehensive, nor are they intended to be. They do not provide concrete lists of dos and don'ts or systematically divide the preacher's sermonic tasks into time spent *conceiving*, *bearing*, or *naming*. They do not provide time-management tools or argue for a particular sermon form. Instead, they describe rhetoric that flows from a living relationship. They are concrete examples of preachers who have stopped avoiding the uneasy borders of their performing bodies and have put their faith in the One who meets them there.

Spirit-Shadowed Performances

We have become accustomed to thinking about performance in terms of excellence and effectiveness. In the vernacular, to *perform* is to embody communal norms or draw attention to one's prowess. But the performance of faith is something different. It is the willingness to show up in one's own skin and risk being changed by the God who has poured out God's Spirit on a blessed and broken world. When placed in God's hands, our preaching performances are also broken and blessed.

Such an approach to body and Spirit resists the manipulations of power that create *dangerous* preachers. It acknowledges that performative norms are always dependent on and permeable to the body of the risen Jesus—which means they are not set in stone. Kenyatta Gilbert reminds homileticians than even the most well-meaning sermonic approach "may be the seat of idolatry."[2] Such idols create a pulpit "built only for some."

But it also speaks to *disappearing* preachers who fear making visible in their sermons the uneasy borders of their lives. There was time when

1. Reflecting on the sermons of Davuilevu pastor spouses, October 2014.

2. Kenyatta Gilbert, "Decolonizing the Homiletical Mind: Religious Hypocrisy and Cultural Invasion," Howard University School of Divinity, April 8, 2019. https://www.youtube.com/watch?v=vNjTmoqSMHE&feature=youtu.be

truth seemed a matter of careful, objective observation or disembodied mysticism. Bodies were meant to be mastered or repressed. A preacher's performance might be useful to promote the purposes of power or illustrate a point. But it was not something to which truth *related*. A body's unease could not be trusted to bear the weight of revelation, which meant that pulpit performance required the disappearance of a preacher's full humanity.

But Jesus embraced the unease of the world so it might be saved.

He chose to become a body *performing*, and his performance continues. This affirmation of faith means that Christ's revelation requires our fully human testimony, for our bodies are the sites of his performative work. Through our *particular, permeable, provisional* creation, Christ's performance becomes visible. Through the Spirit's promise, our bodies witness to—and even mediate—Jesus. "To bear the glory of God cannot mean somehow to deny vulnerability or to escape ambiguity," Kristine Culp argues. But bearing God's glory does mean "real and ongoing change—conversion, repentance, empowerment, healing."[3] Sermon performances make visible this saving work.

Spirit-shadowed performances do more than imitate a Savior. They *relate* to a Savior, and they are changed by that relation. The challenge of practical theology is to give descriptive specificity to that change while maintaining the primacy of the relation itself. I have used the description of Mary's labor in pregnancy—her *conceiving, bearing,* and *naming*—to describe the Spirit-filled labor of preachers who bear Christ to the world. There is a reflexivity in these verbs that foreshadows Christ's cruciform calling. In the unsettling of Mary's identity, certainty is laid aside for the sake of faith. In the unsettling of her agency, struggle is borne for the sake of hope. And in the unsettling of her communal role, risk is embraced for the sake of love. I do not claim that every pregnancy bears this fruit. But I suggest that the labors of those who bear Christ to the world by the power of the Spirit do.

What these uneasy borders mean for the rhetoric of specific preachers in specific communities requires discernment. Rhetoric that responds to a relational God will be diverse in practice. But, finally, the testimonies of Acts and Luke assert that a lived dependence on the living Lord results in performances that bear recognizable marks: the marks of the Cruci-

---

3. Kristine A. Culp, *Vulnerability and Glory: A Theological Account* (Louisville: Westminster John Knox, 2010), 103.

fied One. This cruciformity "interrupts all dominant notions of power and success, [and] turns human visions of grandeur on their head."[4] It refuses to replace the body of Christ with any "human ideal," be those ideals ecclesial, scholastic, political, or pietistic.[5] Instead, it calls those who bear the Word to labors of hospitality, dependence, and discernment in their relationships with Christ and world.

For those who wonder about the value of Spirit-filled, embodied performances for theology (or *as* theology), the reflexivity between Mary's pregnant action and Christ's labor implies something more radical still: that Christ's performance bears a resemblance to hers. Because her conceiving, bearing, and naming are Spirit-born, these labors are like a mirror. They tell us something of the Savior they reflect. Calvin understood the Eucharist as a reflexive act, whereby the believer was taken into Christ's body.[6] I suggest the same. Through a preacher's Spirit-shadowed bearing of Christ, she is taken into *Christ's* womb, reconceived, renamed, and reborn.[7]

"Do You Really Believe It?"

> That pious stuff about "inspiration outside of us" and "God doing the work," do you really believe it?[8]

Trusting in that Spirit and in that reflexivity, I touch a wound near the pulpit's heart. I don't know the identity of the preaching student who scratched the question about "inspiration outside of us" and "God doing the work" on a torn scrap of notebook paper. "Do you really believe it?" the student asks. The question seems brave to me—and honest. It sounds like a question written by a preacher who knows that preaching is hard. It sounds like a *disillusioned* preacher, embarrassed by the unseemly

---

4. Charles Campbell and Johan Cilliers, *Preaching Fools: The Gospel as the Rhetoric of Folly* (Waco, TX: Baylor University Press, 2012), 53.

5. Campbell and Cilliers, *Preaching Fools*, 53.

6. John Calvin, *Institutes of the Christian Religion*, Library of Christian Classics (Philadelphia: Westminster, 1960), 2:1303.

7. Jesus does not only participate in Mary's body. Through the Spirit, Mary participates in his.

8. Submitted anonymously on a small scrap of paper by a seminarian, February 5, 2013.

smudge of her own performative fingerprints. Perhaps she had heard too many sermons that were abusive or exclusionary, and she refused to equate such speech with the work of God. Or perhaps she was tired of feeling inadequate to the task. If God was real, why were her sermons not good enough?

Maybe she had simply stopped believing in what she could not see.

In her classic study of pregnancy and delivery, Emily Martin describes the "very real dilemma" of women who feel a lack of agency in the birth process, alongside a sense of responsibility for that process. The tension is particularly acute when one's birthing does not conform to the expectations or norms of a given community.[9] Women can feel that "I have no control over this situation" and yet "I have failed."

For preachers, the dilemma Martin describes is complicated by a third variable. When preaching does not provide proof of divine intervention through established conventions of purity, power, and authority, it is true that preachers may feel they have no control over a performance in which they have failed. But they may also feel that *God has failed*. Or, perhaps, God never intended to be a part of this broken, messy business of preaching in the first place. "Jesus, stand among us" is not a promise, after all. It is a request. What if God's answer is no?

I have no proof to offer the preacher who finds herself in this difficult place. I do not have rhetorical silver and gold to authenticate one's performance as Spirit-filled or offer techniques that will evoke God's healing presence. But what I have, I give.

I do believe it.

I believe it not only because of theological doctrine or biblical witness, but because, on provisional, performative borders of preaching performance, I have seen signs of an Other. I have seen human preachers who confront the exclusion of their communities with the promise that "Nothing is impossible with God."[10] I have seen preachers who serve tiny congregations with no public recognition, who say, "The Lord takes the simplest—those who don't have, by the world's standards—the most. He sanctifies our gifts."[11] I have heard preachers who describe "a kind of spontaneity, . . . a press of discovery" in the preaching moment, both

9. Emily Martin, *The Woman in the Body: A Cultural Analysis of Reproduction* (Boston: Beacon Press, 1992), 90.

10. Andreta Livena (sermon, Miller Chapel, Princeton Theological Seminary, December 5, 2012).

11. Interview on the joys and challenges of preaching, July 23, 2013.

for themselves and for their congregations.[12] I have heard them describe being "caught off guard by emotion—a tightening in the throat and chest . . . an emotional edge where you are caught by surprise."[13] Alternately, I have heard descriptions of "no special feeling" in the pulpit at all, "but trust in the absence of feeling."[14] I have heard preachers describe the holiness of the moment "when you walk up and ground yourself and get a connection with others before you speak. You breathe out . . . and see that it's not just [you] talking alone."[15]

None of these statements provide proof of a divine Agent. But they bear the unsettled marks of the Spirit's work. They bear the marks of persons whose identity, agency, and communal role have been brought into embodied relation with Christ. These marks do not transform in and of themselves, but they testify to the living presence of a Savior who does. He is present, not in a way that can be proven or guaranteed, yet in a way that is recognizable in human action.

Preaching in embodied relation to the risen Christ is what sermonic labor entails. To conceive, bear, and name the Word within the context of this relation, standing under the shadow of the Spirit who makes it possible, is *what we really do* when we preach. Such a metaphor affirms diverse, bodily performances, without divinizing bodily action. It invites preachers to affirm their human particularity in the pulpit without universalizing their experience. Jesus's crucified body, risen and reigning, provides the corrective and affirmation to contextual theologies that start with the body. When the body of this living Word intersects the performances of human preachers through the power of the Spirit, it calls forth bold humility. It exposes preachers as human persons called to be God's *douloi* and *doulai*, persons who have laid aside false shadows of success and authority to be overshadowed by the Spirit instead.

Such preachers bear witness to the advent of an ascended Savior. Come, Lord Jesus, come.

12. Interview on the joys and challenges of preaching, April 23, 2012.
13. Interview on the joys and challenges of preaching, January 29, 2013.
14. Interview on the joys and challenges of preaching, May 15, 2013.
15. Interview on the joys and challenges of preaching, January 29, 2012.

I sit in the second pew of my congregation. It is several weeks before Easter, but as this community knows little Scripture, the preacher is foreshadowing the story of Easter morning (John 20:1-20). "It bears repeating," he tells us.

He describes Jesus's garden meeting with Mary Magdalene, and he asks us a question. "What is it that Jesus says to her? Do you know?"

An unexpected response comes from the back of the sanctuary. It is a seventh-grade girl, naturally quiet and not prone to speaking in groups. Her voice makes the preacher stop short. The girl's mother does not come to church, so she gets a ride from a neighbor. When she first began attending, she had never held a Bible. Several months ago, she and her sisters decided they wanted to be baptized on Easter morning. The preacher had been coming by their house each week to tell them stories about Jesus.

"He says her name," she says aloud. We turn and look at her, surprised. And then, she leans forward in her pew and repeats herself, like she needs the preacher to understand something very important. "He says her name."

Something happens on the preacher's face. He loses his words and faces her. He swallows hard. It takes him a moment to continue.

Later, he will explain, "We had just talked about that moment at her house the week before, but I didn't think she would say it. It wasn't that she had the right answer. It was like it had happened to her." His eyes fill again. "She got it."

But right now, none of us have language for what has occurred. We only know that our falling-down sanctuary is a garden, and in the shadows, Jesus is here.

Reflections on a Sunday
worship service, March 17, 2013

∽

Bibliography

Adam, Peter. *Speaking God's Words: A Practical Theology of Preaching*. Vancouver: Regent College Publishing, 2004.

Ahmed, Sarah. *Living a Feminist Life*. Durham, NC: Duke University Press, 2017.

Alexander, Loveday. "Reading Luke-Acts from Back to Front." In *The Unity of Luke-Acts*. Edited by J. Verheyden. Leuven: Leuven University Press, 1999.

Althaus-Reid, Marcella. *Indecent Theology*. New York: Routledge, 2000.

Aristotle. *Poetics*. Translated by Ingram Bywater. *Introduction to Artistotle*. Edited by Richard McKeon. Chicago: University of Chicago Press, 1973.

———. *On Rhetoric: A Theory of Civic Discourse*, 2nd ed. Translated by George A. Kennedy. Oxford: Oxford University Press, 2006.

Augustine. *On Christian Doctrine*. Translated by R. P. H. Green. Oxford: Oxford University Press, 1997.

Austin, John L. *How to Do Things with Words*. Cambridge: Harvard University Press, 1962.

———. "Performative Utterances." In *Philosophical Papers*, 2nd ed. Oxford: Clarendon Press, 1970.

Bakhtin, Mikhail. *Rabelais and His World*. Translated by Hélène Iswolsky. Bloomington: Indiana University Press, 1984.

Balthasar, Hans Urs von. *The Glory of the Lord: A Theological Aesthetics*. Vol. 1. Translated by Erasmo Leiva-Merikakis. San Francisco: Ignatius Press, 1982.

Barth, Karl. *Church Dogmatics*. Edited by Geoffrey W. Bromiley and T. F. Torrance. Translated by Geoffrey W. Bromiley. 14 vols. Edinburgh: T&T Clark, 1975.

———. *Homiletics*. Louisville: Westminster John Knox, 1991.

Bartow, Charles. *God's Human Speech: A Practical Theology of Proclamation*. Grand Rapids: Eerdmans, 1997.

Bass, Dorothy, and Craig Dykstra. "Ways of Life Abundant." In *For Life Abundant: Practical Theology, Theological Education, and Christian Ministry*. Grand Rapids: Eerdmans, 2008.

Battles, Ford Lewis. "God Was Accommodating Himself to Human Capacity." *Interpretation* 31, no. 1. (January 1977): 19–38.

Bauer, Walter, William F. Arndt, F. Wilbur Gingrich, and Frederick W. Danker. *Greek-English Lexicon of the New Testament and Other Early Christian Literature*. 2nd ed. Chicago: University of Chicago Press, 1979.

Bentley, Cara. "John MacArthur Says Southern Baptist Preacher Beth Moore Should 'Go Home.'" *Premier*, October 21, 2019. https://www.premier .org.uk/News/World/Pastor-John-MacArthur-says-Southern-Baptist-preacher-Beth-Moore-should-go-home.

Bhagwan, James. "Gratitude." Sermon preached at Girmitiya Welcome Service, Nabudrau Village, Rewa, October 9, 2016.

Birgitta of Sweden. *Revelaciones*. Book 7. Edited by Birger Bergh. Uppsala: Almqvist & Wiksells Boktryckeri, 1967.

Boal, Augusto. *The Rainbow of Desire: The Boal Method of Theatre and Therapy*. New York: Routledge, 2003.

Bolatiki, Maika. "Girmitiyas Accepted as Rewans." *Fiji Sun*, July 10, 2016. http://fijisun.com.fj/2016/07/10/girmitiyas-accepted-as-rewans.

Bourdieu, Pierre. *The Logic of Practice*. Cambridge: Polity Press, 1992.

Bouwsma, William J. *Calvinism as Theologia Rhetorica: Protocol of the Fifty-Fourth Colloquy*. Berkeley, CA: Center for Hermeneutical Studies in Hellenistic and Modern Culture, 1987.

———. *John Calvin: A Sixteenth-Century Portrait*. New York: Oxford University Press, 1988.

Bowler, Kate. *The Preacher's Wife: The Precarious Power of Evangelical Women Celebrities*. Princeton: Princeton University Press, 2019.

Boyle, Marjorie O'Rourke. "Rhetorical Theology: Charity Seeking Charity." In *Calvinism as Theologia Rhetorica: Protocol of the Fifty-Fourth Colloquy*. Berkeley, CA: Center for Hermeneutical Studies in Hellenistic and Modern Culture, 1987.

Bozarth-Campbell, Alla. *The Word's Body: An Incarnational Aesthetic of Interpretation*. Tuscaloosa: University of Alabama Press, 1980.

Brawley, R. L. "Abrahamic Covenant Traditions and the Characterization of God in Luke-Acts." In *The Unity of Luke-Acts*. Edited by J. Verheyden. Leuven: Leuven University Press, 1999.

Brekus, Catherine A. *Strangers and Pilgrims: Female Preaching in America*. Chapel Hill: University of North Carolina Press, 1998.

Bridges-Johns, Cheryl. "Epiphanies of Fire: Para-Modernist Preaching in a Postmodern World." Paper presented at the annual meeting of the North American Academy of Homiletics, Santa Fe, NM, 1996.

Bridget. *The Word of the Angel: Sermo Angelicus*. Translated by John E. Halborg. Toronto: Peregrina, 1996.

Broadus, John A. *On the Preparation and Delivery of Sermons*, 4th ed. Revised by Vernon Stanfield. Vestavia Hills, AL: Solid Ground Christian Books, 2004.

———. *A Treatise on the Preparation and Delivery of Sermons*. Michigan Historical Reprint Series. Ann Arbor: University of Michigan Library, 2006.

Brown, Raymond. *The Birth of the Messiah: A Commentary on the Infancy Narratives in Matthew and Luke*. Garden City, NY: Image Books, 1979.

Brown, Sally A. *Cross Talk: Preaching Redemption Here and Now*. Louisville: Westminster John Knox, 2008.

———. "Exploring the Text-Practice Interface: Acquiring the Virtue of Hermeneutical Modesty." *Theology Today* 66, no. 3 (October 2009): 279–94.

Brown, Sally A., and Luke A. Powery. *Ways of the Word: Learning to Preach for Your Time and Place*. Minneapolis: Fortress Press, 2016.

Brueggemann, Walter. *Theology of the Old Testament: Testimony, Dispute, Advocacy*. Minneapolis: Fortress Press, 1997.

Brummett Wudel, Molly. "Bearing Witness at Table: Not What We Expect, Luke 7:36–50." Sermon dialogue at Emmaus Way Church, Durham, NC, September 2, 2018.

Bultmann, Rudolf. *Kerygma and Myth: A Theological Debate*. New York: HarperCollins, 2000.

Buss, Helen. "Antigone, Psyche, and the Ethics of Female Selfhood." In *Paul Ricoeur and Contemporary Moral Thought*. Edited by John Wall, William Schweiker, and W. David Hall. New York: Routledge, 2002.

Butin, Philip Walker. *Revelation, Redemption, and Response: Calvin's Trinitarian Understanding of the Divine-Human Relationship*. New York: Oxford University Press, 1995.

Butler, Judith. *Excitable Speech: A Politics of the Performative*. New York: Routledge, 1997.

———. "For a Careful Reading." In *Feminist Contentions: A Philosophical Exchange*. London: Routledge, 1995.

Buttrick, David. *Homiletic: Moves and Structures*. Philadelphia: Fortress Press, 1987.

Cadbury, H. J. *The Making of Luke-Acts*. London: SPCK, 1927.

Calvin, John. *Calvin's New Testament Commentaries*. Edited by David Torrance and T. J. Torrance, 12 vols. Grand Rapids: Eerdmans, 1959–1972.

———. *Commentaries on the Book of the Prophet Jeremiah and the Lamentations*. Grand Rapids: Eerdmans, 1950.

———. *Commentary on the Epistles of Paul the Apostle to the Corinthians*. Grand Rapids: Eerdmans, 1948.

———. *Commentaries on the Epistles of St. Paul to the Galatians and Ephesians*. Translated by William Pringle. Grand Rapids: Baker Books, 1989.

———. *Commentary on the Epistle to the Hebrews*. Grand Rapids: Eerdmans, 1949.

———. *Commentary on a Harmony of the Evangelists, Matthew, Mark, and Luke*. Grand Rapids: Eerdmans, 1949.

———. *Commentary upon the Acts of the Apostles*. Grand Rapids: Eerdmans, 1949.

———. *Institutes of the Christian Religion*. Vols. 1–2. Library of Christian Classics 20–21. Philadelphia: Westminster, 1960.

———. *Ioannis Calvini Opera Quae Supersunt Omnia*. Corpus Reformatorum 26. Brunsvigae: C. A. Schwetschke, 1863.

———. *A Selection of the Most Celebrated Sermons of John Calvin, Minister of the Gospel, and One of the Principal Leaders in the Protestant Reformation to Which Is Prefixed a Biographical History of His Life*. Philadelphia: Desilver, Thomas, 1834.

———. *Sermons on 2 Samuel: Chapters 1–13*. Edinburgh: Banner of Truth, 1992.

———. *Songs of the Nativity: Selected Sermons on Luke 1 and 2*. Translated by Robert White. Edinburgh: Banner of Truth, 2008.

———. *Tracts Relating to the Reformation*. Vol. 2. Edinburgh: Calvin Translation Society, 1844.

Campbell, Charles L. "Incarnate Word: Preaching and the Carnivalesque Grotesque." Lyman Beecher Lecture Series, Yale Divinity School, October 19, 2018.

———. *Preaching Jesus: New Directions for Homiletics in Hans Frei's Postliberal Theology*. Grand Rapids: Eerdmans, 1997.

———. Sermon preached in Duke Chapel, Duke Divinity School, May 11, 2019.

———. *The Word before the Powers: An Ethic of Preaching*. Louisville: Westminster John Knox, 2002.

Campbell, Charles L., and Johan Cilliers. *Preaching Fools: The Gospel as a Rhetoric of Folly*. Waco, TX: Baylor University Press, 2012.

Canlis, Julie. *Calvin's Ladder: A Spiritual Theology of Ascent and Ascension*. Grand Rapids: Eerdmans, 2010.

Carroll, John. *Response to the End of History: Eschatology and Situation in Luke-Acts*. Atlanta: Scholar's Press, 1988.

Carter, J. Kameron. *Race: A Theological Account*. Oxford: Oxford University Press, 2008.

Childers, Jana. *Birthing the Sermon: Women Preachers on the Creative Process*. St. Louis: Chalice Press, 2001.

——. *Performing the Word: Preaching as Theatre*. Nashville: Abingdon Press, 1998.

——. "Seeing Jesus: Preaching as an Incarnational Act." In *Purposes of Preaching*. St. Louis: Chalice Press, 2004.

Chodorow, Nancy. *The Reproduction of Mothering: Psychoanalysis and the Sociology of Gender*. Berkeley: University of California Press, 1999.

Chopp, Rebecca. *The Power to Speak: Feminism, Language, God*. Eugene, OR: Wipf & Stock, 1991.

——. "Practical Theology and Liberation." In *Formation and Reflection: The Promise of Practical Theology*. Edited by Lewis Mudge and James Poling. Philadelphia: Fortress Press, 1987.

Cicero. *On Oratory and Orators*. Translated by J. S. Watson. Carbondale: Southern Illinois University Press, 1986.

Coakley, Sarah. "The Identity of the Risen Jesus." In *Seeking the Identity of Jesus: A Pilgrimage*. Edited by Beverly Gaventa and Richard Hays. Grand Rapids: Eerdmans, 2008.

——. "Mariology and Romantic Feminism: A Critique." In *Women's Voices: Essays in Contemporary Feminist Theology*. Edited by Teresa Elwes. New York: Marshall Pickering, 1992.

Cohen, Ted. "Metaphor and the Cultivation of Intimacy." In *On Metaphor*. Edited by Sheldon Sacks. Chicago: University of Chicago Press, 1979.

Collins, John J., ed. *The Origins of Apocalypticism in Judaism and Christianity*. Vol. 1 of *The Encyclopedia of Apocalypticism*. New York: Continuum, 1998.

Congdon, David. "Eschatologizing Apocalyptic: An Assessment of the Present Conversation on Pauline Apocalyptic." In *Apocalyptic and the Future of Theology: With and Beyond J. Louis Martyn*. Edited by Joshua Davis and Douglas Harink. Eugene, OR: Cascade, 2012.

Conquergood, Dwight. "Rethinking Elocution: The Trope of the Talking Book and Other Figures of Speech." In *Text and Performance Quarterly* 20, no. 4 (October 2000): 325–41.

Conzelmann, Hans. *The Theology of St. Luke*. Translated by Geoffrey Buswell. London: Faber, 1960.

Cooke, Sarah. *The Handmaiden of the Lord*. Chicago: T. B. Arnold, 1896.

Copeland, Shawn. "Wading through Many Sorrows: Toward a Theology of Suffering in Womanist Perspective." In *A Troubling in My Soul: Womanist*

Perspectives on Evil and Suffering. Edited by Emilie Townes. Maryknoll, NY: Orbis, 1993.

Craddock, Fred B. *Luke*. Louisville: Westminster John Knox, 1990.

———. *As One without Authority*. Enid, OK: Phillips University Press, 1971.

———. "In Service to the Gospel." Macleod Lectures, Princeton Theological Seminary, October 16, 1996.

Crawford, Evans. *The Hum: Call and Response in African American Preaching*. Nashville: Abingdon Press, 1995.

Crossan, John. "Virgin Mother or Bastard Child?" In *A Feminist Companion to Mariology*. Edited by Amy-Jill Levine. Cleveland: Pilgrim Press, 2005.

Culp, Kristine A. *Vulnerability and Glory: A Theological Account*. Louisville: Westminster John Knox, 2010.

Curl, Leigh. Sermon preached in Goodson Chapel, Durham, NC, October 25, 2018.

Dasenbrock, Reed Way. "Do We Write the Text We Read?" In *Falling into Theory: Conflicting Views on Reading Literature*. Edited by David Richter. Boston: Bedford Books, 1994.

Davis, Ellen. *Preaching the Luminous Word: Biblical Sermons and Homiletical Essays*. Grand Rapids: Eerdmans, 2016.

Davis, Thomas J. *This Is My Body: The Presence of Christ in Reformation Thought*. Grand Rapids: Baker Academic, 2008.

Day, Keri. Pauli Murray/Nannie Hellen Burroughs Lecture on Women and Religion, Duke Divinity School, Durham, NC, March 5, 2018.

Deeg, Alexander. "Imagination and Meticulousness." *Homiletic* 34, no. 1 (2009): 139–51.

Derrida, Jacques. *Acts of Religion*. New York: Routledge, 2002.

———. *Of Grammatology*. Translated by Gayatri Spivak. Baltimore: Johns Hopkins Press, 1974.

———. *Of Hospitality*. Stanford, CA: Stanford University Press, 2000.

Des Vignes, Crystal. "Luke 4:1–13." Sermon preached at CityWell United Methodist Church, Durham, NC, March 10, 2019. https://citywell.org/audio-items/3-10-19-crystal-desvignes.

DeYoung, Curtiss, Michael Emerson, George Yancey, and Karen Chai Kim. *United by Faith: The Multiracial Congregation as an Answer to the Problem of Race*. Oxford: Oxford University Press, 2004.

Dobrin, Sidney I. "Race and the Public Intellectual: A Conversation with Michael Eric Dyson." *Race, Rhetoric, and the Postcolonial*. Edited by Gary Olson and Lynn Worsham. Albany: State University of New York Press, 1999.

Dodd, C. H. *The Apostolic Preaching and Its Developments*. New York: Harper, 1936.

Doherty, Cathal. *Maurice Blondel on the Supernatural in Human Action: Sacrament and Superstition*. Leiden: Brill, 2017.

Donne, John. "Death's Duel." Sermon preached at St. Paul's Cathedral, Whitehall, February 25, 1631.

———. *The Sermons of John Donne*. Edited by Theodore Gill. New York: Meridian Books, 1958.

Douglass, Jane Dempsey. "Calvin's Use of Metaphorical Language for God: God as Enemy and God as Mother." In *Articles on Calvin and Calvinism*. Vol. 6. Edited by Richard Gamble. New York: Garland Press, 1992.

Dube, Musa. "Curriculum Transformation: Dreaming of Decolonization." In *Border Crossings: Cross-Cultural Hermeneutics*. Edited by D. N. Premnath. Maryknoll, NY: Orbis, 2007.

Duff, Nancy. "Mary, Servant of the Lord: Christian Vocation at the Manger and the Cross." In *Blessed One: Protestant Perspectives on Mary*. Edited by Beverly Gaventa and Cynthia Rigby. Louisville: Westminster John Knox, 2002.

Eastman, Susan. *Recovering Paul's Mother Tongue: Language and Theology in Galatians*. Grand Rapids: Eerdmans, 2007.

Ebeling, Gerhard. "The Beginnings of Luther's Hermeneutics." *Lutheran Quarterly* 7 (1993): 315–38.

———. *Theology and Proclamation: A Discussion with Rudolph Bultmann*. New York: HarperCollins, 1966.

Elwood, Christopher Lee. *The Body Broken: The Calvinist Doctrine of the Eucharist and the Symbolization of Power in France, 1530–1570*. Cambridge: Harvard University Press, 1995.

Fant, Clyde E. *Preaching for Today*. New York: HarperOne, 1987.

Farley, Edward. "Theology and Practice outside the Clerical Paradigm." In *Practical Theology*. Edited by Don Browning. San Francisco: Harper & Row, 1983.

Farley, Wendy. *Eros for the Other: Retaining Truth in a Pluralistic World*. University Park: Pennsylvania State University Press, 1996.

Farrow, Douglass. *Ascension and Ecclesia: On the Significance of the Doctrine of the Ascension for Ecclesiology and Christian Cosmology*. Grand Rapids: Eerdmans, 1999.

———. "In Support of a Reformed View of Ascension and Eucharist." In *Reformed Theology: Identity and Ecumenicity*. Edited by Wallace Alston and Michael Welker. Grand Rapids: Eerdmans, 2003.

Faul, Kelsey. Sermon preached at Princeton Theological Seminary, Princeton, NJ, November 5, 2013.

Fiorenza, Elisabeth Schüssler. *In Memory of Her: A Feminist Theological Reconstruction of Christian Origins*. New York: Crossroad, 1983.

Fitzmyer, Joseph. "The Role of the Spirit in Luke-Acts." In *The Unity of Luke-Acts*. Edited by J. Verheyden. Leuven: Leuven University Press, 1999.

Florence, Anna Carter. *Preaching as Testimony*. Louisville: Westminster John Knox, 2007.

———. "Put Away Your Sword! Taking Torture out of the Sermon." In *What Is the Matter with Preaching Today?* Edited by Michael Graves. Louisville: Westminster John Knox, 2004.

Flores, Saul Gastelum. Sermon preached at Duke Divinity School, Durham, NC, November 27, 2018.

Flynn, Meagan. "Feds Deport Undocumented Immigrant Whose Church Supporters Went to Jail to Protect Him." *Washington Post*, November 30, 2018. https://www.washingtonpost.com/nation/2018/11/30/feds-dep ort-undocumented-immigrant-whose-church-supporters-went-jail-p rotect-him.

Foskett, Mary. *A Virgin Conceived*. Bloomington: Indiana University Press, 2002.

Foss, Sonja K., and Cindy L. Griffin. "Beyond Persuasion: A Proposal for an Invitational Rhetoric." *Communication Monographs* 62 (1995): 2–18.

"483 Drown in the Mediterranean While Rescue Ships Are Trapped in Port." *Care4Calais*, July 8, 2018. https://care4calais.org/news/483-drown -mediterranean-rescue-ships-trapped-port.

Freeman, Curtis. "Southern Baptists and Roman Catholics Face Similar Crises." *News and Record*, February 24, 2019. https://www.greensboro. com/opinion/columns/curtis-freeman-southern-baptists-and-roman -catholics-face-similar-crises/article_4fca4890-6613-5705-99b5 -1dc7d1a8ed35.html.

Frei, Hans W. *The Identity of Jesus Christ*. Eugene, OR: Wipf & Stock, 1997.

Fulkerson, Mary McClintock. *Changing the Subject: Women's Discourses and Feminist Theology*. Minneapolis: Fortress Press, 1994.

———. *Places of Redemption*. Oxford: Oxford University Press, 2009.

Fuller, Charles W. *The Trouble with "Truth through Personality": Phillips Brooks, Incarnation, and the Evangelical Boundaries of Preaching*. Eugene, OR: Wipf & Stock, 2010.

Garrett, Susan. *The Demise of the Devil: Magic and the Demonic in Luke's Writings*. Minneapolis: Fortress Press, 1989.

Gaventa, Beverly. *The Acts of the Apostles*. Nashville: Abingdon Press, 2003.

——. "All Generations Will Call Me Blessed." In *A Feminist Companion to Mariology*. Edited by Amy-Jill Levine. Cleveland: Pilgrim Press, 2005.

——. "The Eschatology of Luke-Acts Revisited." *Encounter* 43 (1982): 27–42.

——. "Learning and Relearning the Identity of Jesus from Luke-Acts." In *Seeking the Identity of Jesus: A Pilgrimage*. Edited by Beverly Gaventa and Richard Hays. Grand Rapids: Eerdmans, 2008.

——. *Mary: Glimpses of the Mother of Jesus*. Minneapolis: Fortress Press, 1999.

——. *Our Mother Saint Paul*. Louisville: Westminster John Knox, 2007.

——. "Standing Near the Cross." *Blessed One: Protestant Perspectives on Mary*. Edited by Beverly Gaventa and Cynthia Rigby. Louisville: Westminster John Knox, 2002.

Geertz, Clifford. "Religion as a Cultural System." In *The Interpretation of Cultures*. New York: Basic Books, 1973.

Gerrish, B. A. *Grace and Gratitude: The Eucharistic Theology of John Calvin*. Minneapolis: Fortress Press, 1993.

Gilbert, Kenyatta. "Decolonizing the Homiletical Mind: Religious Hypocrisy and Cultural Invasion." Public lecture at Howard University School of Divinity, April 8, 2019.

——. *The Journey and Promise of African-American Preaching*. Minneapolis: Fortress Press, 2011.

Glancy, Jennifer. *Corporal Knowledge*. Oxford: Oxford University Press, 2007.

Goss, Robert E. "Luke." In *The Queer Bible Commentary*. Edited by Deryn Guest, Robert Goss, and Mona West. London: SCM Press, 2015.

Graham, Elaine. *Transforming Practice: Pastoral Theology in an Age of Uncertainty*. Eugene, OR: Wipf & Stock, 1996.

Grant, Jacquelyn. *White Women's Christ and Black Women's Jesus: Feminist Christology and Womanist Response*. Atlanta: Scholars Press, 1989.

Green, Joel. "The Social Status of Mary in Luke 1,5–2,52: A Plea for Methodological Integration." *Biblica* 73, no. 4 (1992): 457–72.

Griffin, Susan. "Feminism and Motherhood." In *Mother Reader: Essential Writings on Motherhood*. New York: Seven Stories, 2001.

Guerrero, Katherine. Sermon preached at Homegrown North Carolina Women's Preaching Festival, Trinity Presbyterian Church, Durham, NC, October 26, 2018.

Hampson, Margaret Daphne. *Christian Contradictions: The Structures of Lutheran and Catholic Thought*. New York: Cambridge University Press, 2001.

Hartshorn, Leo. "Evaluating Preaching as a Communal and Dialogical Practice." *Homiletic* 35, no. 2 (2010): 13–24.

Harvey, Susan A. "Odes of Solomon." In *Searching the Scriptures: A Feminist*

Commentary. Vol. 2. Edited by Elisabeth Schüssler Fiorenza. New York: Crossroad, 1994.

"Herstory." *Black Lives Matter*. Accessed April 5, 2019. https://blacklivesmatter.com/about/herstory.

Hilkert, Mary Catherine. *Naming Grace: Preaching and the Sacramental Imagination*. New York: Continuum, 1997.

Hitchman-Craig, Kelli. "God Seeking Surrogate (Luke 1:39–55)." Sermon preached at Duke Divinity School, Durham, NC, October 19, 2016.

Hobson, Janell, ed. *Are All the Women Still White? Rethinking Race, Expanding Feminisms*. New York: SUNY Press, 2016.

Hogan, Lucy Lind, and Robert Stephen Reid. *Connecting with the Congregation: Rhetoric and the Art of Preaching*. Nashville: Abingdon Press, 1999.

Howell, William Samuel, trans. *Fenelon's Dialogues on Eloquence*. Princeton: Princeton University Press, 1951.

Hudson, W. D. *Wittgenstein and Religious Belief*. London: Macmillan, 1975.

Isherwood, Lisa. "The Fat Jesus: Explorations in Fleshy Christologies." *Feminist Theology* 19, no. 1 (2010): 20–35.

Jacobsen, David Schnasa. "Promise as an Event of the Gospel in Context: Toward an Unfinished Homiletical Theology of Grace and Justice." In *Toward a Homiletical Theology of Promise*. Edited by David Schnasa Jacobsen. Eugene, OR: Cascade, 2018.

Jennings, Willie. *Acts*. Louisville: Westminster John Knox, 2017.

———. *The Christian Imagination: Theology and the Origins of Race*. New Haven: Yale University Press, 2010.

Johnson, Elizabeth A. *Truly Our Sister: A Theology of Mary in the Communion of Saints*. New York: Continuum, 2003.

Johnson, Luke Timothy. *The Gospel of Luke*. Sacra Pagina. Collegeville, MN: Liturgical Press, 1991.

———. *Scripture and Discernment: Decision Making in the Church*. Nashville: Abingdon Press, 1983.

Jones, Serene. *Trauma and Grace: Theology in a Ruptured World*. Louisville: Westminster John Knox, 2009.

Juel, Donald. *A Master of Surprise: Mark Interpreted*. Minneapolis: Fortress Press, 1994.

Kahl, Brigitte. "Reading Luke against Luke: Non-Uniformity of Text, Hermeneutics of Conspiracy and the 'Scriptural Principle' in Luke 1." In *A Feminist Companion to Luke*. Edited by Amy-Jill Levine. London: Sheffield Press, 2002.

Kamitsuka, Margaret. *Feminist Theology and the Challenge of Difference*. Oxford: Oxford University Press, 2007.

Käsemann, Ernst. "Ephesians and Acts." In *Studies in Luke-Acts*. Edited by Leander Keck and J. Louis Martyn. Nashville: Abingdon Press, 1966.

Kay, James F. "Preacher as Messenger of Hope." In *Slow of Speech and Unclean Lips: Contemporary Images of Preaching Identity*. Edited by Robert Reid. Eugene, OR: Cascade, 2010.

———. *Preaching and Theology*. St. Louis: Chalice Press, 2007.

———. "The Word of the Cross at the Turn of the Ages." *Interpretation* 53, no. 1 (January 1999): 44–56.

Kienzle, Beverly. "The Prostitute Preacher: Patterns of Polemic against Medieval Waldensian Women Preachers." In *Women Preachers and Prophets through Two Millennia of Christianity*. Edited by Beverly Mayne Kienzle and Pamela J. Walker. Berkeley: University of California Press, 1998.

Kiran, Sashi. "For Peace Which Is True." *Fiji Times*, September 29, 2016. https://www.fijitimes.com/for-peace-which-is-true.

Kisliuk, Michelle. "The Poetics and Politics of Practice: Experience, Embodiment and the Engagement of Scholarship." In *Teaching Performance Studies*. Edited by Nathan Stucky and Cynthia Wimmer. Carbondale: Southern Illinois University Press, 2002.

Klein, Ellen R. "Birth of a Woman." *The Spirit of Pregnancy*. Edited by Bonni Goldberg. Chicago: Contemporary Books, 2000.

Knight, Jonathan. *The Ascension of Isaiah*. Sheffield: Sheffield Academic, 1995.

Kristeva, Julia. "Stabat Mater." In *Tales of Love*. Translated by Leon Roudiez. New York: Columbia University Press, 1987.

Kuecker, Aaron. *The Spirit and the "Other": Social Identity, Ethnicity and Intergroup Reconciliation in Luke-Acts*. New York: T&T Clark, 2011.

Kwok, Pui-Lan. "Feminist Theology as Intercultural Discourse." In *The Cambridge Companion to Feminist Theology*. Edited by Susan Frank Parsons. Cambridge: Cambridge University Press, 2002.

Laurentin, René. "Mary and Womanhood in the Renewal of Christian Anthropology." *Marian Library Studies* 1 (1969): 77–95.

Lazarre, Jane. "Excerpt from *The Mother Knot*." In *Mother Reader: Essential Writings on Motherhood*. New York: Seven Stories, 2001.

Lee, Dorothy. *Symbol, Gender and Theology in the Gospel of John*. New York: Crossroad, 2002.

Lee, Jarena. *The Life and Religious Experience of Jarena Lee, a Coloured Lady, Giving an Account of Her Call to Preach the Gospel*. In *Sisters of the Spirit: Three Women's Autobiographies of the Nineteenth Century*. Edited by W. Andrews. Bloomington: Indiana University Press, 1986.

Lee, Peace. Sermon preached in Goodson Chapel, Duke Divinity School, Durham, NC, October 30, 2018.

Lévinas, Emmanuel. *Totality and Infinity*. Dordrecht: Kluwer Academic, 1992.

Lewis, Ralph L. *Speech for Persuasive Preaching*. Wilmore, KY: Asbury Theological Seminary, 1968.

Lindbeck, George A. *The Nature of Doctrine: Religion and Theology in a Postliberal Age*. Louisville: Westminster John Knox, 1984.

Lischer, Richard. *The Company of Preachers*. Grand Rapids: Eerdmans, 2002.

——. *The End of Words: The Language of Reconciliation in a Culture of Violence*. Grand Rapids: Eerdmans, 2005.

Livena, Andreta. Sermon preached in Miller Chapel, Princeton Theological Seminary, December 5, 2011.

Lorde, Audre. "The Master's Tools Will Never Dismantle the Master's House." In *Sister Outsider*. Berkeley, CA: Crossing Press, 1984.

Lorensen, Marlene Ringgaard. *Dialogical Preaching: Bakhtin, Otherness and Homiletics*. Bristol, CT: Vandenhoeck & Ruprecht, 2014.

Lonergan, Bernard. *The Subject*. Milwaukee: Marquette University Press, 1968.

Long, Thomas G. *The Witness of Preaching*. Louisville: Westminster John Knox, 1990.

Lose, David J. *Confessing Jesus Christ: Preaching in a Postmodern World*. Grand Rapids: Eerdmans, 2003.

Lowry, Eugene L. *The Homiletical Plot: The Sermon as Narrative Art Form*. Louisville: Westminster John Knox, 2001.

Lunsford, Andrea, and Cheryl Glenn. "On Rhetoric and Feminism: Forging Alliances." *On Rhetoric and Feminism 1973-2000*. New York: Routledge, 2015.

Luther, Henning. *Religion und Alltag: Bausteine zu einer Praktischen Theologie des Subjekts*. Stuttgart: Radius, 1992.

Luther, Martin. "Commentary on the Magnificat." *Luther's Works* 21. St. Louis: Concordia, 1956.

——. *Luther's Works*. Vol. 36. Edited by Helmut Lehman and Jaroslav Pelikan. Philadelphia: Fortress Press, 1955.

Macpherson, Ian. *The Burden of the Lord*. London: Epworth Press, 1955.

Macy, Gary. *The Hidden History of Women's Ordination: Female Clergy in the Medieval West*. Oxford: Oxford University Press, 2008.

Ma'ilo, Mosese. *Bible-ing My Samoan: Native Languages and the Politics of Bible Translating in the 19th Century*. Apia, Samoa: Piula Publications, 2016.

Malcolm, Lois. "What Mary Has to Say about God's Bare Goodness." In *Blessed One: Protestant Perspectives on Mary*. Edited by Beverly Gaventa and Cynthia Rigby. Louisville: Westminster John Knox, 2002.

Marshall, I. Howard. *Luke: Historian and Theologian*. Exeter: Paternoster Press, 1970.

Martin, Emily. *The Woman in the Body: A Cultural Analysis of Reproduction*. Boston: Beacon Press, 1987.

Martyn, Dorothy. "A Child and Adam: A Parable of the Two Ages." In *Apocalyptic and the New Testament: Essays in Honor of J. Louis Martyn*. Edited by Joel Marcus and Marion Soards. Sheffield: JSOT Press, 1989.

Martyn, J. Louis. "Apocalyptic Antinomies in Paul's Letter to the Galatians." In *Theological Issues in the Letters of Paul*. Nashville: Abingdon Press, 1997.

Matthews, Shelly. *Perfect Martyr: The Stoning of Stephen and the Construction of Christian Identity*. Oxford: Oxford University Press, 2010.

McClure, John. *Otherwise Preaching: A Postmodern Ethic for Homiletics*. St. Louis: Chalice Press, 2001.

McCormack, Bruce L. "Participation in God, Yes, Deification, No: Two Modern Protestant Responses to an Ancient Question." In *Denkwürdiges Geheimnis: Beiträge zur Gotteslehre, Festschrift für Eberhard Jüngel zum 70. Geburtstag*. Tübingen: Mohr Siebeck, 2004.

———. "Union with Christ in Calvin's Theology: Grounds for a Divinization Theory?" In *Tribute to John Calvin: A Celebration of His Quincentenary*. Edited by David W. Hall. Philipsburg, NJ: Presbyterian & Reformed, 2010.

McCray, Donyelle. "Pauli Murray: Preaching in Many Voices." Public lecture at Duke Divinity School. Durham, NC. April 1, 2019.

———. "Sweating, Spitting and Cursing: Intimations of the Sacred." *Practical Matters* 8 (April 2015): 62–72.

McCullough, Amy. "Preaching Pregnant: Insights into Embodiment in Preaching." Paper presented at the Academy of Homiletics, Chicago, IL, November 15–17, 2012.

McFague, Sally. *Metaphorical Theology: Models of God in Religious Language*. Philadelphia: Fortress Press, 1982.

McKeon, Richard. "Rhetoric in the Middle Ages." *Speculum* 17 (1942): 1–32.

McNamara, Jo Ann. *Sisters in Arms: Catholic Nuns through Two Millennia*. Cambridge: Harvard University Press, 1996.

Merleau-Ponty, Maurice. *Phenomenology of Perception*. Translated by Colin Smith. New York: Humanities Press, 1962.

Miller-McLemore, Bonnie. "Pondering All These Things." In *Blessed One: Protestant Perspectives on Mary*. Edited by Beverly Gaventa and Cynthia Rigby. Louisville: Westminster John Knox, 2002.

Minear, Paul. "Luke's Use of the Birth Stories." In *Studies in Luke-Acts*. Edited by Leander Keck and J. Louis Martyn. Nashville: Abingdon Press, 1966.

Moessner, David. "'The Christ Must Suffer': New Light on the Jesus-Peter,

Stephen, Paul Parallels in Luke-Acts." *Novum Testamentum* 28 (1986): 220–56.

Moltmann, Jürgen. *Theology of Hope: On the Ground and Implications of a Christian Eschatology*. New York: Harper & Row, 1965.

Montoya, Alex. *Preaching with Passion*. Grand Rapids: Kregel, 2007.

Morrison, Toni. *The Nobel Lecture in Literature, 1993*. New York: Alfred Knopf, 1994.

Moule, C. F. D. "The Christology of Luke-Acts." In *Studies in Luke-Acts*. Edited by Leander E. Keck and J. L. Martyn. Nashville: Abingdon Press, 1968.

Muller, Richard A. "The Foundation of Calvin's Theology." In *Biblical Interpretation in the Era of the Reformation: Essays Presented to David C. Steinmetz in Honor of His Sixtieth Birthday*. Grand Rapids: Eerdmans, 1996.

Noordmans, Oepke. *Gestalte en Geest*. Haarlem: Uitgeversmaatschappij Holland, 1956.

Økland, Jorunn. "'The Historical Mary' and Dea Creatrix: A Historical-Critical Contribution to Feminist Theological Reflection." In *A Feminist Companion to Mariology*. Edited by Amy-Jill Levine. Cleveland: Pilgrim Press, 2005.

O'Meara, Thomas. *Mary in Protestant and Catholic Theology*. New York: Sheed & Ward, 1966.

Osmer, Richard. "Rhetoric and Practical Theology: Toward a New Paradigm." In *To Teach, Delight, and to Move: Theological Education in a Post-Christian World*. Edited by David S. Cunningham. Eugene, OR: Cascade, 2004.

Overy, Chalice. "Planted (Jeremiah 17:5–7)." Sermon preached at Goodson Chapel, Durham, NC, February, 12, 2019.

Paintner, Christine Valters. "Please Can I Have a God." In *Dreaming of Stones: Poems*. Orleans, MA: Paraclete, 2019.

Pardue, Megan. "Dialogic Preaching." Lecture at Duke Divinity School, Durham, NC, November 6, 2018.

Pasewark, Kyle A. "The Body in Ecstasy: Love, Difference, and the Social Organism in Luther's Theory of the Lord's Supper." *Journal of Religion* 77, no. 4 (1997): 511–40.

Pasquarello, Michael. *Sacred Rhetoric*. Grand Rapids: Eerdmans, 2005.

Pelias, Ronald. *Performance Studies: The Interpretation of Aesthetic Texts*. New York: St. Martin's Press, 1992.

Pidwell, Ruth. "The Word Made Flesh: Gender and Embodiment in Contemporary Preaching." *Social Semiotics* 2, no. 2 (2001): 177–92.

Piercy, Marge. "For Strong Women." In *The Moon Is Always Female*. New York: Knopf, 1980.

Pius IX. *Ineffabilis Deus*. Apostolic Constitution of Pope Pius the IX on the Immaculate Conception, 1854.

Powery, Luke A. *Dem Dry Bones: Preaching, Death, and Hope*. Minneapolis: Fortress Press, 2012.

———. "Groaning for Love." Sermon preached in Miller Chapel, Princeton Theological Seminary, May 2, 2012.

———. *Spirit Speech: Lament and Celebration in Preaching*. Nashville: Abingdon Press, 2009.

Quinn, Margie. Sermon preached at Duke Divinity School, Durham, NC, March 19, 2019.

Raitt, Jill. "Calvin's Use of Persona." In *Calvinus Ecclesiae Genevensis Custos: Die Referate des Congrès International des Recherches Calviniennes vom 6–9 September 1982 in Genf*. Frankfurt: Lang, 1984.

Ravuvu, Asesela. *The Fijian Way of Life*. Suva, Fiji: University of the South Pacific Press, 1983.

Reid, Barbara E. *Choosing the Better Part? Women in the Gospel of Luke*. Collegeville, MN: Liturgical Press, 1996.

Rice, Charles. *The Embodied Word: Preaching as Art and Liturgy*. Minneapolis: Augsburg Fortress, 2010.

Rich, Adrienne. "Of Woman Born: Motherhood as Experience and Institution." In *Mother Reader: Essential Writings on Motherhood*. New York: Seven Stories, 2001.

Richert, Scott P. "Why Can't Women Be Priests?" *About.com Catholicism*. Accessed September 11, 2012. http://catholicism.about.com/od/beliefs teachings/f/Women_Priests.html.

Ricoeur, Paul. "Between Rhetoric and Poetics." In *Essays on Aristotle's Rhetoric*. Edited by Amélie O. Rorty. Berkeley: University of California Press, 1966.

———. *Hermeneutics and the Human Sciences: Essays on Language, Action and Interpretation*. New York: Cambridge University Press, 1981.

———. "The Hermeneutics of Testimony." In *Essays on Biblical Interpretation*. Edited by Lewis Mudge. Philadelphia: Fortress Press, 1980.

———. "The Model of the Text: Meaningful Action Considered as a Text." In *From Text to Action: Essays in Hermeneutics*. Translated by Kathleen Blamey. Evanston, IL: Northwestern University Press, 1991.

———. *Oneself as Another*. Translated by Kathleen Blamey. Chicago: University of Chicago Press, 2002.

———. *The Rule of Metaphor: Multidisciplinary Studies in the Creation of Meaning in Language*. Translated by Robert Czerny. Toronto: University of Toronto Press, 1977.

Rienstra, Debra. *Great with Child: Reflections on Faith, Fullness, and Becoming a Mother*. New York: Penguin Putnam, 2002.

Rigby, Cynthia. "Mary and the Artistry of God." In *Blessed One: Protestant Perspectives on Mary*. Edited by Beverly Gaventa and Cynthia Rigby. Louisville: Westminster John Knox, 2002.

Riggs, John. Review of *Homiletic: Moves and Structures*, by David Buttrick. *Journal of Religion* 69, no. 2 (April 1989): 270–71.

Roloff, Leland. *The Perception and Evocation of Literature*. Glenview, IL: Scott, Foresman, 1973.

Rorem, Paul. "Lover and Mother: Medieval Language for God and the Soul." In *Women, Gender, and Christian Community*. Edited by James F. Kay and Jane Dempsey Douglass. Louisville: Westminster John Knox, 1997.

Rose, Lucy Atkinson. *Sharing the Word: Preaching in the Roundtable Church*. Louisville: Westminster John Knox, 1997.

Rosenblatt, Louise. *The Reader, the Text, and the Poem*. Carbondale: Southern Illinois University Press, 1978.

Ross, Janell, and Wesley Lowery. "Black Lives Matter Shifts from Protests to Policy." *Chicago Tribune*, May 4, 2017. https://www.chicagotribune.com/nation-world/ct-black-lives-matter-trump-20170504-story.html.

Rowe, C. Kavin. *Early Narrative Christology: The Lord in the Gospel of Luke*. Grand Rapids: Baker Academic, 2009.

———. *World Upside Down: Reading Acts in the Graeco-Roman Age*. Oxford: Oxford University Press, 2009.

Ruiz, Alma Tinoco. "La Entrega o Presentación del Sermón." Spanish language preaching manual, Asbury Theological Seminary, forthcoming.

Ruiz, Alma Tinoco, and Tito Madrazo. "Preaching from Sanctuary." Paper presented at *Societas Homiletica*. Durham, NC, August 5, 2019.

Rush, James. *The Philosophy of the Human Voice: Embracing Its Physiological History; Together with a System of Principles, by Which Criticism in the Art of Elocution May Be Rendered Intelligible, and Instruction, Definite and Comprehensive*. 7th rev. ed. Philadelphia: J. B. Lippincott, 1879.

Sacks, Jonathan. *The Dignity of Difference*. London: Continuum, 2002.

Schaberg, Jane. "Feminist Interpretations of the Infancy Narrative of Matthew." In *A Feminist Companion to Mariology*. Edited by Amy-Jill Levine. Cleveland: Pilgrim Press, 2005.

Schechner, Richard. *Performance Theory*, 2nd ed. New York: Routledge, 1988.

Schrag, Calvin. *The Resources of Rationality: A Response to the Postmodern Challenge*. Bloomington: Indiana University Press, 1992.

Segovia, Fernando. "Toward a Hermeneutics of the Diaspora: A Hermeneutics of Otherness and Engagement." In *Reading from This Place: Social Location and Biblical Interpretation in the United States.* Vol. 1. Edited by Fernando Segovia and Mary Ann Tolbert. Minneapolis: Fortress Press, 1995.

Seibert, Sarah. Sermon preached in Goodson Chapel, Durham, NC, February 7, 2019.

Shepherd, William Henry. *The Narrative Function of the Holy Spirit as a Character in Luke-Acts.* Atlanta: Scholars Press, 1994.

Shoop, Marcia Mount. *Let the Bones Dance: Embodiment and the Body of Christ.* Louisville: Westminster John Knox, 2010.

Sleeman, Matthew. *Geography and the Ascension Narrative in Acts.* Cambridge: Cambridge University Press, 2009.

Simons, Herbert. *The Rhetorical Turn: Invention and Persuasion in the Conduct of Inquiry.* Chicago: University of Chicago Press, 1990.

Smith, Ted. "Theories of Practice." In *The Wiley Blackwell Companion Guide to Practical Theology.* Edited by Bonnie Miller-McLemore. Oxford: Blackwell, 2012.

Snider, Phil. *Preaching after God: Derrida, Caputo and the Language of Postmodern Homiletics.* Eugene, OR: Cascade, 2012.

Soskice, Janet. *Metaphor and Religious Language.* Oxford: Clarendon Press, 1989.

Spillers, Hortense. "Moving on Down the Line." *American Quarterly* 40, no. 1 (1988): 94–95.

Spivak, Gayatri Chakravorty. "Can the Subaltern Speak?" In *Marxism and the Interpretation of Culture.* Edited by Cary Nelson and Lawrence Grossberg. London: Macmillan, 1988.

Springer, Carl. *Cicero in Heaven.* Boston: Brill, 2018.

Stanley, Susie C. *Holy Boldness: Women Preachers' Autobiographies and the Sanctified Self.* Knoxville: University of Tennessee Press, 2002.

Steinmetz, David. "The Eucharist and the Identity of Jesus in the Early Reformation." In *Seeking the Identity of Jesus: A Pilgrimage.* Edited by Beverly Roberts Gaventa and Richard B. Hays. Grand Rapids: Eerdmans, 2008.

Stern, Carol Simpson, and Bruce Henderson. *Performance: Texts and Contexts.* New York: Longman, 1993.

Stiver, Dan. *Theology after Ricoeur: New Directions in Hermeneutical Theology.* Louisville: Westminster John Knox, 2002.

Strong, James. *The New Strong's Exhaustive Concordance of the Bible.* Nashville: Thomas Nelson, 2003.

Stronstad, Roger. *The Charismatic Theology of St. Luke.* Grand Rapids: Baker Academic, 1990.

Suchocki, Marjorie. *The Whispered Word.* St. Louis: Chalice Press, 1999.

Suleiman, Susan Rubin. "Writing and Motherhood." In *Mother Reader: Essential Writings on Motherhood*. New York: Seven Stories, 2001.

Sutton, Jane. "The Taming of the Polos/Polis: Rhetoric as an Achievement without Woman." In *Contemporary Rhetorical Theory: A Reader*. Edited by John Louis Lucaites, Celeste Michelle Condit, and Sally Caudill. New York: Guilford Press, 1998.

Talbert, Charles H. *Reading Acts: A Literary and Theological Commentary on the Acts of the Apostles*. Macon, GA: Smyth & Helwys, 2001.

Tannehill, Robert C. *Luke*. Nashville: Abingdon Press, 1996.

———. *The Narrative Unity of Luke-Acts*. Vol. 2. Minneapolis: Fortress Press, 1989.

———. *The Shape of Luke's Story: Essays on Luke-Acts*. Eugene, OR: Cascade, 2005.

Tanner, Kathryn. "Christian Claims." *Christian Century*, February 23, 2010.

Tarabe, Akanisi Sobusobu. "Re-Assessing Gender Roles: A Study of Indigenous Fijian Women's Role in Funerals." Master's Thesis, School of Social Science, University of the South Pacific, September 2015.

Taylor, Barbara Brown. *Leaving Church: A Memoir of Faith*. San Francisco: HarperSanFrancisco, 2006.

Thompson, Lisa. *Ingenuity: Preaching as an Outsider*. Nashville: Abingdon Press, 2018.

Tilling, Chris. *Paul's Divine Christology*. Tübingen: Mohr Siebeck, 2012.

Timpane, Pilar. "After Samuel Oliver-Bruno's Deportation, a Sanctuary Community Suffers Together." *Sojourners*, December 3, 2018. https://sojo.net/articles/after-samuel-oliver-brunos-deportation-sanctuary-community-suffers-together.

Townes, Emilie. *In a Blaze of Glory: Womanist Spirituality as Social Witness*. Nashville: Abingdon Press, 1995.

Tuckett, C. M. "The Christology of Luke-Acts." In *The Unity of Luke-Acts*. Edited by J. Verheyden. Leuven: Leuven University Press, 1999.

Turner, Mary Donovan. "Reversal of Fortune." In *Performance in Preaching*. Edited by Jana Childers and Clayton Schmit. Grand Rapids: Baker, 2008.

Tuwere, I. S. *Vanua: Towards a Fijian Theology of Place*. Suva, Fiji: University of the South Pacific Press, 2002.

Vaai, Upolu Luma. "Relational Hermeneutics: A Return to the Relationality of the Pacific Itulagi as a Lens for Understanding and Interpreting Life." In *Relational Hermeneutics: Decolonizing the Mindset and the Pacific Itulagi*. Edited by Upolu Luma Vaai and Aisake Casimira. Suva, Fiji: University of the South Pacific Press, 2017.

———. "A Theology of Talalasi: Challenging the 'One Truth' Ideology of the Empire." *Pacific Journal of Theology* 55 (2016): 1–19.

Van den Hengel, John. "Miriam of Nazareth: Between Symbol and History." In

The Feminist Companion to Mariology. Edited by Amy-Jill Levine. Cleveland: Pilgrim Press, 2005.

Verheyden, J. "The Unity of Luke-Acts." In *The Unity of Luke-Acts*. Edited by J. Verheyden. Leuven: Leuven University Press, 1999.

Wakeley, Joseph Beaumont. *The Prince of Pulpit Orators: A Portraiture of Rev. George Whitefield: Illustrated by Anecdotes and Incidents*. New York: Carlton & Lanahan, 1871.

Walker-Barnes, Chanequa. *Too Heavy a Yoke: Black Women and the Burden of Strength*. Eugene, OR: Wipf & Stock, 2014.

Wallace, Michele. *Black Macho and the Black Superwoman*. New York: Dial Press, 1978.

Walton, Steve. "Jesus: Present and/or Absent? The Presence and Presentation of Jesus as a Character in the Book of Acts." In *Characters and Characterization in Luke-Acts*. Edited by Frank Dicken and Julia Snyder. London: T&T Clark, 2016.

Ward, Graham. *Radical Orthodoxy: A New Theology*. Edited by John Milbank, Catherine Pickstock, and Graham Ward. London: Routledge, 1999.

Ward, Richard. "Finding Your Voice in Theological School." In *Preaching and Performance*. Edited by Clayton Schmit and Jana Childers. Grand Rapids: Baker Academic, 2008.

Warner, Marina. *Alone of All Her Sex: The Myth and the Cult of the Virgin Mary*. New York: Vintage, 1983.

Waters, Claire M. *Angels and Earthly Creatures: Preaching, Performance, and Gender in the Later Middle Ages*. Philadelphia: University of Pennsylvania Press, 2004.

Webb, Stephen H. "A Hyperbolic Imagination: Theology and the Rhetoric of Excess." *Theology Today* 50 (April 1993): 56–67.

Weems, Renita. *Just a Sister Away: A Womanist Vision of Women's Relationships in the Bible*. San Diego: Lura Media, 1988.

———. *Showing Mary*. New York: Warner Books, 2002.

Weir, Allison. *Sacrificial Logics: Feminist Theory and the Critique of Identity*. London: Routledge, 1996.

Welker, Michael. "A Problem of Experience in Today's World." In *God the Spirit*. Minneapolis: Fortress Press, 1994.

West, Cornell. *Hope on a Tightrope: Words and Wisdom*. Carlsbad, CA: Smiley, 2008.

Whitenton, Michael R. "Rewriting Abraham and Joseph: Stephen's Speech (Acts 7:2–16) and Jewish Exegetical Traditions." *Novum Testamentum* 54, no. 2. (2012): 149–67.

Williams, Delores. *Sisters in the Wilderness: The Challenge of Womanist God-Talk*. Maryknoll, NY: Orbis, 1993.

Williams, Marva. "Tarry Service—Is It Still Needed?" *Pentecostal Family*, March 16, 2017. https://www.thepentecostalfamily.org/blog/tarry -service-is-it-still-needed.

Williams, Rowan. "'The Seal of Orthodoxy': Mary and the Heart of Christian Doctrine." In *Say Yes to God: Mary and the Revealing of the Word Made Flesh*. London: Tufton, 1999.

Willis, David E. "Rhetoric and Responsibility in Calvin's Theology." In *The Context of Contemporary Theology: Essays in Honor of Paul Lehmann*. Atlanta: John Knox, 1974.

Wilson, Brittany E. *Embodied God: Seeing the Divine in Luke-Acts and the Early Church*. New York: Oxford University Press, forthcoming.

———. *Unmanly Men: Reconfigurations of Masculinity in Luke-Acts*. Oxford: Oxford University Press, 2015.

Winters, Joseph. "The Gift, and Death, of Blackness." *Journal of Africana Religions* 6, no. 1 (2018): 1–26.

Wright, David. "Calvin's Accommodating God." In *Calvin as Protector of the Purer Religion*. Edited by Welhelm Neuser and Brian Armstrong. Zurich: International Congress on Calvin Research, 1997.

Yong, Amos. *Hospitality and the Other: Pentecost, Christian Practices, and the Neighbor*. Maryknoll, NY: Orbis, 2008.

Young, Frances, and David Ford. *Meaning and Truth in 2 Corinthians*. Eugene, OR: Wipf & Stock, 2008.

Young, Iris Marion. "Pregnant Embodiment." In *On Female Body Experience: "Throwing Like a Girl" and Other Essays*. Oxford: Oxford University Press, 2005.

Young, Pamela D. "Encountering Jesus through the Earliest Witnesses." *Theological Studies* 57 (1996): 513–21.

Zachman, Randall C. *John Calvin as Teacher, Pastor, and Theologian: The Shape of His Writings and Thought*. Grand Rapids: Baker Academic, 2006.

Zappen, James P. "Francis Bacon and the Historiography of Scientific Rhetoric." *Rhetoric Review* 8, no. 1 (1989): 74–88.

Index of Authors

Subject Index

apocalypticism: in Luke/Acts, 62, 93–94; in the preaching performance, 128–31. *See also* Holy Spirit: eschatology, relation to

ars predicandi (medieval preaching handbooks), 14, 27–29, 194

ascension, significance for practical theology, 5, 13, 18, 84–85, 106, 211. *See also* body of Christ; absent and present in ascension

authenticity in pastoral role, 17, 29, 49–50, 135, 191–97

biblical exegesis: as "carrying," 170–75; historical critical study, 172; "otherness and engagement," 172–73; as performance, 140–41; as staging, 61; as *talanoa*, 173–74; as testimony, 148–50

birthing the sermon: reflexivity of labor, 150, 157, 159–60, 165, 184–85, 213–14; as risk, 145, 178–84; role of lament and struggle in, 179–81, 183

body (embodiment), 10, 13, 31, 33, 41, 56, 128, 134, 135, 136; Bakhtin and, 134; defined (i.e. particular, permeable, provisional), 10–14; forgetful of, 10–11, 12, 16–17, 26, 30–31, 33, 44–45, 51–52, 84, 136–37; practical theological approaches to, 7, 9n19, 29, 30–31, 33, 41–42, 128–29, 133n29, 136–37, 147; as revelatory sign, 56–57, 65, 69, 74, 84–85, 99–100, 103, 108, 120, 123, 131–35, 141, 214

body of Christ: absent and present in ascension, 4–6, 14, 19, 54, 84; crucified/resurrected, 3–5, 55–56, 123; ecclesiology, significance for, 4, 47–48, 57, 61–62, 67, 72–73, 77, 80, 147; homiletics, underexplored in, 50–52, 65, 84; postliberalism/radical orthodoxy and, 73–74, 147; practical theology, significance for, 13, 18, 57, 73, 80–81, 84, 123, 133, 191, 213; preaching, significance for, 14, 16–17, 19, 33, 54, 56, 65, 123, 127, 133–34, 190–91, 212; pregnant, 125–26, 125nn8–12; sacraments, significance for, 6, 63–64, 74, 124–25, 126. *See also* Eucharist; Word of God, as body of Christ

243

Scripture Index